D0367638

DISCARDED
From Nashville Public Library

Property of
The Public Library of Nashville and Davidson County
225 Polk Ave., Nashville, Tn. 37203

Regarding
KARL BARTH

Toward a Reading of His Theology

Trevor Hart

DISCARDED
From Nashville Public Library

InterVarsity Press
Downers Grove, Illinois

InterVarsity Press
P.O. Box 1400, Downers Grove, IL 60515-1426
World Wide Web: www.ivpress.com
E-mail: mail@ivpress.com

©*Trevor Hart 1999*

Published in the United States of America by InterVarsity Press, Downers Grove, Illinois, with permission from Paternoster Press.

All rights reserved. No part of this book may be reproduced in any form without written permission from InterVarsity Press.

InterVarsity Press® is the book-publishing division of InterVarsity Christian Fellowship/USA®, a student movement active on campus at hundreds of universities, colleges and schools of nursing in the United States of America, and a member movement of the International Fellowship of Evangelical Students. For information about local and regional activities, write Public Relations Dept., InterVarsity Christian Fellowship/USA, 6400 Schroeder Rd., P.O. Box 7895, Madison, WI 53707-7895.

All Scripture quotations, unless otherwise indicated, are taken from the Holy Bible, New International Version®. NIV®. *Copyright* ©*1973, 1978, 1984 by International Bible Society. Used by permission of Hodder and Stoughton Ltd. All rights reserved. "NIV" is a registered trademark of International Bible Society. UK trademark number 1448790. Distributed in North America by permission of Zondervan Publishing House.*

ISBN 0-8308-1564-3

Printed in the United States of America ∞

Library of Congress Cataloging-in-Publication Data

Hart, Trevor A.
  Regarding Karl Barth: toward a reading of his theology / Trevor Hart.
    p. cm.
  Originally published: Carlisle, Cumbria, UK: Paternoster Press, 1999.
  Includes bibliographical references and index.
  ISBN 0-8308-1564-3 (pbk.: alk. paper)
    1. Barth, Karl, 1886-1968   I. Title.
BX4827.B3 H295 2000
230'.044'092—dc21
                                                                          00-057543

24	23	22	21	15	14	13	12	11	10	9	8	7	6	5	4	3	2	1
15	14	13	12	11	10	09	08	07	06	05	04	03	02	01	00			

CONTENTS

Acknowledgments _____ vi

Abbreviations _____ viii

Preface _____ ix

1 Was God in Christ? Revelation, History and the
   Humanity of God _____ 1

2 The Word, the Words and the Witness: Proclamation
   as Divine and Human Reality _____ 28

3 Christ and God's Justification of Creation _____ 48

4 Mapping the Moral Field and Mediating the
   Promise: A Study in Barth's Ethics _____ 74

5 Person and Prerogative in Perichoretic Perspective:
   The Triunity of God _____ 100

6 Truth, the Trinity and Pluralism _____ 117

7 The Capacity for Ambiguity: Revisiting the
   Barth-Brunner Debate _____ 139

8 Speaking of God's Love: Analogy, Reference
   and Revelation _____ 173

Index of Names _____ 195

Acknowledgments

All of the chapters in this book originated in invitations to read papers to conferences or colloquia. While all have been revised (some very considerably) in the preparation of this volume, earlier versions of some have appeared in print elsewhere.

Chapter One is based on a paper read to the Tyndale Christian Doctrine Group in Cambridge, July 1998. It appears in print here for the first time.

Chapter Two originated with an invitation to speak at the first Karl Barth Colloquium held at Eastern Baptist Seminary in Philadelphia, November 1993. The current text is based on the Tyndale Christian Doctrine Lecture for 1994, an earlier version of which was published in *Tyndale Bulletin* 46.1 (1995), pp. 81–102.

Chapter Three is based on a paper read to the Tyndale Christian Doctrine Group in Cambridge, July 1990. An earlier version was published as 'Barth and Küng on Justification: Imaginary Differences?' in *Irish Theological Quarterly* 59.2 (1993), pp. 94–113.

Chapter Four is based on a paper read to a meeting of the Karl Barth Society of North America in Philadelphia, June 1996. It appears in print here for the first time.

Chapter Five is based on a short paper read to the trinity and christology seminar at the Society for the Study of Theology in Cambridge, April 1991. An earlier version was published as 'Person and Prerogative in Perichoretic Perspective: An Ongoing Dispute in Trinitarian Ontology Observed' *Irish Theological Quarterly* 58.1 (1992), pp. 46–57.

Chapter Six is based on a paper read to the Fifth Edinburgh Dogmatics Conference in Edinburgh, August 1993. An earlier version was published as 'Karl Barth, the Trinity, and Pluralism', in K.J.

Vanhoozer (ed.), *The Trinity in a Pluralistic Age: Theological Essays on Culture and Religion* (Grand Rapids: Eerdmans, 1997), pp. 124–142.

Chapter Seven is based on a paper read to a meeting of the Tyndale Christian Doctrine Group in Cambridge, July 1993. An earlier (much shorter) version was published as 'A Capacity for Ambiguity? The Barth-Brunner Debate Revisited', in *Tyndale Bulletin* 44.2 (1993), pp. 289–305.

Chapter Eight is based on a paper read to the Sixth Edinburgh Dogmatics Conference in Edinburgh, August 1995.

I am grateful to those whose invitations first afforded the opportunity to prepare these chapters, and to Tyndale House in Cambridge, Wm. B. Eerdmans Publishing Company and the editors of the *Irish Theological Quarterly* for permission to reprint some of them in a revised form.

Abbreviations

CD   *Church Dogmatics*, Bromiley, G. and Torrance, T.F. (eds) (Edinburgh: T & T Clark, 1956–76)

GD   *The Göttingen Dogmatics: Instruction in Christian Religion, Volume 1* (Edinburgh: T & T Clark, 1991)

KD   *Die kirkliche Dogmatik* (Munich: Chr. Kaiser Verlag, 1932 and Zurich: TVZ, 1938–65)

UCR1   *Unterricht in der christlichen Religion, Erster Band* (Zurich: TVZ, 1985)

UCR2   *Unterricht in der christlichen Religion, Zweiter Band* (Zurich: TVZ, 1990)

Preface

Some books are a long time in the writing. The origins of this particular volume lie some twenty years back in a lecture hall in Durham where a Professor of Divinity encouraged his first year students early in their studies to identify a prominent theologian whose writings they might use thenceforth as a sounding board on a wide range of theological questions. The names cast out like pearls included many notable British, European and American scholars who were familiar as yet only from reading lists hurriedly perused but largely unused. Perhaps it was a simple matter of alphabetical order which led one student in particular to alight on the name of Karl Barth and, later that same day, to lift a hefty black-spined volume from the college library shelf.

I cannot now remember exactly which part-volume of *CD* it was. I do recall, though, the sense of surprise mingled with excitement which my first venture into this physically and intellectually daunting text evoked. I had not been studying systematic theology long; but long enough at least to have noticed that some practitioners of it seemed nervous about tackling the key themes of the Christian tradition too directly, or drawing too openly on the resources offered by the scriptural, liturgical and practical heritage of that tradition in doing so. Much of what I had found myself reading hitherto had had an anaemic feel about it, or communicated a sense of apologetic timidity, even a sort of intellectual shame where the ownership of a distinctively Christian identity and vision was concerned. This was, admittedly, the perspective of a novice who was still learning what a properly theological question was, let alone how to go about answering one. The lines in my personal picture of the theological cosmos would eventually be drawn with a less thick pencil. But what I got right in my first impulsive reaction to Barth's writing was that here was a Christian theologian who, rather than prioritising 'relevance' and seeking it through the abandonment or total reconstruction of Christian identity, or making a show of having stepped outside the Christian tradition in order to consider it 'critically', was actually convinced that it was necessary to pursue the critical dialogue and hence to rejuvenate that same tradition un-ashamedly *from within*, and doing so precisely in order to address the wider intellectual, social, political and ethical concerns and challenges of his day. That was surprising and exciting to me twenty years ago, and it is still so today.

The years since have been ones during which, like many others, I have found Barth to be a more than worthy dialogue partner on almost any and every theological question. The index volume in my set of *CD* is one of the most heavily thumbed books on my shelves, having been consulted time and again for the purposes of preparing lectures, papers and sermons, or simply in the urgent process of re-solving some problem which has lodged itself as an irritant in my consciousness. If I offer the obvious qualification that I have not always agreed with what I have found in the text, it is equally true that I have rarely come away from the reading without some bene-fit. To engage with a theological mind of such dimensions, to allow that mind to pose fundamental questions and to explore possible routes to answering them, is in itself a worthwhile and enriching ex-perience intellectually.

This book is written in the assumption that the project of regarding (paying respectful heed to) Karl Barth is an intrinsically worthwhile and even an important one for Christian theology at the end of the twentieth century, no matter how vigorously we may wish subsequently to insist upon theological strategies and conclu-sions other than (even incompatible with) Barth's own. That Christian theology today should be 'post-Barthian' is doubtless true in at least one and probably a variety of senses. Barth himself would not have wanted it otherwise. Thus there can be no uncritical return to Barth's theology as if he identified all the relevant questions, let alone held all the answers. To suggest this is not to limit or to under-estimate the greatness of Barth's achievement but to acknowledge something of which Barth himself was well aware; namely, that as a human activity theology is inherently partial and provisional, and

must constantly be redone in the light of ever changing circumstances, as an attempt to hear and respond to the Word of God
speaking anew every morning. Yesterday's answers, while they may
serve as a helpful set of guidelines and clues, can never satisfy a theology which is concerned with a living and dynamic God. But there is
one sense in which one may not properly claim to be post-Barthian.
The prefix 'post-' presupposes a serious encounter with the contribution which Barth has made to theological discussion in this
century, and my impression is that there are many who have not yet
availed themselves properly of such an encounter. Doubtless this is
due in part to the sheer expenditure of energy and time required to
do so. It is for this reason that the recent renaissance of interest in
Barth in Britain and North America which, among other things, has
spawned a string of publications introducing and responding to
various aspects of his theology, is so welcome.

This book is offered as part of an ongoing dialogue with Barth's
own writings and with other interpreters of and respondents to his
work. Its purpose is to allow Barth's voice to be heard more clearly,
and to respond to some of the theological challenges which that
voice articulates. As its subtitle makes clear, it lays no claim either to
comprehensiveness or to finality. It is precisely a series of essays aris-
ing out of an engagement with various aspects of Barth's theology.
Its various chapters are all substantially based on papers or invited
lectures written and delivered in Britain and America since 1990.
Some have already appeared in print in earlier versions. Others
appear here for the first time. The coherence of the volume reposes
on the close relationships existing between the themes addressed
within Barth's own corpus, and on my own developing but largely
continuous responses to it. The original contexts of some of the
pieces account for slight differences of style and length between
them.

There are many people without whose patience, encourage-
ment, stimulus and interest these pieces would never have been
written. Teaching undergraduate classes on Barth in Aberdeen and
St Andrews over the last thirteen years has provided the happy excuse
to spend so much time immersed in reading and discussing his writings, as well as a source of fresh critical questioning of and response to
his theology. Among those postgraduates with whom I have enjoyed
extended dialogue and whose own learning has taught me much

about Barth are Baxter Kruger, Sam Clark, Scott Rodin, John Yates and Li Jen Ou. I am grateful, also, to those groups and institutions who have graciously invited me to speak at conferences and thereby forced me to commit most of what is contained in this volume to paper: the Tyndale Christian Doctrine Group, Rutherford House, the Karl Barth Society of North America, and Eastern Baptist Seminary. Finally, my thanks are due to Pieter Kwant, Jeremy Muddit and Tony Graham at Paternoster Press for their willingness to publish this volume and their remarkable patience in awaiting its completion.

Trevor Hart
St Mary's College
St Andrews

1

Was God in Christ?
Revelation, History and the
Humanity of God

About half a century ago a distinguished British theologian spoke of
the loss of concern for the recovery of the historical Christ as the
most distinctive and determinative element in modern christology.
The theologian was Donald Baillie, whose book *God was in Christ*
(to which generations of apprentice British theologians and teachers
of theology since have owed a quiet but substantial debt) was published 50 years ago.[1] It is fitting that we should mark this anniversary
by allowing Baillie to pose the question which this chapter will seek
to address, and to do so in both general and specific terms.

1. Was the Word made flesh in vain?

In general terms, Baillie's concern in 1948 was with a trend in
christology towards a practical (if not a theoretical) Nestorianism[2]:
in other words, an effective separation of Jesus (the man from
Nazareth whose mummified remains two centuries of histori-
cal-critical archaeology had attempted to uncover in the textual
sand of the gospels) from the divine Word with whom the gospel
and faith allegedly have to do. Baillie acknowledges that such
dualisms were in large measure a reaction to the poverty of the
nineteenth-century Quest for the Jesus of history and its eerily

---

[1] D.M. Baillie, *God Was in Christ: An Essay on Incarnation and Atonement*
(London: Faber, 1948).
[2] This is my, rather than Baillie's, way of describing it.

proto-postmodern outcomes. No matter, then, that the most
expert critical attention to the sources available had rendered only
a bewildering series of identikit images having in common at most
the fact that they looked remarkably unlike the figure portrayed by
the evangelists. Faced with this veritable identity parade of 'fully
human' figures from the imagined past Christian faith need not
despair when the real Jesus of history repeatedly refused to step forward. For faith as such, it was now insisted, is not and could never
be contingent upon the results of historical scholarship. Its roots lie
elsewhere, in (in Martin Kähler's phrase) a *sturmfreies Gebiet*, an
invulnerable area. History and belief do not belong within the
same sphere of influence and consideration. Fact and faith, whatever the positive relation between them may be held to be, must
constantly be disentangled in order for faith to be liberated from
historical scepticism and theology properly orientated towards its
true object. Historical study can neither render nor falsify faith.
Faith is not rooted in the conclusions of the historian, but in an
encounter with the living God, a phenomenon of which the historian as such knows and can say nothing at all. That 'the Word
became flesh' need not be questioned: but *faith's* proper concern is
ever with the divine Word who addresses it in the here and now
rather than the historical 'flesh' which he once became. Therefore
history cannot become the basis of constructive theology (which
has to do precisely with the concerns of faith). There is, then, a sort
of reciprocal kenoticism operating here: the Word of God, in giving himself for and to us, empties himself of all that is proper to
him as God and assumes the form of a contingent and corrigible
datum of historical research; while we, for our part, empty ourselves of the felt need or the possibility of knowing this datum in
any clear or unambiguous manner, content for our Christian faith
and our theology to rest instead on less intellectually secure but
nevertheless genuine foundations.

Baillie's judgement on this christological trend and its consequences for Christian faith and theology is harsh. There is, he
argues, 'no stability in a position which accepts to the full the
humanity of Christ but has no interest in its actual concrete manifestation and doubts whether it can be recaptured at all; which
insists on the "once-for-all-ness" of this divine incursion into history, but renounces all desire or claim to know what it was really

like'.[3] Far from securing the doctrine of incarnation from the acids of criticism (as Baillie supposes this approach might be intended to do) such a bracketing off of the Jesus of history in order to concentrate on a logically distinct Christ of faith actually stultifies it and constitutes its effective abandonment. In such a scenario the Word does not really 'become flesh' at all, we might say, but hovers above the level of the flesh, at least in all those respects which are significant for faith. To those who advocate such an approach the question must be put whether 'Christ lived for nothing, and the Word was made flesh in vain' since the particular shape of this enfleshing is held to be either unknowable or irrelevant or both.[4] In either case the logic of incarnation as such is seriously eroded. Baillie's call in the middle of our century was thus for a christology which took with renewed seriousness the question of the significance of Jesus' humanity, the precise form and content of the Word's enfleshed existence under the conditions of history, for faith and theology, without collapsing back into the sort of optimistic romantic historicism which first launched the Quest on its fateful voyage. In broad terms Christian New Testament scholarship has heeded his call, the advent of the so-called Third Quest being the most recent initiative in this direction.

This brings us to the more precise focus for this chapter, namely, to inquire into the significance of the humanity of Christ in Karl Barth's theology of revelation with particular reference to his development of that doctrine in the 1924 Göttingen lectures in dogmatics and the first volume of *CD*. If justification for this particular line of inquiry be sought then three main considerations may be advanced in mitigation: First, Barth is the systematic theologian in whose writings the themes of christology and knowledge of God find their most serious and extensive treatment in the twentieth century. Second, his treatment of these themes is one which tackles head-on the very issue which Baillie raises: the peculiar place of the *humanitas Christi* in the mediation of our knowing of God. Third, and not entirely unrelated to the preceding, while Barth is not the sole culprit he is prominent among

---

[3] Baillie, *God Was in Christ*, p. 28.
[4] Ibid. p. 54.

those on whom Baillie's sights are firmly fixed.[5] Thus, Baillie writes, in its severe reaction to the failure of the Jesus of history movement '[Barth's] theology has become so austerely a theology of the Word that . . . it is hardly a theology of the Word-made-Flesh.'[6]

This is a serious charge indeed if it can be made to stick. That there is certainly a question to be answered is indicated by the essentially similar charge laid at Barth's door (or, perhaps, skilfully wrapped around a rhetorical brick and thrown through his window) some 30 years later by Richard Roberts in relation to Barth's handling of the relationship between time and eternity.[7] After a marathon overview of *CD* Roberts offers the following judgement on its complex theo-logic: 'Wherever the content of revelation and its time draws close to the reality common to humanity, ambiguity results because the "reality" of revelation must both affirm and deny, recreate and annihilate at the same moment.' But, 'if the God of the orthodox Christian Gospel is prized apart from the structures of contemporary human life' in this way, Roberts concludes, 'The ontological dogma of the Incarnation loses its roots in the shared and public reality of the world in which we live; it hovers above us like a cathedral resting upon a cloud.'[8] The point here is essentially similar to Baillie's. If Barth's *Logos* truly becomes *sarx*, the particular way in which the 'becoming' or the union between the two is consistently construed in his theology nonetheless risks reducing it to the point where it loses all purchase in the real world, thereby robbing it of genuine redemptive and revelatory force, and finally robbing theology of both its theme and its form as talk about God.

In what follows I wish to explore what truth there may be in such charges. Unsurprisingly the evidence is far from unambiguous. Yet I believe the ambiguity to lie in the critical *reception* of what Barth says rather than being inherent in what he says. The

---

[5] Ibid. esp. pp. 17–18, 36–37, 48–50, 53.

[6] Ibid. p. 53.

[7] R.H. Roberts, 'Barth's Doctrine of Time', in S.W. Sykes (ed.), *Karl Barth: Studies of His Theological Methods* (Oxford: Clarendon Press, 1979), pp. 88–146.

[8] Ibid. pp. 144, 145.

latter is certainly marked by *dialectic*, but this is not the same thing. Therefore I side neither with Roberts' spirited attack nor with Graham Ward's recent defence of Barth from the standpoint of a Derridean philosophy of language.[9] As both Roberts and Ward recognize, it is with Barth's espousal of the so-called 'analogy of faith' that the capacity for ambiguity arises. One suspects, however, that any attempt to make sense of this analogy in terms of a general philosophy of language or anything else, however well intentioned, would provoke a thundering denial from Barth himself. The point is (as Roberts certainly sees but Ward may not have) that for Barth the *analogia fidei* is and must be *sui generis* and arises precisely and only as a result of the very particular conditions of human speech about God, conditions which can by definition apply to no other object of human knowing and speaking. Behind this device, therefore, there lies a very particular ontology of divine-human relatedness, an ontology which is itself decisively shaped and informed by the structure of Chalcedonian christology. It is, in effect, an analysis of the linguistic implications of believing that when God becomes human his presence in the world is to be understood and confessed in terms of the transcendental category of *hypostasis*, and does not involve any mixing or modification of either creaturely or Creatorly 'natures'. It is this dialectic at the level of being which renders the concomitant dialectic at the level of speaking, and to subsume the *analogia fidei* under any wider linguistic pattern is thus precisely to miss its primary point.

I shall suggest that one key to a more sympathetic reading of Barth than either Baillie or Roberts are able to offer lies in inquiring not just into the implications of the fifth-century epithets 'unconfused' and 'unchanged' which his theology certainly reinforces, but also into the other two Chalcedonian epithets 'undivided' and 'unseparated' which his explicit embrace of the two natures doctrine equally implies. What, in other words, does it mean for Barth to say that the humanity of Jesus is inseparable from the presence of the Word in the world? or (by inference) that the 'flesh' of this particular historical man cannot legitimately be excluded from the

---

[9] G. Ward, *Barth, Derrida and the Language of Theology* (Cambridge: CUP, 1995), esp. Ch. 11.

picture where our knowledge of God is concerned? These are both
claims which Barth makes; yet they are not ones which sit comfort-
ably with the supposition that he dehistoricizes revelation or sees
the humanity of Jesus as in any sense incidental to it. Is there, then,
inherent and irresolvable ambiguity here? If there is, then it must be
said that this is not so much a problem with Barth's theology as such
as one which he shares with the ancient architects of Chalcedonian
theology and perhaps with Christian theology as a whole in the
mainstream of its attempts to make sense of the mode of God's presence in the man Jesus of Nazareth and the implications of this for
our thinking about his relatedness to creation more widely. I hope
to suggest, though, that Barth's interpretation and deliberate
deployment of Chalcedonian categories is far from ambiguous, and
that attention to his use of the categories *hypostasis* and its Alexan-
drian elaboration *anhypostasis* in particular furnish a consistent and
coherent pattern within which to locate and make good sense of his
various statements.

2. Eutyches resuscitated? Revelation and Barth's theological turn from the subject

Consideration of the wider theological context within and in
response to which Barth's distinctive theological emphases developed makes his persistent leaning towards a dualism between the
divine and the human, the infinite and the finite, the eternal and
the temporal easier to appreciate. Baillie's appeal to the failed history of the Quest in this regard is relevant but scarcely adequate.
The bid to secure faith by uncovering the facts about Jesus was only
part of a much broader and more complicated pattern of theological
development in the nineteenth century, a pattern in which Barth
discerned the danger of a thoroughgoing blurring and even loss of
the proper boundaries between Creator and creature, God and the
realm of the 'flesh'. Thus, Baillie's quip, writing in the christological
wake of that century, that 'Eutyches . . . is dead, and he is not likely
to be as fortunate as Eutychus in finding an apostle to revive him!'[10]

---

[10] Baillie, *God Was in Christ*, p. 20.

was and is only partially true. To be sure, it is unlikely that a crudely docetic account of Jesus will ever escape unscathed again (although it is worth noting Stephen Sykes' insistence that just what 'full humanity' means in the case of Jesus is a question demanding investigation rather than a signal for dogmatic extrapolation from our own experience of being human).[11] But there is more than one variety of monophysitism, and the nineteenth century may be construed from another angle precisely as a breeding ground for a form of Eutychian error in which, in one way or another, the divine was constantly brought down to earth, and the created (at least in some of its aspects) exalted and celebrated as *homoiousios* if not *homoousios* with it.

The Romantic idealism which discovered God lurking in and under every leaf, stone and organism, and which interpreted history itself as a mode of divine self-expression or self-realization, is only the most explicit (and for that reason arguably the least pernicious) form of this. There were lots of other versions of it: ways in which theology was led (as Barth believed) to abandon its own proper object (God himself) and shift its attention to and locate its own ultimate source and possibility within some aspect of the sphere of nature, history, the phenomenal, 'the flesh'. It was not in Hegelianism alone that there was, in effect, an adoption of the incarnation of the Logos as a metaphysical principle rather than a contingent fact. The essential unity between God and the world was a truth as widely adhered to in one form or another as it was subversive of the doctrine of revelation in anything like its traditional versions. By the late nineteenth century the most significant streams of Christian theology had either quietly pushed this doctrine aside and substituted for it some other (more 'natural') basis for their endeavour, or else had refashioned the concept in ways which served effectively (if not intentionally) to relocate it within the sphere of human (natural) rather than divine (supranatural) possibilities. Into the first category we may place Kant's concerted bid to limit the range of reason in order to make room for faith and Schleiermacher's appeal to a general and innate human

---

[11] See, S.W. Sykes 'The Theology of the Humanity of Christ', in S.W. Sykes and J.P. Clayton (eds.), *Christ, Faith and History* (Cambridge: CUP, 1972).

God-consciousness as both the basis and the object of theological reflection. Into the second must go many of Barth's Ritschlian teachers who eschewed the notion of religion being rooted in any general human capacity whatsoever, and insisted instead upon the positive and particular revelation of God in the historical person of Jesus; yet in doing so they tended mostly to identify the content of that revelation directly with historically locatable phenomena (the teaching, or the moral and spiritual example, or the personality of Jesus to cite just a few familiar instances). Thus 'revelation', whatever its ultimate source, was effectively reduced to those this-worldly phenomena from Jesus' life which remained once the vultures of academe had picked over the corpus of the New Testament.

As a mature teacher of theology Barth adopted the habit of having his students begin by reading Feuerbach. For in Feuerbach's accusation that talk about God is, in the end, only talk about humanity Barth identified the most complete and telling judgement on the nineteenth-century theological project. For all the varied emphases which may be identified, the chief characteristic of that project was in one way or another to seek to found religion, and the theological reflection which attaches to it, on some aspect of a human nature and experience *which belongs to history and may be understood within its terms*. We should note that the largely pre-critical appeal of Protestant Orthodoxy to possess an inspired and inerrant biblical text and of Roman Catholicism to an infallible human magisterium fared little better in this respect under Barth's scrutiny. In all these ways, Barth believed, theology had effectively already capitulated to Feuerbach's charge and had left itself no way of locating its final source in a God whose reality and activity utterly transcends the sphere of the human. It was in the task of reaffirming this essential difference that Barth immersed himself.

The only way to secure what must be secured here, Barth insisted from his earliest writings, was from the outset to be unequivocally clear about the proper logic of theological statements (i.e. their claim to speak *about God* and not about some dimension or feature of the human) and this in turn would mean being quite clear about the conditions under which alone such speech is possible. Christian faith and speech are essentially response and not essentially source. God produces faith, and not vice versa. It is this concern which lies behind

Barth's relentless appeal to the category of revelation and his particular way of interpreting what is involved in revelation. The account which he offers of the doctrine, therefore, is a properly post-critical version of it.

It is important to note that this issue of the vital differentiation of God from the world is not an issue about God's presence within or immanence to his creation, but rather about the mode of this presence. Barth, as is apparent from first to last in his writings (and not least his account of revelation) believed God to be radically present and active in the world through the agency of the Spirit; but, equally, to be so transcendent of the world which he fills with his presence that it would be mistaken and dangerous to point to any part of the created cosmos (physical or spiritual) and identify it with or as being 'like' God. The alternative to Romantic pantheism and the Liberal Protestant identification of 'divine' principles and virtues enfleshed in human nature and culture was certainly not Deism. Rather, it was a more subtle and theologically adequate differentiation of modes of divine presence and absence.

That one might or ought properly to think and speak of a perichoretic penetration of all created things by the God who calls them into existence and sustains them is not a problem for Barth. Transcendence is not a spatial or temporal category, but an attempt to articulate the wholly and holy otherness of the God in whom we live and move and have our being. But this general presence of God to the world, precisely because it is the presence of the transcendent and wholly other God, is not accessible to human knowing and experiencing. It is transcendent with respect to the objects of human experience and cognition. Barth had certainly learned from Kant that God cannot be treated as if he were just another phenomenon within the sphere of human knowing. Thus 'We have to admit that we cannot see, hear, feel, touch, or either inwardly or outwardly perceive the one who reveals himself, not because he is invisible or pure spirit, but because he is God . . . the subject that escapes our grasp, our attempt to make him an object (*Objekt*).'[12] Again, 'God does not belong to the world. Therefore he does not belong to the series of objects (*Gegenstände*) for which we have categories and words by

---

[12] *GD* p. 136; *UCR1* p.166.

means of which we draw the attention of others to them, and bring them into relation with them.' The implication of this is clear enough: in general terms 'it is impossible to speak of God, because he is not a "thing", either natural or spiritual'.[13] God, precisely because he is God, is not a possible object of human knowing or speech. This is not, we should reiterate, because God is remote or absent from the world, but because his mode of presence within it is one of radical transcendence.

Thus Barth eschews every form of what he refers to as 'Christian Cartesianism';[14] namely the assumption that the possibility of a human knowing and experiencing of God is one which either is or ever becomes 'man's own, a predicate of his existence, a content of his consciousness, his possession', that it rests at some point decisively upon something located within and accountable for in terms of the potentialities of natural and historical existence. To think thus is to have missed the point about God entirely. But, of course, in order to grasp the point about God, in order to grasp any point about God, there must already be some knowledge or experience of God actualized in the human sphere. This is the careful irony of Barth's insistence that knowledge of God is impossible: we can only know that it is (ordinarily) impossible because in actual fact the possibility of it has (surprisingly and extraordinarily) been established and realized. This is no a priori anthropological analysis, then, but an a posteriori reflection on the implications of the fact that and the way in which God has actually made himself known.

For Barth knowledge of God is both impossible and possible for particular human beings; but the impossibility and possibility do not exist on the same level. In general terms, and in terms of natural human capacities, knowledge of God is wholly impossible; yet God's own capacities transcend and bracket this truth without invalidating or even modifying it, calling forth faith and acknowledgement from the side of the particular creature in an event every bit as miraculous as the virgin conception and the resurrection with which Barth repeatedly compares it.[15] Should the miracle, the

---

[13] *CD* 1/2, pp. 750, 839.
[14] *CD* 1/1, pp. 214, 224.
[15] *CD* 1/1, p. 238; 1/2, p. 246.

enabling, the determination of our existence in the creation of faith cease from God's side, then the truth of our natural incapacity would remain unscathed. Faith and obedience, which are an integral part of what Barth intends by the word 'revelation', are the granting by the Spirit of a 'capacity of the incapable', a capacity called into being *ex nihilo* and held in being by God in accordance with his own choosing.

3. Crossing the boundary? Epistemic and hypostatic union

The 'radical dedivinization (*radikale Entgötterung*) of the world, of nature, of history'[16] which Barth commends is thus not at odds with the claim that God may be and is actually known and experienced in the world, but is in fact established by this claim:

> Revelation and it alone really and finally separates God and man by bringing them together. For by bringing them together it informs man about God and about himself . . . it tells him that this God (no other) is free for this man (no other) . . . The man who listens here, sees himself standing at the boundary where all is at an end . . . The revelation that crosses this boundary, and the togetherness of God and man which takes place in revelation in spite of this boundary, make the boundary visible to him in an unprecedented way.[17]

What is at issue, then, is not the *fact* of God's knowable presence and activity in history, but the question of the *mode* of this presence. And here, Barth is quite clear, we have to do with a distinct mode of presence which is not general but specific, not available to all everywhere and always, but only to some in particular times and places. 'Always in all circumstances the Word of God is reality in our reality *suo modo, sua libertate, sua misericordia.* Consequently it is present and ascertainable only contingently – again, *suo modo.*'[18] The revealing

---

[16] *GD* p. 144; *UCR1* p 177.
[17] *CD* 1/2, p. 29.
[18] *CD* 1/1, p. 158.

presence of God in the world in the mode of his Word is, in other words, a matter and a function of God's election, a matter of contingency at both the divine and the human levels.[19] Thus revelation as such is 'not a condition (*ein Zustand*), not an opening through which any Tom, Dick or Harry may look into heaven, but a happening (*ein Geschehen*)'.[20] God does not render himself into the epistemic custody or control of humanity in general. Indeed, even in the case of those to whom he *does* reveal himself God does not do this, but remains from first to last the *Subjekt* as well as the *Objekt* in the knowing relation which is established. His mode of presence, Barth constantly insists, is never direct but always indirect.[21] It is a presence which is paradoxically both immediate and mediated, and in which God is both known and yet remains hidden in his proper transcendence. We must not misunderstand the mode of his presence. There is, at the level of the flesh, no fixed and unambiguous *Offenbarheit* to which the few any more than the many may turn and lay claim.

From the first edition of *Der Römerbrief* (1919) onwards a singular concern may be identified in Barth's writing on the theme of revelation: namely, to give an account of the reality of this happening or event in which the proper (and vital) distinction between God and the world is maintained at every point. God is known in the midst of historical existence. That, as we have seen, is the miracle. But in the midst of this miracle God remains the one who is wholly other than us, and we, for our part, remain human.[22] The radical boundary between God's existence and ours, between the uncreated Lord and the creature is, that is to say, in some sense transcended in the event of knowing, yet without any concomitant loss or compromising of either God's identity or ours. Furthermore, the one who does not and could never belong to the world of 'objects' locates himself within that world, giving himself over to us as an *Objekt* of our knowing, yet doing so (crucially) in such a manner that he remains in control (*das Subjekt*) of this knowing from first to last. How, then,

---

[19] See *GD* p. 444.

[20] *GD* p. 366; *UCR2* p. 66.

[21] *GD* p. 151.

[22] See, e.g., 'The Preface to the Second Edition', in *The Epistle to the Romans* (Oxford: OUP, 1933), pp. 10f.

are we to think of this? How can it be possible for God genuinely to be known in the world without yet being *of* the world? What must happen in order for this to be possible?

The answer to these questions, Barth realized, lay somehow in the christological insistence that in Jesus God himself has 'taken flesh' and entered into the sphere of creaturely existence which is also the sphere of human knowing. The boundary which separates God's existence from ours may ordinarily be an absolute barrier to our knowing God, but it is no obstacle to God himself in his freedom and his desire to cross the line and make himself known to us.[23] For this to be possible he must assume a knowable form, and this he has done in Jesus Christ. God has entered the world of our conceptuality,[24] become an object of our knowing.[25] God, in other words, has become a part of the world of phenomena within which human knowledge ordinarily arises. Thus Barth inquires, 'What if God' (the one who as such even in his immanence within the world can never ordinarily be an object of human knowing) 'be so much God that without ceasing to be God he can also be, and is willing to be, not God as well. What if he were to come down from his unsearchable height and become something different. What if he, the immutable subject, were to make himself an object (*sich selbst zum Objekt machte*)'?[26] In this case God would be present in the world in a new and distinctive way, and in such a way as to be accessible to ordinary human modes of perception and knowing. It is in this sense that the incarnation is the primary condition for the objective possibility of God's self-revelation in the world. The Word has 'become flesh'.

Yet this unqualified profession of divine inhomination raises more questions than it answers, and Barth was well aware of the convoluted history of its interpretation, not least in ways which would betray rather than secure the points he deemed to be so vital to a healthy reorientation of theology in the modern period. Specifically, there are ways of thinking about the *Menschwerdung*

---

[23] *CD* 1/2, p. 31.
[24] *GD* p. 359.
[25] ibid. p. 329.
[26] *GD* p. 136; *UCR 1* p. 166.

Gottes in the modern period which amount in practice to a mild monophysitism, and thereby compromise all that Barth was seeking to safeguard. To begin with (and arguably most seriously) such monophysite trends put at risk the boundary between God and creation itself, a boundary which Barth insists is reinforced rather than transgressed in the crossing of it from above by the Word. They risk the location of 'revelation' as such (and thereby the ultimate basis and source for human talk about God) within the sphere of history and the human, and thus hand Feuerbach the keys to the kingdom. They risk the loss of faith's and theology's proper nature and object (namely, a sharing in communion with God himself) and settle instead for a two-dimensional 'knowing' which terminates at the level of familiarity with a figure in history or a character in a story. In Barth's own terms, by mistaking the veil of the flesh for that which it veils, such approaches fail to inquire into what really matters, and shut themselves off from the possibility of the veil becoming an open door. Finally, by thinking of revelation in terms of a revealedness at the level of the flesh, such monophysitisms fail to account for the particularity of revelation as a function of divine election, and for the activity of the Spirit in the creation of faith and obedient response to the divine Word. Thus the bare assertion that God has taken flesh and entered our world as a human being is necessary but crudely insufficient to account for the actual mode of God's revelatory presence and activity. The nature and implications of this 'assumption' and 'becoming' would, Barth perceived, need to be pinned down much more precisely.

As early as the 1924 Göttingen lectures in dogmatics[27] Barth came to see that this modern set of theological problems had its ancient counterpart, and that the classical doctrine of hypostatic union espoused at the Council of Chalcedon in AD 451 offered resources to enable him to make sense of the peculiar claim that in Jesus God 'becomes not-God as well' and, through this 'secondary objectivity' and the creation of faith by the Spirit gives himself to be known by men and women of his choosing. The precise function of the 'two natures' doctrine (in the incarnation there is one *hypostasis* to be

---

[27] For a discussion of the earlier writings see B.L. McCormack *Karl Barth's Critically Realistic Dialectical Theology* (Oxford: OUP, 1995), esp. 130f. and 207f.

discerned subsisting in two distinct 'natures') was to insist on the personal presence of God in a particular human life while yet differentiating the content of that life at every point from God's own existence as God. Within this context the term *hypostasis* (the rendering of which into Latin as *persona* and subsequently the English 'person' is only partially helpful depending on the precise connotations of its particular use) serves as a transcendental category. It is deliberately differentiated from the category 'nature'. In other words, *hypostasis* is not a predicate of nature, either God's or ours. Rather it is, in Rowan Williams' words, a category referring to 'a subject beyond all its predicates, . . . the unique ground of the unity of its predicates, or, as you might say, the "terminus" of its predicates.'[28] *Hypostasis* is not something which someone (God, Jesus or us) *has*; it is precisely the grammatical subject (as we might say) who *has*, possesses or is characterized by the various predicates of the relevant 'nature' (including, we should note, personality, mind, and consciousness with which the category is frequently confused, as in the numerous ill-targeted objections so often found in contemporary christological works against the category *anhypostasia*).

We can see how this finely tuned categorial distinction suited Barth's purposes perfectly. God becomes the man Jesus; yet this becoming entails the addition of a human level of existence ('nature') to who and what God eternally is, an existence which thus remains logically distinct at every point from his divine 'nature'. The logic of divine becoming in the incarnation is a logic of addition (that is, the addition of humanity) to God's eternal existence, and does not entail the predication of either loss or change to God's nature as Creator. Thus the mode of God's presence in the world in incarnation and revelation is certainly not one which renders God as such available for inspection or apprehension by human knowers. God enters the world and is present within it hypostatically while yet remaining utterly distinct from it by nature. In apprehending the man Jesus, we do not as such and without further ado lay hold of God. We are, after all, beholding God's *humanity* which serves, as Barth repeatedly reminds us, as

---

[28] R.D. Williams, 'Person and "Personality" in Christology', in *Downside Review* 94 (1976), p. 255.

much to veil God (*kata physin*) as to render the possibility of his
knowability (*kat' hypostasin*) in the world.

To repeat, then: since *hypostasis* is a transcendental category
rather than a predicate of either divine or human natures as such
there is nothing of God's *nature* present phenomenally. It is not
'God' as such, but rather God as/having become 'not-God'
who/which is present in the world and available to the normal
channels of knowing. God is both present and yet hidden in the
flesh of Christ. Revelation is both immediate and mediated, for
while God is truly 'in Christ' God also transcends and does not
'become' the *humanitas Christi* (which is yet also the *humanitas Dei*).
The inhomination of God is thus not itself revelation, according to
Barth, but simply the condition for the objective possibility of revelation. To be sure: revelation needs a physical event, a genuine
presence of God in the sphere of phenomena; but revelation itself is
and must be much more than an epistemic event at this level, for
revelation is a knowing of God himself in his nature as God, and the
God who is known transcends his own humanity.[29]

The self-objectification of God for our sakes in Jesus Christ,
therefore, is not the terminus but only the starting point and the
vital means for God's self-disclosure to his creatures. In order for
this same human form to become transparent with respect to God's
own being there must be a corresponding reception, hearing and
response within the human sphere.[30] Faith and obedience, as the
form of all true human knowing of God are a gift bestowed by God
in the event of revelation itself. Here too, though, we are dealing
not with a permanently bestowed condition of receptivity and
response, but with a capacity created in the happening of divine
self-giving. God, through the creative agency of the Spirit, draws us
into communion with himself, and in doing so lifts us up beyond
the limits of our own natural capacity into the self-transcending circle of the knowledge of God. Faith, that is to say, as and when it
arises, is not a capacity which we bring to and with which we meet
and respond to God's revelation: faith is itself the form which that
revelation assumes within the reality of historical existence. No

---

[29] *CD* 1/1, p. 133.
[30] *GD* p. 168; *CD* 1/2, p. 204.

satisfactory account can be given of its possibility in purely human or historical terms. Apart from God's creative and redemptive act it has no existence. It is, we might say, anhypostatic, and enhypostatic in God's revelatory drawing of people to himself.

In the event of revelation, therefore, the proper boundary between uncreated and created, infinite and finite, eternal and temporal, God and humanity, is crossed from both sides. In the words of a Scottish liturgy '[God] has made his home with us that we might for ever dwell in him.' But the nature of God's incarnate presence among us and of our corresponding being in his presence is one in which the boundary itself is not transgressed or called into question. God's becoming is not to be identified at the level of nature but is hypostatic. Correspondingly, our knowing, which begins with the humanity of God in Christ, is indirect and mediated, but is one in which we are enabled to transcend the natural limits of our knowing by an act of the Creator Spirit from above, and are opened up to commune with God himself. In doing so we are not deified or supernaturalized, but our humanity is drawn into a creaturely correspondence with the reality of God. Revelation is thus not a phenomenon within the world, but an event, happening or action in which, through our knowing of certain this-worldly realities, we are drawn into a relationship with a reality lying beyond this world altogether.

4. Analogy, correspondence and the historicity of revelation

In this section we effectively return to the question with which we began, namely, does the humanity of Jesus really matter in the event of revelation in anything more than the purely formal sense that we have identified? Given that we need a phenomenal stepping stone in order to make cognitive contact with the God whose reality utterly transcends the realm of phenomena, that is to say, does the actual shape or content of the phenomenon itself matter very much? Or can Christian faith, to which in some sense the figure of Jesus must be deemed central, rest easy where questions about what this Jesus was actually like, what he did and said, what happened to him and so on, are concerned? Approaching the same problem from a different angle, we might inquire whether, in order to support a christology at all, God's presence in Jesus must not make (and be seen to make) some empirically identifiable difference at the level of the flesh. This is not at all the same thing as saying that 'revelation' could be read off from his facial expression or was contained in his teaching and actions: it is simply to suggest that the most likely starting point for christology (as the gospels themselves indicate) was a question about Jesus, a question which arose naturally enough from simply having been in his presence or even hearing the stories told about him by those who had.

This, it must be admitted, is where the two-natures doctrine is vulnerable if it be adopted as a satisfactory christological framework in and of itself. In itself it does not offer any clear framework for identifying and evaluating what in positive terms it might mean for the flesh that here God is in it. This, of course, was not its purpose. It was purely a formula of careful analytic differentiation, intended to ascribe christological statements to the relevant level of discourse: statements about Jesus' humanity on the one hand, and those pertaining to him as God on the other, holding on meanwhile to the principle of hypostatic identity which holds both levels inseparably together. In order to serve this purpose adequately, though, its interest in the humanity of Jesus tends ever towards the general and the shared, that 'humanity' which all humans indwell rather than the particular human character of the man from Nazareth. Furthermore, in its constant careful segregation of Jesus' 'human' from his 'divine' predicates this doctrine shifts attention away from the role of the humanity of Jesus in revealing God to us. For, if everything that may be said of the man Jesus can and must properly be ascribed to the category of his human nature, and as such is radically differentiated from what is true of him 'as God', then there is no very strong basis for supposing what we see in Jesus' character and actions as a man is also to be true, in some sense, of God, or to be a reflection or function of his secret divine identity (the sort of thing which is true of God when God is 'enfleshed'). Whether we point to Jesus' goodness, his love, his table-fellowship with sinners, his hunger, his fear, his suffering or whatever, the two natures scheme itself furnishes no basis for assuming or arguing that some (and not others) of these human characteristics are directly related to the fact of his being 'God with us'. In each case the response must be strictly the same – these things are true of him *humanly*, and do not pertain to his existence as God. This is a response which, taken alone, rather short-circuits the revelatory role of his humanity as such.

As we have seen, Barth does not think of revelation as such as in any way containable within the humanity of Jesus; yet we may still ask whether the suitability of that humanity to refer us beyond itself in the event of revelation is related in any way to its particular shape? Flesh and blood may not reveal God to us in and of themselves; but is the relation between the flesh and blood which God actually assumes and the purpose for which he assumes it arbitrary? If God is so wholly other and there is no natural analogy between him and anything at the level of the human, is it anything more than a matter of sheer caprice for God to 'reveal' himself in the man Jesus rather than, say, Ivan the Terrible or a dead dog? If we suppose it to be so, then, of course, the question of what Jesus was really like ceases to be of any serious significance and (in a way reminiscent of Bultmann's appeal to the singular moment of the cross) we are liberated to let the fires of history burn: all that is needed is the bare assertion that God entered hypostatically into union with our humanity once (a claim famously, and in terms of its subsequent interpretation unfortunately, made by Kierkegaard).

There are elements in what Barth has to say on this theme which certainly lean in this direction. Thus, for example, he insists that the form of revelation is related to its content not simply by a relationship of difference or otherness but actually by contradiction.[31] Elsewhere he is less vigorous in his efforts to overthrow the idea that knowledge of God's nature could be translated into flesh and blood terms by virtue of a general *analogia entis*, and alludes simply to the essential ordinariness of Jesus as a man among men. The alternative suggestion is delightfully captured in a claim in one of Gerard Manley Hopkins' sermons that, since we know that God is beautiful, Jesus himself must have been the incarnation of physical beauty: 'Moderately tall, well-built and slender in frame, his features straight and beautiful, his hair inclining to auburn, parted in the midst, curling and clustering about the ears and

---

[31] *CD* 1/1, p. 166.

neck.'[32] Barth, who generally preferred to take his cue from Isaiah's 'he had . . . nothing in his appearance that we should desire him', was quite clear that this was not what it meant to claim that 'the fulness of the Godhead dwelt in him bodily'.

Yet while Barth demurred on every possible occasion from what he took to be a theologically unhealthy interest in and focus upon the humanity of Jesus as such, and even once insisted that theology must finally dare not to be too christocentric (*etwas weniger christozentrisch*[33]) since it is with God and not with Jesus that it is finally concerned, he nonetheless also eschewed any form of docetic lack of interest in Jesus, his character, teaching, actions and passion. Christian thought about God, he insists, and much else besides must be decisively shaped by what it finds at this point, rather than importing preconceived notions from elsewhere.[34] Similarly, while he insists that revelation is an event, a happening, and not a body of truths or principles which may be codified and systematically applied (in philosopher John Macmurray's terms it is a matter of personal rather than abstractive knowledge), nonetheless Barth is absolutely clear that there is a vital conceptual and verbal component in revelation, and he has no time at all for the sort of nebulous, non-cognitive encounter with infinity much beloved of post-Schleiermacherian trends in theology. The following citation suffices to make the point:

> Faith and obedience vis-à-vis revelation stand face to face first of all with this historical, self-explicating revelation, or else they do not stand before revelation. It would be a comfortable conjuring away of the offence but no more and no less than the conjuring away of revelation itself, if we were to say that we will cling to God himself but will have nothing whatever to do with all the astonishing things that are linked to our being able to cling to God himself. Faith means not only believing in God but also believing in this and that. To put it with all the offence that it involves, it means believing in the trinity, or in the

[32] See on this Richard Harries, *Art and the Beauty of God* (London: Mowbray, 1993), pp. 6–7.
[33] *GD* p. 91; *UCR1* p. 110.
[34] *CD* 1/2, p. 17.

NT miracles, or in the virgin birth. And obedience means not only uniting our own wills with God's but, for example, keeping the ten commandments.[35]

And so it continues. It is not, then, that the objective form in which revelation comes to us is unimportant but simply that it is not suffi- cient and is not in itself the object of our knowing of God, but merely its creaturely and phenomenal vehicle. And from the above and many other similar passages it is clear that the particular content of this divine self-objectification is non-negotiable. Talk about God is demanded of us by God's address in Christ and the Spirit, and the terms in which we are to engage in *Nachdenken* and *Nachreden* are mapped out for us by a consideration of the man Jesus within his proper context in the history of Israel. With specific reference to Jesus himself, while Barth will have nothing to do with any idealiz- ing of his humanity, he is also content to admit that there is that about it which reflects the unique presence of God which is its secret. Thus, for example, he says:

> In becoming the same as we are, the Son of God is the same in quite a different way from us; in other words, in our human being what we do is omitted, and what we omit is done. This Man would not be God's revelation to us, God's reconciliation with us, if He were not, as true Man, the true, unchangeable, perfect God Himself . . . How can God sin, deny Himself to Himself, be against Himself as God? . . . Therefore in our state and condition He does not do what underlies and produces that state and condition, or what we in that state and condition continually do. Our unholy human existence, assumed and adopted by the Word of God, is a hallowed and therefore a sinless human existence.[36]

So, then, there is little mileage in maintaining that the enfleshing of the Logos makes little or no identifiable difference to the flesh itself in Barth's christology. It clearly does. But it is important to grasp the *nature* and the *source* of the difference which it makes.

---

[35] *GD* pp. 192–193.
[36] *CD* 1/2, pp. 155–156.

Jesus' humanity is not different because it is (to use a misleading phrase) 'the incarnation of God', that is to say, the rendering or replication of what God is, scaled down conveniently to the dimensions of our historical existence. To think thus, Barth supposes, is to risk obscuring the essential otherness of God and to encourage the sort of speculative scaling of the heights of heaven rooted in a general 'analogy of being' which he so disdains. In *this* sense, he insists, *finitum non capax infiniti*. The presence of God in Christ is under the mode of the hypostatic becoming of the Word who becomes, precisely, not-God, and not 'micro-God'. What we do *not* have in the *humanitas Christi*, therefore, is a representation or icon of the divine *ousia* under the form of human *ousia*. Rather, what we have is the hypostatic presence of God among us humanly, and in such a way as to reconcile our fallen and estranged flesh to God, renewing and transforming the flesh until it corresponds in terms proper to its own 'nature' to who and what God is in his. This, then, is the primary reason for Jesus' humanity being essentially other than ours: not that it is a snapshot of God, and made-over to 'look like' God; but rather that it is the firstfruits of a new, redeemed humanity in correspondence with God. When God speaks his Word into the realm of flesh, we might say, it results not in an echo, but precisely in a reply, a response from the side of the creature to the Creator's call. In other words, attention must be granted here in christology to the enhypostatic as well as the anhypostasic aspect of incarnation. The eternal Word of God becomes the particular man Jesus, born of Mary and Joseph; and it is precisely in his particularity and not in spite of it that his universal significance, his concrete fulfilling of the covenant between God and humankind, is to be identified. It is precisely here that the particularity of Jesus' humanity as reflected in the Gospel stories of his life and ministry can and must be accommodated, therefore; for we cannot begin to answer the question 'What does it mean to be the man who corresponds to God, who fulfils the covenant from the human side?' by speaking in general terms (in terms of the general category 'human nature') but only by retelling those same gospel stories, making sense of them out of their Old Testament background, considering the ways in which Jesus lived, the particular things which he did and said, and allowing these to issue their own very particular challenge to us as their outlines overlap, cross and conflict with the patterns of our own particular lives.

It must be admitted that Barth's christology suffers from a relative lack of development in this respect. For reasons having to do
largely with his absolute determination to avoid all forms of
subordinationism he fails to develop the model of divine self-
communication as inherently relational. A relationality which in
Jesus embraces humanity into the network of its own rich dynamics, and witnesses God not just as a human *speaker* of the Word, but
also as its *hearer* and *respondent* from the human side. Although the
basic milieu for nurturing such an Antiochene emphasis are clearly
all present in Barth's theology (he repeatedly affirms the radical
assumption by God of a 'complete' humanity even in its 'fallen' state
and, as we have already seen, tends towards an insistence on the
relation of radical otherness between the two 'natures' of Christ) his
own inclinations at this point are nonetheless finally in an Alexan-
drian direction, ever insisting on the hypostatic identity between
Jesus and God and so stressing the essential *Einigkeit* within the
Dreieinigkeit Gottes that it is hard for him to accommodate any
developed focus on Jesus as a person who is a respondent to the
Father and the Spirit.[37]

To return to our main point: if we ask on what basis Jesus'
humanity is able to serve as a fit vehicle or medium of God's
self-disclosure then, following Barth, we must say several things:
First, that like all flesh in the first instance and in and of itself it has
no capacity to do so at all. It is only as God is present to and active
within it not just hypostatically as the Word but also as the
indwelling Spirit who creates human response, that it acquires any
such capacity, being lifted up 'from above' to a self-transcending
correspondence to God's own being and activity. Thus it is not
because it is 'super-natural' or in some sense 'like God', but in so
far as Jesus' is a truly natural human existence which corresponds to
the nature and will and calling of the God who is wholly other
than it *even in this correspondence*, that the flesh of Christ functions in
a revelatory (or perhaps proto-revelatory) way. Of course we may
infer certain things about God on the basis of what we apprehend

---

[37] This criticism is made and substantiated by Alan Torrance. See A.J.
Torrance, *Persons in Communion: An Essay on Trinitarian Description and
Human Participation with Special Reference to Volume One of Karl Barth's
Church Dogmatics* (Edinburgh: T. & T. Clark, 1996), pp. 100–119.

at the level of his humanity: that he is capable of becoming what he becomes (*Infinitum capax finiti*) and that he wills to become this for our sakes. This in itself suggests certain things about God's character, things which we can only make sense of in terms of human characteristics such as love, faithfulness and so on. Furthermore, within the assumption by the Son and adaptation by the Spirit of our sinful humanity into faithful correspondence with God, we may consider that we have reason to suppose certain analogies between Jesus' human character and his character as God to exist. When Jesus forgives and accepts sinners and outcasts, for example, we may reckon that this tells us something of who God is and what God is like, and that this is part of the purpose of God's becoming human at all. And, so long as we do not slide into any easy generalization of such particular claims (so that Jesus' hunger and tiredness lead us equally to predicate these traits of God) we may be right to suppose this. But the extraordinary human love, faithfulness, forgiveness and so on of Jesus do not 'show us' God directly: rather they point beyond themselves to the reality of God, and the nature of this 'pointing beyond', and the precise points at which it does and does not occur, are not knowable in isolation from the relationship of faith in which we are properly related to God himself. The particular form of Jesus' humanity as 'sanctified flesh' is vital in this task; but it is very definitely penultimate rather than ultimate.

A similar logic can and must be applied, of course, to the subsequent adaptation and determination of those to whom God speaks and discloses himself through this self-objectifying economy. Here, too, there is both a fully human and a fully divine presence and activity to be discerned. There is, that is to say, a union and mutual indwelling of human and divine in the event of faith,[38] a union not now of natures at all but of activity. Here, there is no hypostatic assumption by the Word of the flesh. The relevant flesh here, that is to say, is ours and not his. But the Spirit is present and active from first to last in our flesh, taking *our* broken, fallen and alienated humanity and lifting it up way beyond any 'natural' capacity which it might be supposed to have and rendering it *capax infiniti*. This capacity never belongs to us as such: rather it is the

---

[38] *CD* 1/1, p. 242.

fruit of (a function of) a relationship in which we are held from above by the Spirit from moment to moment.

This leads on to a vital point about the way in which our language and conceptuality functions in revelation (for language and conceptuality there must be, as we have seen). The substance or reality of what we 'know' as we commune with God himself cannot be captured or communicated adequately in language itself. Another way of putting this formally is to say that the *modus significandi* of our analogical predication can never be specified, a fact of which Aquinas, it must be said, was fully aware. Were it able to be specified, then the analogy would not be necessary in the first place. Yet speak of this reality we can and must, and in doing so Barth is clear that we are constrained by faithfulness to the conceptual tools furnished in God's self-objectifying in Christ. In other words, we allow the story of Jesus and its wider context in the story of Israel to shape the pattern of our thinking, speaking and testifying. But in doing so we are constantly aware that our words are merely 'knocking at the gates' of the truth which we seek to express.[39] The dialectic between God's existence and ours (including our language and its ordinary semantic range) remains and is never resolved. That our thinking and speaking should, as it were, overreach itself or transcend its natural range and in some indefinable sense refer appropriately to God, this again is entirely a matter of God's adoption and adaptation of that which pertains to the flesh. In the event of revelation, the moment in which the veil of the flesh is rendered transparent, we 'know' how our language refers because we are in relation with that to which it refers (a relation which, contrary to much post-Wittgensteinian analysis, is not entirely mediated by language; we frequently know more than we can say). That we cannot say it is part of what it means to recognize that God remains mysterious and wholly other, a fact which becomes more and not less apparent as we are drawn closer to him.

All this, then, is the force of the so-called analogy of faith of which Barth was so fond of speaking. In the event of God's own personal self-disclosure both the media and the recipients of that disclosure are lifted up beyond the limits of their natural capacities

---

[39] *GD* p. 374.

and established within an epistemic triangulation the third term in which is God himself. Thereby God is truly known and may properly be spoken of. But in the knowing God remains mysterious: the mystery is never fathomed but rather indwelt.

5. Was God in Christ?

So, was God 'in' Christ? Is revelation 'historical' in any sense? Does the castle ever rest on *terra firma*, or remain suspended tantalizingly but largely irrelevantly in the clouds? What we have seen is that, for Barth, revelation is not a thing, a condition or an aspect of some nature, but rather a relationship between the reality of God and our created world. As such 'revelation' can and could never be apprehended or laid hold of at the level of nature or history although, as we have seen, it certainly is apprehended from within nature and history (where else could it be if it is actually to reveal anything to anyone?). The attempt to lay hold of revelation 'in' the phenomena of fleshly existence is, to use one of Barth's own images, like trying to scoop the moon's reflection from the surface of a pond.[40] It is to mistake the historical coordinates of revelation with a relation or event which embraces and yet necessarily transcends them. God 'touches' history and the flesh in the hypostatic becoming of the Word and the creative indwelling of the Spirit; but never *kata physin*. There is, we might say, no physical contact, but a divine relating to us which is proper to the integrity of God's own nature and which creates, calls into being *ex nihilo*, a reciprocal relating from our side. So revelation is historical in the sense that it happens within history, embracing and transforming particular features of created, fleshly existence. But it is *not* historical in the sense that its happening can be accounted for in terms of the normal cause and effect processes of nature and history. That it happens at all is pure miracle. It is in the world but not of it. Apart from God's action 'from above' it has no being, no independent existence or reality. As a reality in the world, therefore, it is, to use a christological metaphor, anhypostatic. Were it not so, it would

---

[40] *CD* 1/1, p. 216.

not really *be* revelation at all; we would not be knowing God but one of the many surrogates which, as Feuerbach saw, humans are prone to gather or fashion from the world of objects and to throw up towards the clouds from below to see which, if any, will stick. The loss of any genuine sense of transcendence (and thus of a proper understanding of immanence) in much contemporary theology suggests that the problems which Barth faced are just as live at the end of the twentieth century as they were at its outset, and that the emphases which he adopted and the categories upon which he drew in facing these problems may well be worthy of further careful consideration.

2

The Word, the Words and the Witness: Proclamation as Divine and Human Reality

Karl Barth's entire theological project might legitimately be described as a 'theology of proclamation'. The assumption upon which it is predicated and with which Barth concerns himself as (he insists) the only legitimate starting point for truly *theological* activity, is the claim made by faith that God has spoken, that he has proclaimed his Word to humankind, that he has revealed himself. This divine speaking occurs, according to Barth, in the enhumanization of God's own Word as the man Jesus of Nazareth, in the prophetic and apostolic testimony to this in Scripture, and in the preaching of the church. This threefold exposition of the doctrine of the Word of God is informed by and developed in terms of both trinitarian and incarnational analogies and insights. In each of the three forms of God's Word there is a paradox and scandal of identity between the divine and the human to be grasped. The relationships between these three, and the peculiar duality in unity which each manifests, will be explored in this chapter in relation to Barth's characteristic understanding of revelation as event.

1. The significance of proclamation in Barth's theology

As we have already seen, Barth sets himself from the outset firmly against all accounts of Christian knowledge of God which trace the proper basis of that knowledge to some inherent capacity for

the divine, sense of absolute dependence, experience of the ultimate or the numinous, or whatever. Such accounts of the matter,
he insists, cannot finally avoid capitulating to the accusation of
Feuerbach that talk about God is in the end only talk about humanity. To seek to found talk about God, as much nineteenth-century
theology did, by pointing to the possibility and actuality of such
anthropological phenomena was to invite the reduction of theological assertions to anthropological ones. It was to focus in the wrong
place, to become preoccupied with the human organ of response
rather than that objective reality which stimulates it. Christian talk
about God is no more intended to be talk about a certain variety of
religious or spiritual experience than talk about a glorious sunset is
intended to be an indirect way of speaking about a complex chemi-
cal and physiological process taking place in our eyes, our optic
nerves and our brain, or talk about the feel of polished wood an
indirect way of speaking about the activity of the nerve endings in
our fingers. Both levels of discourse may be appropriate. But in the
first our intention in speaking is to refer to the reality beyond
the experience, that which provokes or evokes the experience, and
not the experience itself.

'God has turned to us', Barth writes, 'in such a way that we can
answer only with faith. We may not give this answer, but when we
do it is an answer to God, an answer to this confidential turning
and address of his. The address is not an expression of faith. Faith, if
it is faith, finds its generative basis in it.'[1] Thus the proper basis of
Christian talk about God, of knowledge of God, is precisely this
unexpected and undeserved address of God: God's own proclamation to humanity, his speaking of the divine Word. And the proper
form of all theological endeavour is that of response. Christian
preachers, says Barth, dare to speak about God. But they can do so
only on the presupposition that God himself has spoken first, that
he has addressed human beings, has addressed them as human subjects, and that his address compels them also to speak. Otherwise
their speech would be the ultimate presumption.

The point which Barth makes here is not concerned simply with
the objective reference of theological statements, but, more

---

[1] *GD*, p.12.

strongly still, with the epistemic incapacity of humans in and of themselves to know or to speak of the particular object concerned, and the gracious initiative of God which alone bridges this gap by a supreme atoning and revelatory self-giving in the redemptive economy of the Son and Spirit together. 'Only revelation in the strict sense,' Barth urges, 'overcomes the dilemma which haunts all religious philosophy, namely, that the object escapes or transcends the subject. Revelation means the knowledge of God through God and from God. It means that the object becomes the subject. It is not our own work if we receive God's address, if we know God in faith. It is God's work in us.'[2]

When God reveals himself, furthermore, it is precisely in the form of Word, that is to say with attendant cognitive and linguistic form and content, and not via some mysterious and nebulous feeling or sense of ultimacy. In this event of revelation God himself is both the object of our knowing, and yet mysteriously the subject. He is the one who initiates and brings to completion the act of knowing by, on the one hand, positing himself objectively to be known, and on the other, entering into us as the Holy Spirit and creating the faith which responds appropriately to this self-manifestation. Thus (and it is vital that we bear this point in mind throughout what follows) the term revelation refers *not to the objective self-manifestation alone, but equally to the act of faith in which it is heard and received and obeyed*. Revelation for Barth, as Christina Baxter has put it, 'straddles objectivity and subjectivity, and is never completed or finished, for the relationship between God who is giving Himself to be known, and the "human subject" who is receiving the capacity to know God is a continuing relationship: it has to be "new every morning" or it is not knowledge of God at all.'[3]

That this happens, that God's Word is heard, rests, therefore, not in the realms of human capability or responsibility, but utterly with God in his sovereign freedom. But *happen* is precisely what it does. Revelation, the Word of God, is an event in which actual humans find themselves drawn into a circle of knowing in which

[2] Ibid. p. 61.

[3] Christina Baxter, 'The Nature and Place of Scripture in the Church Dogmatics', in John Thompson (ed.), *Theology Beyond Christendom* (Allison Park, PA: Pickwick Publications, 1986), p. 35.

they are given to share God's own knowledge of himself. As such it can in no way be abstracted from this happening and frozen or codified, any more than it can be provoked or coerced by human effort. As event or happening we can no more hold on to it or recreate it than we can cause it. We can only live in faith, recollecting that it has happened in the past, and trusting God's promise that it will happen in the future. We can even identify the places where it has happened and where we trust it will happen again. But we can no more confuse those places with the event itself than we would confuse an empty concert hall with the rapturous symphony which we heard performed there or the site of some long distant romantic encounter with the love which once infused it. To employ the word revelation to refer to any reality other than the dynamic happening itself is, for Barth, to confuse the issue, and to mistake purely human realities for that which is of God alone.

2. The threefold and twofold form of God's self proclamation

I want to turn now to consider the precise form which Barth understands the self-proclamation of God to have taken and to take. And I suggest that we can look at the matter through two specifically theological analogies, the relationship of which to the matter in hand is far from accidental – namely, the triunity of God as Father, Son and Holy Spirit, and the hypostatic union of human nature and the reality of God himself in the person of the Son or Word in the incarnation. Both of these represent patterns or figures which Barth himself employs in discussing this matter as early as *GD*.

For Barth the proclamation of God in which he speaks his Word to humans and reveals himself to them takes three basic forms which are yet mysteriously one Word. Each of these three forms, we should note, manifests a duality in unity, having both a fully human and a fully divine aspect, and united, more or less, by a radical becoming of God himself in which he takes on human form. The three forms are, of course, the man Jesus of Nazareth, the text of Scripture, and Christian preaching.

The way in which Barth speaks of the relationships pertaining between these three are at once complex and highly ambiguous, or perhaps we should say rather dialectical. He seems to speak in different places, and sometimes even in the same places, in ways which entail contradiction and self-referential incoherence. And yet when the substance of what he has to say is considered it becomes apparent that this same dialectical aspect is precisely parallel to that which is to be found in the theological speech of every age concerning the reality of Jesus Christ as the incarnate Son, and concerning the triune identity in distinction of God Father, Son and Holy Spirit. My contention, then, would be that in order to grasp the logic of Barth's thought concerning God's proclamation it is most helpfully approached via these perichoretic and incarnational patterns, carefully distinguishing the sense in which these various realities are one from the sense in which they are yet three distinct realities, and equally carefully differentiating their human and their divine aspects.

There is, Barth affirms, an important distinction to be drawn between the realities to which we have referred. Thus the preacher must not confuse himself and his words with those of the apostles and prophets, which are the source of and the authority for his preaching. Likewise the human words of Scripture are not to be confused with that historical self-manifestation of God in the human history of Jesus to which it is their self-declared and unremitting responsibility to point and direct the church. Here, then, there is both difference and order to be perceived. If we think in terms of the order of our knowing, then it is with preaching that the church must begin. We hear the gospel expounded or proclaimed from the pulpit, or in some other context. Behind such preaching lies the given text of Scripture with which the preacher must wrestle, and the meaning of which she must seek to unpack for her hearers. But the text is not, in this sense, the ultimate referent of her words. For there is another more ultimate authority to which Scripture itself points, which lies beyond its words, and which engendered and called forth those words of witness in the first place. This other reality is, of course, the event in which God acted decisively for our salvation in the life, death and resurrection of his Son Jesus Christ. It is this which is the real object of Christian preaching. Thus the ontic order, the order of being, is the precise reverse of the noetic. It begins with Christ whose saving economy in due course calls forth Scripture as a witness, and this in turn leads to the preaching ministry in the church. To fail to draw these careful distinctions and to maintain the relationships of order would be fatal for the church's life, for it might entail, for example, either an absolutizing of Scripture as the ultimate referent of preaching (in which case it would become opaque, rather than serving as the transparent witness to the risen Christ which it is intended to be), or else a failure by the preacher to stand under the authority of the apostles and prophets (to confuse his words with theirs), and thence, rather than an absolutizing, a *relativizing* of the biblical text.

On the other hand, however, Barth insists that these three forms of existence (modes of being?) of the divine proclamation are yet one perichoretic reality, namely, the Word of God, incarnate as the man Jesus Christ, and, we might legitimately say, incarnate (albeit in a distinct sense) in both the text of Scripture and the human verbiage of preaching. Viewed thus, he maintains, there can be no ascribing of a greater or lesser significance to any one over the others. Inasmuch as the same Word of God is present in each of the three there can be no question of making distinctions of value or importance, or of thinking of a gradual weakening or dilution of God's Word, supposing the order of being to reflect a hierarchy of power. For Barth Jesus Christ is God's Word, holy Scripture is God's Word, and the preaching of the church is God's Word. God speaks in each of these three places, and we cannot discern any greater or lesser among them in this respect. How, then, are we to understand this? Is the preaching of the church really to be placed on the same level as the man Jesus? Are the words of Paul and Isaiah, let alone the words which Christian preachers utter on a Sunday morning, really of equal standing and revelatory significance with the personal presence of God among us in Jesus himself? And if so, how are we to hold on to what Barth has already said concerning the need for a strict ordering of authority between the three?

The answer, I suggest, lies in the need to draw a careful distinction between the humanity of the three forms and what we might legitimately term their divinity. Each of the three forms has a human aspect: the particular human story of Jesus, the texts which the church acknowledges as Scripture, and the all too human words of the preacher. But in each case what must be recognized is that this human aspect as such, in and of itself, does not reveal God, but conceals him. There is nothing about this human being as such, nothing about these words as such, nothing about this preaching as such, which compels faith or reveals God in any straightforward or obvious manner. It is entirely possible for intelligent humans to see and hear these human realities and not to find themselves in the grip of a revelatory encounter. Every preacher knows that. Those who followed Jesus around Palestine knew it. In order for these human realities to reveal God, therefore, they must, as it were, be accompanied by or infused with something more, with an activity of God which employs them as the instruments and agents of his self-revealing activity. It is this and this alone which grants men and women the 'eyes to see and ears to hear' of which Jesus so often spoke. But this something, this presence of God is not to be confused with the human realities as such. The fathers of Chalcedon made that clear enough in the case of Jesus: in the incarnate union we have both fully human and fully divine reality in genuine union, but equally importantly, in genuine and continuing contradistinction. The humanity of Jesus does not become divine or even semi-divine. It comes to be the humanity of the Word. Likewise, for Barth, the words of Scripture and those of the preacher do not cease to be fully human, but enter into a union with the Word of God who speaks through them.

To return, then, to the dialectic stated above, what Barth is saying is that if we think of the *humanity* of these three forms of the Word of God there is an immediate need to draw a threefold distinction, and to impose a clear order of importance and function. There is first an important distinction to be drawn between Scripture and preaching. It has seemed good to God, Barth insists, to provide the church with an objective and abiding rule by which to measure its ongoing proclamation of God's Word, and this rule consists in the witness of Scripture. As a historically constituted and literary phenomenon Scripture has a permanence of form which enables it to stand identifiably over against and above the church, and thereby to act as an index or gauge of the church's faithfulness to the Word of God witnessed to within its pages. Thus Scripture constitutes an authority for the preacher: it stands in the place of Jesus himself, since we have no direct access to him either in his historic or his risen form, except as these are mediated to us by the text of Scripture. But an altogether more drastic distinction yet must be drawn which sets this first distinction in the shade. For between the humanity of Jesus Christ on the one hand, and the text and words of Scripture and preaching on the other, there is an absolute distinction. Barth expresses it thus: The man Jesus is the revelation of God himself. In this divine speaking there is no other subject but God involved. Jesus is the reality of God's revelation in history. But Scripture and preaching are not this reality as such. Considered as human realities they stand as witnesses to this revelation, and derive any meaning or authority which they have from their relationship to it. They are witnesses; Jesus is the one to whom they bear witness.

The point here is sharpened if we develop it in terms of the christological model. In Jesus Christ, God himself becomes a human person, identifies himself fully with this human life and history. Jesus' humanity, as the fathers put it, was anhypostatic, it had no prior or independent existence apart from the incarnation of the Son of God. Here, then, we have a simple and permanent relationship of personal identity between the Word and Jesus Christ. But it is not at all like this in the cases of Scripture and preaching. Here what we have are human realities which do have a prior and independent human existence and which the Word of God 'becomes' in the sense that he enters into union with them in the event of revelation. It is not a union of identity, but one of indwelling, and it is not permanent but temporary. In christological terms, we might say, the sort of relationship between the humanity and divinity of Scripture and preaching which Barth has in mind is more of a Nestorian union than a Chalcedonian one. This, it seems to me, is precisely why, when he is thinking of the human aspect of these things, Barth prefers the figure of John the Baptist to that of the humanity of Christ. John's role is to point away from himself to Christ and to bear witness to his hidden identity. Thus, I would contend, for Barth, Scripture and preaching considered in their human aspect act precisely as witnesses to God's revelation in Jesus Christ. The differences between them, however significant, are purely functional. Both constitute human talk about God, human witness to him, and as such are set decisively over against 'revelation itself', namely, the reality of Jesus Christ in his human and divine aspects.

When, though, we consider the *divine* aspect of these three forms of God's proclamation, then we must confess that all of them constitute God's own address. The same revelatory event happens, whether it happens in and through the flesh of Jesus, the text of Scripture or the words of the preacher. There are distinct modes of becoming involved: The flesh of Christ 'becomes' God's Word precisely because it is already God's Word, because the Word of God has become Jesus Christ; whereas the words of Scripture and of the preacher become God's Word because this same Word which was in Jesus Christ enters into a moral and temporary rather than a hypostatic and permanent union with them, but a real and revelatory union nonetheless. Thus, Barth affirms, 'holy Scripture is God's Word in exactly the same sense in which we have said this of the event of . . . proclamation,'[4] namely, that it becomes it through the miracle of God's willingness to become these words, to make his own Word known through them.

3. The scandal of identity

Grasping the nettle of the full humanity of the incarnate Word has always been the occasion for scandal and offence in the Christian church. This is so in christology, where there is the constant temptation to allow a subtle docetism to creep into our thinking about, for example, the limitations of Jesus' knowledge and understanding, or the genuine integrity and ferocity of his experiences of temptation. The same temptation arises in our understanding of Scripture where, it seems, for many Christians an acknowledgement of the mundaneness, the contingency, the ordinariness and maybe even the weakness and folly of the texts as they have been transmitted to us, and viewed in their purely human aspect, is just too much to take. And so we have the emergence and popularity of doctrines of the infallibility and even inerrancy of the text *as text* which, it may be argued, seek successfully to avert the offence, but in doing so, it can hardly be denied, elevate the text *even in its human aspect* way above the level of anything recognizable as human textuality.

We do not, of course, on the whole, have quite the same problem with the third form of God's self-proclamation – i.e. human preaching. Why not? Perhaps we should? For what we are forced to

---

[4] *CD* 1/1, p. 109.

reckon with here is an alleged Word of God which nonetheless is spoken through the limitedness, the weakness and even the *sinfulness* of a human agency. We cannot deny it. If there is not a sense of offence or scandal here then I suspect that it is because we do not have a high enough view of the preacher's task, a high enough 'christology of preaching' as it were, to *make* our own weakness and sinfulness and base fleshliness as preachers a cause of offence and scandal.

In practice what we often do is to bracket off two forms of the Word of God (Jesus himself and holy Scripture) from the other (preaching) which we think of perhaps as in some sense *less* fully identifiable with God's own Word. If we do so then, doubtless unconsciously, we risk a betrayal of the Reformed heritage. For while the Reformers with their so-called Scripture principle firmly identified the human text of the biblical writers as the Word of God, Barth suggests, they *no less surely* identified the human words of the preacher with this *same* Word, and in the same sense. Thus, for example, the words of Bullinger in the Second Helvetic Confession: 'The preaching of the Word of God *is* the Word of God.'

It is this small word, this '*is*' which, if we take it seriously, and if we face up to the full humanness of that to which it refers (the best and worst of Christian preaching), can only be the occasion of paradox, scandal and offence.

Barth, as we have seen, takes as his starting point this strong view of the *identity* of the text of Scripture and the words of Christian preachers with God's own Word. And for him there is a scandal, an offence not just in the case of preaching, but in the case of Scripture also. For, as we saw in the previous section, if he will have us draw a line between these three forms of God's Word then it is *not* between Jesus and Scripture on the one hand and preaching on the other. Rather, Jesus himself as the human form of God's personal (hypostatic) presence among us in history is decisively set apart from Scripture and preaching, both of which are to be understood as *witness* to that same historical and supra-historical reality.

So too for Barth the scandal and offence of identity in the case of Scripture is not 'How can this divine reality be thought of or treated in the same basic categories as purely human realities?' but, as in the case of preaching, 'How can this weak, sinful and errant human reality be identified with God's Word?' Whereas all too often we seek to remove the cause of offence, either (in the case of Scripture) by qualifying the humanity of the text and pruning away those aspects which might make its assumption by God problematic, or (in the case of preaching) by weakening the 'is' and not taking fully seriously the identity of our human words with God's Word, Barth sees this as a false response which *denies* the scandal rather than facing up to and grasping it. Thus he *both* insists upon the full deity of Scripture and preaching, *and* upon their full humanity, even to the point of conceding their sinfulness, a step which places him decisively beyond the christological analogy.

Thus we find once again a certain dialectical quality in what Barth has to say on this topic. Both Scripture and preaching are to be likened to the humanity of the Logos which remains fully human in the event of incarnation and even in its glorified state. There is no mystical fusion or change whereby the humanity becomes something which, in and of itself, is possessed of revelatory power or glory.[5] Considered humanly there is nothing about the logical form, the material content, the religious profundity or the personal power of any portion of Scripture or any preacher's discourse which could serve as such to reveal God. In both cases there are varying degrees of all these things. But, as the words of Isaiah are applied to the flesh of Jesus so they might well be applied to the 'flesh' of text and proclamation: 'He had no beauty or majesty to attract us to him, nothing in his appearance that we should desire him . . . like one from whom men hide their faces he was despised, and we esteemed him not.'[6]

Barth goes further still. What we must say, he insists, is that in the case of Scripture just as surely as in preaching '*fallible* men speak the Word of God in *fallible* human words'.[7] There is the scandal of identity in all its stark offence. Fallibility and God, we tend to suppose, don't mix – any more than passibility and God, ignorance and God, crucifixion and God. Yet for Barth in both Scripture and preaching (and here as elsewhere as we have seen they stand and fall together –

---

[5] See *GD*, p. 271.
[6] Isa. 53: 2–3.
[7] *CD* 1/2, p. 529.

they are both human entities in the same sense and Word of God in the same sense) the two are clearly juxtaposed and, by that problematic '*is*', identified. Preaching is human talk about God (thus far we might agree) in and through which God speaks about himself,[8] and to which God commits himself absolutely 'in such a way that like the existence of Jesus Christ himself *it is God's own proclamation*'.[9] Here, then, is the other side of the dialectic. These human words (of even the best of which, Barth insists, it remains true that, as Paul says, 'all men are *liars*')[10] *are* yet God's own words, words which he himself adopts and speaks. On the one hand we must ever distinguish the human from the divine, the Word which God speaks from the words which Paul speaks and which you or I speak. 'These', Barth affirms, 'are two different things'.[11] And yet, on the other hand, we must insist with equal vigour and in the strongest possible sense that 'they are not two different things but become one and the same thing in the event of the Word of God'.[12] They are *both*: human witness to revelation, *and* the very Word of God, revelation itself.[13] There is both identity in difference, and difference in identity. But that there is identity at all is a source of scandal and offence.

In relation to Scripture in particular Barth finds himself compelled to spell out this offence in the face of infallibilist and inerrantist views which, as he sees it, fail to face up to the offence by failing to face up to the scandalous humanity which the Word of God, as it were, assumes in this form of divine self-proclamation, and which seek to identify the revelatory capacity of Scripture in some facet of the text as such – its literal propositional truth, its theological orthodoxy or whatever. This he considers tantamount to seeking Jesus' *divinity* at the level of his humanness, in his miracles, his teaching, his ethical example and so on. In reality, Barth insists, as a human entity Scripture really is treatable like any other – although that includes taking genuine and full account of the historical *intentions* of the human authors as they

---

[8] *CD* 1/1, p. 95.
[9] *CD* 1/2, pp. 745–746 (my italics).
[10] Rom. 3:4; see *CD* 1/2, p. 734.
[11] *CD* 1/1, p. 113.
[12] Ibid.
[13] See *CD* 1/2, p. 473.

appear to have understood their task under God including their intention to speak of, and sometimes on behalf of God. In one important sense, therefore, we certainly cannot treat it just like any other human text. To do so would be bad literary practice as well as bad theology. The Bible is not any other human text, but this particular text; and we must attend with integrity to the specificity of this text, its *Sitz im Leben* and *Sitz im Denken*, and the particular world of meaning which it therefore evokes. Nonetheless, to do this is precisely to recognize, as we can and *must*, that it is a human book, and that when we handle it, print it, translate it, edit it, read it and so on, we are handling a piece of human literature. Whatever else we may want to say about the Bible we must certainly say this much. And part of what that entails, Barth argues, is recognition of a genuinely human textuality with all its attendant weaknesses and problems.

Why does Barth insist that it is thus? One answer to that question might be that the advent of modern historical and critical methods as applied to the biblical text have made views of its infallibility and inerrancy impossible to sustain without a *sacrificium intellectus*, or else only by qualifying these to the point where they seem to have lost their basic intent. That case is one which must be faced seriously, and no doubt it played its part in shaping Barth's mind; for, whatever may sometimes be said about his attitude to biblical criticism, he was able to take its learning fully on board. He considered the way in which it had often been *used* to be an irrelevance for the task of Christian proclamation, but that is another matter altogether, and one which we do not have time to pursue. Yet I want to end this section by suggesting that the real reason for Barth's insistence upon the full humanity of the biblical text – along with the full humanity of Jesus and that of preaching – was that his particular understanding of the nature of revelation as *event* drove him to do so.

4. Revelation and concealment: an essential paradox

From his earliest writings till his latest, Barth maintains that there is an implicit paradox in the very nature of revelation. God *reveals* himself, yet he does so in such a way and in such a form that in the midst of his revealedness he remains hidden. Thus in the Romans commentary, citing Kierkegaard and Luther for moral support, Barth writes:

The Gospel requires – faith . . . It can therefore be neither directly communicated nor directly apprehended . . . it can appear among us, be received and understood by us, only as contradiction. The Gospel does not expound or recommend itself. It does not negotiate or plead, threaten or make promises. It withdraws itself always when it is not listened to for its own sake . . . 'Indeed only when that which is believed on is hidden, can it provide an opportunity for faith. And moreover, those things are most deeply hidden which most clearly contradict the obvious experience of the senses' (Luther).[14]

The same precise point undergirds Barth's view of Scripture and preaching as developed in *GD* and *CD*. Thus, 'To deny the hiddenness of revelation even in Scripture is to deny revelation itself, and with it the Word of God. For God's Word is no longer God's Word when the truth that is new every morning . . . is made into a sacred reality, when the miracle of God that is encircled with the possibility of offense is made into a marvel to which one may quietly point.'[15] What is being said here, then, is precisely that at the level of the human reality of Jesus, text and sermon these things possess 'no form or comeliness . . . that we should desire' them, but act as much to *veil* the reality of God (as that which is truly not God inevitably must) as to reveal him. In the event of revelation God tears the veil away, and makes known the incomprehensible, but as the event is precisely *that*, something which happens and passes and is gone, the veil itself remains formally in place. For those with 'eyes to see' it becomes transparent, but for others it is and remains utterly opaque.

Behind this view of things lies an epistemological and ontological assumption which permeates Barth's theology from the days of his so-called dialectical period through to the very end of *CD* and beyond. Namely, that God is by definition utterly transcendent, that he can be neither known nor spoken about by human beings as such. He cannot be posited as an object. Put the other way around, human beings are quite incapable of knowing or speaking about God. Thus 'we have to admit', Barth writes, 'that we cannot

---

[14] Barth, *Romans* (London: OUP, 1933), p. 39.
[15] *GD*, p. 59.

see, hear, feel, touch or either inwardly or outwardly perceive the one who reveals himself, not because he is invisible or pure spirit, but because he is God, because he is wholly himself, "I am who I am," the subject that escapes our grasp, our attempt to *make* him an object.'[16] Again, 'God does not belong to the world. Therefore he does not belong to the series of objects for which we have categories and words by means of which we draw the attention of others to them, and bring them into relation with Him. Of God it is impossible to speak, because He is neither a natural nor a spiritual object.'[17]

The source of this radical dualism need not concern us at length. In part, at least, it seems to be a response to the somewhat optimistic and imperialistic epistemology of Neo-Kantian philosophy in which something is known as it is 'objectified' or 'made into an object', that is to say, classified and labelled by the mind in accordance with universally given sets of categories. God, Barth, together with Bultmann and others of his generation, wants to insist, cannot be dealt with like that. He cannot be seized and subjected to a confident process of analysis by human reason, put in a box and defined, and thereby effectively tamed. Unlike Bultmann, however, Barth wants equally to insist that this does not mean in the final scheme of things that God is unknowable, that is, restricted within human experience to some ahistorical, non-cognitive and purely moral existential encounter, but rather gives himself to be known precisely in cognitive, verbal, and even fleshly-historical terms. 'What if', he asks, 'God be so much God that without ceasing to be God he can also be, and is willing to be, not God as well? What if he were to come down from his unsearchable height and become something different?'[18] In this case we must say two things. First, that the form which God assumes in this radical self-objectifying is itself not God. Thus 'what we see, hear, feel, touch, and inwardly and outwardly perceive [whether it be the man Jesus, the text of Scripture or human preaching] is always something different, a counterpart, a second thing.'[19] It is what Barth refers to as the 'secondary objectivity' of God's word. But in, with,

---

[16] Ibid. p. 136.
[17] *CD* 1/2, p. 750.
[18] *GD*, p. 136.
[19] Ibid.

and under this creaturely self-objectification, and not apart from it, the Word of God himself may be known. 'On this objective condition', Barth writes, '. . . revelation is possible. Note', he continues, 'that I do not say more than "possible." Through the transparency of this concealment . . . the light of God's revelation can be seen. We cannot take it for granted that it really is seen. This still rests with God.'[20] The veil, in other words, must still be lifted, and lifted by God himself alone. By entering into the realm of human being and knowing in these three forms, the flesh of Christ, the text of Scripture, the words of the preacher, the Word of God becomes that which is knowable by us. But in order that he may be known as Word of God, recognized in the midst and in spite of his concealment, this objective, given, humanly recognizable form must be accompanied by the Spirit whose activity 'straddles objectivity and subjectivity' and creates the event, the 'happening' of revelation and faith.

That this happens in spite not only of the creatureliness of the form which the Word assumes but (in the instances of Scripture and preaching at least) in spite of its inherent fallibility and sinfulness, this, Barth insists, is miracle, a miracle of the same sort if not the same magnitude as the creation *ex nihilo*, the resurrection of Jesus out of the despair of death, and the conception of the embryonic Christ in the virgin's womb. The paradox is the same in each case.

To return fleetingly, then, to the question of the doctrine of biblical infallibility or inerrancy, Barth's objection to it is that it denies this essential miracle. It cannot bear the paradox, the scandal of the audacious affirmation that weak and errant human words *are* the very Word of God himself. This identification is too much for it, so in order to cope with it, it shifts the scene of the miracle to another place, to an earlier place, positing a miraculous 'preparing of the ground,' the furnishing of a sinless and flawless textual humanity for the Word of God to be identified with and incarnate in. As such (the comparison is mine not Barth's) one might say that the logical force of the doctrine is much the same, and posited for the same reasons, as that of the Catholic doctrine of the immaculate conception of Mary. The assumption is that for the Word of God to enter into any genuine union with the human, the human must be purged in

---

[20] Ibid. p. 140.

advance of its imperfections, since these would be unfitting for God to identify himself or his activity with. Pursuing the same logic it might be asked whether, if our view of preaching were as high as Barth's, we might not be forced to develop some parallel notion in this relation too, some account of how our human verbiage is, prior to being assumed into the task of proclamation, specially purged of its inherent human sinfulness as a necessary condition of its adoption by God as his speech.

For Barth, the *scandalon* must be allowed to stand, for all the reasons outlined thus far. God's Word comes to us in fully human form. It is veiled from us by this very creatureliness, and becomes 'visible', as it were, only in the event of revelation. The real presence of the Word in human words cannot be guaranteed, coerced, pinned down or held on to. As in the sacrament, it can only be prayed for and received by faith in, with and under the creaturely elements. There is no magical transubstantiation.

It is precisely *this* that provokes the question 'How, in this case, is preaching possible?' It is to Barth's answer to this question that I want to turn very briefly in the next and final section.

5. Inspiration as event: the Word, the flesh and the Spirit

Notwithstanding the kenotic aspect of the humanity of the Word, its historically conditioned nature, its contingency, its theological contradictions and limitations, nonetheless, Barth affirms, God's Word is pleased to identify himself with it, to commit himself to it, and, in what can only be described as a miraculous event, to speak through it to human beings. In this event, wrought by Word and Spirit together, the one as the 'objective possibility' of revelation, the other as its 'subjective possibility', these human words actually *become* the Word of God. God speaks here in such a way that he is heard, as he has spoken here many times before, and promises to do so again and again. As such, both Scripture and preaching may be called Word of God in a straightforward and unqualified manner.

But such a description refers not to an attribute which the words possess in and of themselves, nor even one which they come to possess through grace, but precisely to the event in which they are taken up, assumed, and in which God's Word becomes incarnate once again with revealing and redeeming effect. Thus God is himself the subject of this event as well as the object made known. And as we are drawn into it, actively engaged in knowing, what is in effect taking place is a drawing of us into the very inner heart of God's triune life, into his own self-knowledge, as he posits himself as the Son to be known and loved by the Father in the Holy Spirit. The event of revelation thus has a profoundly trinitarian structure, although in our case it is a trinity rooted firmly in the historical realm: we are drawn to know God as Father in and through our knowing of and sharing in the life of the human Son, the *Christos*, empowered and sustained by the anointing Spirit. That this miracle should occur, this reconciling and atoning knowing should happen to us or to others is never, of course, within our sphere of influence or responsibility. We are not called upon to conjure it up genie-like, even from a book rather than a bottle: but simply to point away from ourselves to Christ, to bear witness, to tell the story of redemption. 'Only God can talk about God,' Barth asserts. 'To this extent, in appropriate application of a christological formulation, we might say of preaching as the Word of God that it is "conceived by the Holy Ghost." '[21]

Hence we arrive at Barth's understanding of the term 'inspiration' in relation to Scripture and its interpretation. There was, he insists, a special activity of the Spirit upon both the prophets and the apostles, commissioning them for their particular task of human witness, even in the midst of their 'capacity for errors.'[22] Furthermore, God renders the words of Scripture theologically reliable so that 'the message which Scripture has to give to us, even in its most debatable and less assimilable parts, is in all circumstances truer and more important than the best and most necessary things that we ourselves have said or can say.'[23] But the notion of inspiration need not (*cannot* for reasons which we have rehearsed) be construed in such a way as to involve an inerrant text as such; and nor can it be limited to some past phenomenon resulting in a revelation which is subsequently to be had in codified and textually fossilized form.

---

[21] *GD* p. 272.

[22] *CD* 1/2, p. 508.

[23] Ibid. p. 719.

Rather, 'we have to say that we must view inspiration as a single, timeless – or rather, contemporary act of God . . . in *both* the biblical authors *and* ourselves.'[24] In this single event of the Spirit, then, the biblical witnesses themselves are in a sense made contemporary with us, and we are given to see and hear what they saw and heard for themselves.

6. Conclusion

Real proclamation, therefore, is in essence for Barth 'human talk about God on the basis of the self-objectification of God which is not just there, which cannot be predicted, which does not fit into any plan, which is real only in the freedom of His grace, and in virtue of which He wills at specific times to be the object of this talk, and is so according to His own good pleasure.'[25] Furthermore, 'It must be solely the truth and miracle of God if his Logos, as he does not regard the lowliness of his handmaiden . . . or view the unclean lips of Isaiah as an obstacle . . . does not think it impossible to pitch his tent in what is at best our poor and insignificant and stammering talk about God.'[26]

The practical implication of this is that we are *absolved* from every and any attempt to force this event to happen, liberated from the responsibility of generating it, set free from the pressure created by those who, week in and week out, hear and yet do *not* hear the message. Alan Lewis writes as follows:

> The word of the cross itself liberates the community of faith from compulsive, worldly models of success, effectiveness and power; and her conviction that preaching is the Word of God itself, though anything but antinomian, lifts from the church the crushing burdens of 'relevance' and popularity. Preaching may continue in a culture which humiliates the word, because the riskiness which lays an offensive

---

[24] *GD* p. 225.
[25] *CD* 1/1, p. 92.
[26] *GD* p. 271.

message on unfashionable messengers reposes firstly and finally in God's own accommodation and commission.[27]

Barth encourages us, therefore, to think of the task of preaching as a human task, to be sure; as a response to the prior word of divine grace, certainly; but much more than this, as that which is possible only on the basis of its objective *and* subjective conditions, the self-giving of the Son as Jesus Christ, and the here and now presence of the Spirit of Christ at work in the hearts and minds of both preacher and congregation. Jesus Christ is the Proclaimer as well as the proclaimed, and our ministry of proclamation is, therefore, precisely a sharing in his divine and human ministry before the Father through the Spirit, a ministry which for him led only via the suffering and rejection of the cross to resurrection and triumph. It is with this trinitarian perspective firmly in mind that the awesome task of preaching the foolishness of the gospel can be faced with confidence as, each week afresh, we prepare again to embrace the Gethsemane, Calvary and empty tomb which marked the first Friday, Saturday and Sunday morning of the Christian era.

---

[27] Alan Lewis, 'Kenosis and Kerygma: The Realism and the Risk of Preaching', in Hart and Thimell (eds.), *Christ in Our Place* (Exeter: Paternoster Press, 1989) p. 88.

3

Christ and God's Justification of Creation

'Protestants speak of a declaration of justice and Catholics of a
making just. But Protestants speak of a declaring just which
includes a making just; and Catholics of a making just which supposes a declaring just. Is it not time to stop arguing about imaginary
differences?'[1] This provocative question, posed by Hans Küng in
the 1950s prior to the new ecumenical mood engendered in the
West by Vatican II, remains a significant focus for contemporary
ecumenical discussion. Küng answered his own question with an
exposition of Barth's theology. His basic case, that centuries of
mutual suspicion and terminological confusion since the Reformation could now be cut away to reveal not so much a difference of
substance as of emphasis, is an important one worthy of further
exploration. Whether it claims rather too much on the basis of
rather too little: whether Küng and Barth may legitimately serve as
typical of the Catholic and Protestant traditions in relation to the
doctrine of justification, are matters equally deserving of consideration. In this chapter, however, my goals are more modest. I want
simply to examine some key points in Barth's theology of justification using Küng's book as an occasional source of comparison.
This exercise will, I suspect, reveal some basic and determinative
differences between their respective understandings of the doctrine. Since each speaks as a critical and creative voice within his
tradition, the direct implications of any such demonstration for
ecumenical relations may nonetheless be relatively slight.

---

[1] H. Küng, *Justification: The Doctrine of Karl Barth and a Catholic Reflection*
(London: Burns & Oates, 1981), p. 221.

1. Justification, creation and covenant

According to Alister McGrath the Christian doctrine of justification 'constitutes the real centre of the theological system of the Christian Church, encapsulating the direct and normative consequences of the historical revelation of God to mankind in Jesus Christ. There never was, and there never can be, any true Christian Church without the doctrine of justification.'[2] Significantly neither Barth nor Küng sees the doctrine of justification as such as *articulus stantis et cadentis ecclesiae*. Both urge upon us the importance of looking beyond this particular doctrine (vital though it may be) to the broader context within which it takes its place, and in relation to which, therefore, it is properly to be understood. Thus for Barth the article by which the church stands or falls is 'not justification as such, but its basis and culmination: the confession of Jesus Christ . . . the knowledge of his being and activity for us and to us and with us.'[3]

Notwithstanding this general agreement between our two theologians concerning the relative significance of justification within the constellation of Christian doctrines, there is nonetheless a difference from the outset over the meaning of the term, and it is one which we should bear in mind throughout our discussion. For Küng justification (*iustitia, dikaiosyne*) entails God *making* humans righteous (*iustus, dikaios*) not simply in a forensic (extrinsic) sense, but in an ontological (intrinsic) sense. God *declares* us to be righteous, certainly; but in so doing he *makes* us righteous in our being.[4] The divine Word actualizes that which it proclaims.[5] Hence humans are themselves involved (albeit on the basis of grace alone) in the subjective aspect of this divine work; they are themselves made righteous, and since they are neither puppets nor machines this must involve their (graced) cooperation. For Barth too, we will

---

[2] A. McGrath, *Iustitia Dei* 1 (Cambridge: CUP, 1986), p. 1.

[3] *CD* 4/1, p. 527.

[4] Küng, *Justification*, p. 200: 'Grace, as the favor and benevolence of God, is not oriented toward a vacuum. It is not impotent in regard to the sinner, but omnipotent – Verbum Dei efficax . . . Grace accomplishes something in man. It transforms him inwardly. It is grace upon *man*' (italics original). See further pp. 208f.

[5] Ibid. p. 213.

argue, justification is 'ontological' and not a matter of mere verbal assertion. But his use of the term is significantly different from Küng's, which trespasses, from Barth's perspective, unforgiveably into the realm of 'sanctification', and thereby risks undermining the very heart of the gospel of grace. For Barth justification is never something which involves the Christian in any cooperation or active involvement ('graced' or otherwise). It is, in this sense, wholly objective, standing over against us as a finished work. In what sense, then, can it be an 'ontological' reality? The answer will become clear as we proceed. For now let us simply lay down this marker, noting that, whatever Küng may believe to be the case, the two are already at odds even at this most basic level of the discussion.

When, however, in his 'attempted Catholic response' to Barth, Küng outlines three major areas of dogmatic understanding which he sees as 'foundations' of the particular doctrine of justification (namely, creation, harmartiology and christology)[6] he finds himself in basic agreement with him. Indeed it is the latter's way of setting justification within the matrix of creation, covenant and christology that lends to his treatment its distinctive shape. It is important, therefore, to recall the relationship between creation and covenant as Barth articulates it in §41 of *CD*.[7] The two are held closely together in a strong protest against tendencies to detect two different orders or dispensations in the relationship between God and humankind, one according to 'nature' and the other according to 'grace'. Thus, for Barth, creation is the external basis for the covenant, and the covenant the internal basis for creation. Neither, of course, can properly be understood apart from the perspective afforded us by their common *telos* in the self-revelation of God in Jesus Christ.[8] He is the fulfilment of the covenant, both from the side of God and from the side of humanity; and he is the fulfilment

---

[6] Ibid. p. 193.

[7] *CD* 3/1, pp. 42f.

[8] See ibid p. 42: 'the purpose and therefore the meaning of creation is to make possible the history of God's covenant with man which has its beginning, its centre and its culmination in Jesus Christ. The history of this covenant is as much the goal of creation as creation itself is the beginning of the history'.

of creation, both from the side of the Creator and from the side of the creature.[9]

It is within this context that the theme of 'justification' first appears in *CD*. Thus in §42 Barth develops the notion that in some sense justification is analytic in creation itself. That is to say, the very fact that God creates carries with it the implication that what he creates is 'justified'. The repeated refrain of Genesis 1, 'and God saw that it was good', means, says Barth, that the existence of what he has made is justified, not, clearly, in relation to the law or to any external moral or legal standard, but rather in relation to God's purpose in creating.[10] Insofar as it is possessed of rightness (*Gerechtigkeit*) in relation to the divine purpose, so it is the object of *Rechtfertigung*.

Is this, however, not a rather peculiar use of the term 'justification', somewhat removed from the more familiar sense in which Barth employs it in §61, 'The Justification of Man', and hence irrelevant for our discussion? At first sight it may seem to be so. But there is certainly an important link between the two sections, and Barth's quite deliberate (and rather awkward) use of *Rechtfertigung* in the former context may provide an important clue for our interpretation of the latter.

First, we may note that the judgement 'it is good' uttered by God in the beginning is made not in relation to some unknown divine blueprint, but precisely in relation to the fulfilment of His purpose in creation and covenant *as that has taken place in Jesus Christ*.[11] The creation is *recht*, that is to say, precisely insofar as it is *capax infiniti*, able to be taken up by God in the incarnation and brought concretely to its *telos* in fulfilment of the covenant. The divine

---

[9] See ibid. p. 365.

[10] '[T]he Creator justifies the creation . . . only because the latter is created according to his will and plan, and therefore with the purpose of instituting and fulfilling the covenant between the divine Creator and man . . . The created world is, therefore, right (*recht*) as it is, because in its essence and structure it is an appropriate sphere and instrument of the divine activity' (ibid. pp. 369–370).

[11] 'Its rightness, goodness, worth and perfection spring from its correspondence to the work of God's own Son as resolved from all eternity and fulfilled in time' (ibid. p. 370).

judgement is thus proleptic. The creation is *gerechtfertigt* due to its *Gerechtigkeit* in relation to God's action in Jesus Christ.

Second, the description of the justification of humanity in §61, while it is certainly bound up with the themes of law, sin and justice (it is the 'sentence' and the 'pardon' of God),[12] is nonetheless at the same time fundamentally determined by this same (extra-forensic) notion of *Rechtfertigung* in relation to creation and covenant. God the Creator, who is also the Lord of the covenant, has a right (*Recht*) to human beings as his creatures and covenant partners, and establishes their *Recht* to existence precisely *by putting to death that which contradicts his purpose in creation and replacing it with the new creation.*[13] Humans, through their sin, have made themselves impossible as the creatures and covenant partners of God: they have desecrated that which in the beginning God made and saw that it was good. They have compromised their existence, and put themselves in the wrong as opposed to the right.[14] Yet God's initial judgement on what he has made still stands, and he exercises his *Recht*, his right and authority as Creator over his creation by rising up in opposition to this rebellion and rendering it powerless.[15] He will not tolerate the spoiling of that which he has made; he will not allow evil to prevail over it.[16] Human beings, as the doers of wrong, meet with God's wrath which consumes evil.[17] Their evil nature is circumcised, and they emerge as renewed creatures, worthy to be the covenant partners of the Lord.[18] Thus God *justifies* his creation precisely by demonstrating concretely, because of and in spite of human sin, the veracity of his age-old 'justification' of it in the judgement of Genesis 1.

Justification, then, is to do not simply with the law and our standing before it, but fundamentally with God's purpose as Creator and Lord of the covenant, and our fulfilment of the same. Sin is an ontological condition and not merely an external forensic relation. God judges us in our sinfulness and finds us wanting, executing that

---

[12] *CD* 4/1, pp. 515f.
[13] Ibid. p. 542.
[14] Ibid. p. 528.
[15] Ibid. pp. 534f.
[16] Ibid. p. 563.
[17] Ibid. p. 535.
[18] Ibid. p. 597.

judgement in the cross. Yet the sentence of God is revealed in the resurrection as well as the cross: the old Adam must die, but precisely in order that the new Adam might take his place. Justification is thus an ontological as well as a forensic reality, since in justifying us God actually raises up and establishes the new creature and the faithful covenant partner of whom it can truly be said that he is 'good'. The existence of this new humanity is no hypothetical or merely potential reality, any more than the death of the 'man of sin' is hypothetical. 'In the one case, as in the other,' Barth writes, God 'does not fashion a mere *quid pro quo*, a mere "as if," but actualities (*Realitäten*).'[19]

2. Justification as transition: the *simul iustus et peccator*

According to Barth, then, justification is effected at the level of the ontological and not merely the forensic. Our *being* is changed as a result of what occurs; we *are* just, we are not simply treated as if we were just. The old is put to death; the new has come. But this is not all that must be said about us. Equally true is the affirmation that we are yet sinners, those deserving of judgement and death, and who know themselves to be such. Just as the verdict and sentence of God executed in the death and resurrection of Christ present a twofold aspect, on the one hand the 'rejection of the elect man' and on the other the 'election of the reject man',[20] so too our present existence as *die Gerechtfertigten* reflects this same tension. We are in fact (in reality) both: *simul iustus et peccator*.[21] How, then, are we to understand this? With what degree of seriousness can we take the *simul*?

Küng, following the Council of Trent, approaches this problem from the assumption of our essential righteousness. How, he asks, can the one who is through the justifying activity of God truly *iustus* yet be said to be sinful?[22] The answer which he proffers is that the

---

[19] Ibid. pp. 542f.
[20] Ibid. p. 515.
[21] Ibid. p. 516.
[22] Küng, *Justification*, p. 237.

justified 'remains capable of sin', remains in the danger zone, so to
speak, where sin is an ever-present option. Küng cites approvingly
Schmaus who writes, 'The justified man, who is free from sin, and
yet always tempted towards it, approaches a condition in which he
is freed also from temptation to sin.'[23] Is this, then, the way in which
we are to make sense of the *simul iustus et peccator*, by arguing that it is
still possible for the justified to (be the man or woman of) sin, but
equally possible for them to choose not to (be)?

Certainly Barth would not rest content with any such formulation of the matter. To say this is to fail to take the *peccator* fully
seriously. His own exposition of Luther's phrase is structured around
the dialectic of Romans 7:24–5 which he (rightly or wrongly) takes
as a reference to Paul's Christian experience.[24] Thus Barth
approaches the problem of the *simul* from the other end to Küng.
Notwithstanding his repeated insistence that justification is no mere
'as if ', he poses the problem thus: '[Man] is *homo peccator* . . . How can
he be seriously in the wrong before God . . . and yet also before the
same God, and in the same sentence and judgement come to be and
be seriously, in the right',[25] that is to say, justified? The answer to this
question he perceives to lie in the eschatological aspect of justification, the tension between the 'already' and the 'not yet'. He does not,
however, as Küng seems to think,[26] so overemphasize the 'not yet' as
to rob the 'already' of any basis in reality. To argue thus is to misunderstand the sense in which, for Barth, we are already *iustus*. Whereas
Küng is thinking of justification in terms of a process initiated within
our being, which is heavily front-loaded and gradually works itself
out in the Christian life as our progress towards perfection, Barth has
something altogether different in mind.

Justification is not, for Barth, a process taking place in us which at
any given stage could be adjudged more or less complete. The *simul*
in *simul iustus et peccator* does not, therefore, refer to an imbalanced
proportionality in which we are *in ourselves* gradually more *iustus*
and less *peccator*. Rather it is to be taken in its full force, as implying

[23] M. Schmaus, *Katholische Dogmatik* 3/2, 5 vols, 4th edition, (Münschen,
1949) pp. 117f.
[24] *CD* 4/1, p. 589.
[25] Ibid. p. 517.
[26] Küng, *Justification*, p. 237.

that we are completely and utterly both in the same instant. Yet the existence of the justified is not to be understood as the static co-existence of two ontological or forensic states, but as a transition, an existence determined by the relationship of our prior existence (*totus peccator*) to our future hope (*totus iustus*) and caught up in the eschatological dialectic between the two.[27] Thus Barth refers to justification as a 'history' rather than a 'state', a history in which our present is determined by the assurance of things hoped for and the conviction of things not seen just as surely as it is by our continuing sinfulness. In this present moment, 'as [man's] past as a sinner is *still his present*, so his future as a righteous man is *already his present*.'[28] Both things are true. Both things are real. We are on a 'pilgrimage from an ever new past through an ever new present to an ever new future.'[29] Meanwhile we live in hope of the removal of the contradiction which characterizes our present existence. Our wrong and death is decisively behind us; yet it is still our present: our right and our existence as the new humanity are part of our present; yet they are so as our promised future. The problem and the puzzling thing, Barth admits, is that we are unable to experience or to perceive ourselves as those who are dead to sin, or as active participants in the righteous new humanity.[30] Insofar as our experience is our guide and our gauge the *totus peccator* seems to overwhelm the *totus iustus*.

At this point Küng lodges a protest and poses a question. Barth seems, after all, to be relegating the *totus iustus* to a future existence, to being an object of hope rather than a present reality. What then, are we to say of the present state of the justified? What is the truth concerning their being *today*? What *are* they, righteous or sinful? In what sense is their sinful past really their past if it is still present? In what sense is their righteous present really present at all, if it is still the object of hope for the future? Is the justification which Barth claims as determinative of our existence, setting us free from our past and directing us to our future, really anything more than a verbal pronouncement after all?

---

[27] *CD* 4/1, pp. 545, 576, 595.
[28] Ibid. p. 595.
[29] Ibid. p. 602.
[30] Ibid. pp. 548f.; esp. 552, 554.

3. In search of the real: Barth's ontology of justification

Küng's questions concerning the *simul iustus et peccator* reflect very well the terms in which the age-old debate over justification has been couched. Both sides in the debate have framed their questions and responses in terms of what we might call an 'ontology of the actual'; that is to say, an unquestioned identification of that which is true or real with *that which is actually the case* in relation to individual human beings considered in and of themselves. If I am said to be 'justified', what exactly does this imply about my being? What is actually the case? Am I, as Catholic theologians have generally insisted, 'just' in the very depths of my being, and in spite of all appearances to the contrary? Is this the actuality of my situation? Or am I, as Protestants have for the most part responded, in reality (actually) still very much a sinner in need of forgiveness, so that the 'justification' spoken of, if it is to apply to me in any sense in my present actuality, must be understood as an objective, non-intrinsic (and probably purely forensic) thing?

These relative terms presuppose an identification of the real with the actual. The Protestant doctrine has tended to identify the actual with the empirical, with that which we experience of ourselves and our situation. Catholicism, on the other hand, has presented a more transcendental account of actuality, in which what we really *are* may not correspond to our experience at all. But both are essentially at one in identifying reality and truth with that which is intrinsic to our being as individual human persons. What is real and true is what I am now in and of myself. Within such a framework it is not possible to assert in any meaningful way that anyone is *simul totus iustus et totus peccator*. If sense is to be made of the *simul* at all, then it is in terms of some sort of dualism or proportionality (Küng) between the two, or else an eschatological projection of one into the future as an anticipated reality ('not yet' – Protestantism). There is seemingly no third option.

There are, of course, other answers to the question concerning the locus of the real. Eberhard Jüngel[31] challenges the traditional

---

[31] 'The world as possibility and actuality. The ontology of the doctrine of justification', in J.B. Webster (ed.), *Eberhard Jüngel: Theological Essays* (Edinburgh: T & T Clark, 1989), pp. 95–123.

western post-Aristotelian identification of the real with the actual, and suggests that a more fruitful approach to the ontology of justification might be to attribute greater reality to the possible than to the actual. This proposed 'ontology of the possible' would alter decisively the centre of gravity in the eschatological dimension of the doctrine, making the future which God has established as a possibility for me *more* real in relation to me than the present in which, along with the rest of creation, I groan and travail, waiting for the revelation of the sons of God.

Another answer to the question 'Where is reality to be located?' might be framed in terms of the will or mind of God. That which is ultimately true and real in relation to us, it might be argued, is not the actual (empirical or transcendent) but rather that which is true of us in the mind of God, or in his eternal divine decision concerning us. Again this 'ontology of divine intention' would provide an interesting new perspective within which to pose and answer the traditional questions concerning justification.

There is a sense in which both of these latter alternatives have been approximated to in traditional Protestant doctrines of justification, emphasizing on the one hand the eschatological nature of justification, and on the other the declaration of human righteousness by God as that wherein our justification is located. Yet in the final analysis none has taken the step of identifying the real with anything other than our present actuality, with the result that Catholic theologians have constantly resorted to the charge of either a legal or an ontological *fiction* (i.e. something not possessed of full reality).

Where, then, does Barth locate 'reality' or truth concerning men and women? When he refers to us as really and totally justified, notwithstanding our self-understanding as the sinner deserving of judgement, is he verging on the sort of transcendental/metaphysical reference preferred by Küng and the Catholic tradition, or is he adopting some other ontological basis for his statement? Is it, perhaps, in the eternal decree of God, or the eschatological future that reality is located, and hence we are *really* justified? This is a crucial question if we are to understand what Barth says concerning justification properly and fairly.

Strictly speaking, the answer is that none of these constitutes the locus of reality for Barth. To be sure, all of them play important roles in his theology, but none is ultimately determinative of the real. If we would deal with truth and reality, then for Barth we must turn not to our own empirical experience, nor to some metaphysical sphere beyond that experience, nor to God's future, nor to divine intention *per se*; rather we must consider *the concrete history of the one man Jesus of Nazareth.*[32] It is here, Barth insists, that the divine intention for humankind has been actualized (not just anticipated); it is here that the eschatological future of God has broken decisively into history; it is here that our experience of ourselves and our situation is called radically into question as we are called upon to discover ourselves 'in him' and in his situation.

How are we to understand this? Simply as a piece of theological chicanery perhaps, or an excursion into a dogmatic Wonderland in which familiar values and assumptions are turned on their head, and in which our common spatio-temporal experience is threatened or arbitrarily set aside? If so, then we must reckon seriously with the fact that it is no mere aberration from the straight and narrow, but rather, as Ingolf Dalferth[33] suggests, the very weave of the fabric of Barth's entire theological enterprise, the *scandalon* which underlies every section of *CD*, whether it is explicitly mentioned or not. Hence it is certainly no ill-considered or contrived piece of

---

[32] 'We have found (justification) at the place where it is reality and truth, the reality and truth which applies to us and comprehends us, our own reality and truth. We have found it where we ourselves are and not merely appear to be . . . It is all true and actual in Him and therefore in us. It cannot, therefore, be known to be valid and effective in us first, but in Him first, and because in Him in us. We are in Him and comprehended in Him, but we are still not He Himself. Therefore it is all true and actual in this Other first and not in us. That is why our justification is not a matter of subjective experience and understanding. That is why we cannot perceive and comprehend it. That is why it is so puzzling to us' (*CD* 4/1, p. 549). 'It is not a mere figure of speech to say that in faith man finds that the history of Jesus Christ is his history, that his sin is judged in Him, that his right is established in Him, that his death is put to death and his life is born in Him, that he can regard himself as justified in His righteousness because it is his own righteousness, because his faith is a real apprehension of his real being in Christ (*seiner realen Seins in Christus*)' (ibid. p. 636).

[33] See I. Dalferth, 'Karl Barth's Eschatological Realism', in S.W. Sykes (ed.), *Karl Barth: Centenary Essays* (Cambridge: CUP, 1989), pp. 14–45.

rhetoric, but rather a carefully worked out alternative ontology which we must seek to take into consideration in interpreting Barth at every stage, whether or not we find ourselves able to concur with it. To do otherwise is to engage in interpretative mischief and inevitably to misrepresent the substance of his thought.

Behind Barth's insistence in *CD* 4/1 that the truth concerning human beings and their justification is not to be located in the histories of individual men and women *per se*, but rather in the particular history of the one man Jesus Christ, we may trace the development of his doctrine of election in *CD* 2/2 in which Jesus is presented as the Elect Man in whom God's purposes for the human race are decisively focused, and with whom our very 'being' as human persons is somehow mysteriously bound up.[34] In seeking some theological rationale for this idea we might look to Barth's conviction that this one man is indeed to be identified (*homoousios*) with the one in whom all things were created in the beginning, and in whom all continue to live and move and 'have their being'.[35] In other words, as creatures we are inevitably bound up with our Creator. We exist, we have our being, only in relation to him; a relationship which we cannot deny without deceiving ourselves, and out of which we cannot opt without ultimate consequences. When this same Creator himself takes flesh and becomes a human person, therefore, and comes, furthermore, to fulfil his own creative and covenantal purposes, to be the very peak or crisis point in human history, a further and deeper level of relationship between him and us is established. Now what we are and who we are are matters no longer determined simply by our relationship to God as such, but precisely by our relationship to this man, *Deus incarnatus*, in such a way that 'his particular history is the pre-history and post-history of all our individual lives'.[36]

For Barth, then, the divine intention is no abstraction, but concrete historical actuality in Jesus Christ. The eschatological future *has been realized* historically, and our future rests decisively upon this past and present reality. Importantly, Dalferth observes that Barth

---

[34] See, e.g., *CD* 2/2, pp. 310f.
[35] See, e.g., *CD* 3/1, pp. 29f.
[36] Ibid. p. 27.

does not see the realm of our experience as relegated to the level of unreality by this reversal of perspective. Rather, he writes: '. . . our world of common experience is an *enhypostatic reality* which exists only insofar as it is incorporated into the concrete reality of God's saving self-realization in Christ. Taken by itself, natural reality is an anhypostatic abstraction, unable to exist on its own, and systematically at one remove from the texture of concrete reality.'[37] Insofar as we address our questions about justification (or anything else)[38] to reality, therefore, precisely what we must not do, for Barth, is simply to ask after our own intrinsic or natural state, what we *are* considered in and of ourselves apart from Jesus Christ, since reality proper, the 'really real', is not be found here. Instead we must ask what we are considered in our ontological relatedness to Jesus Christ, whose history is our history, whose death is our death, and in whose resurrection and exaltation we share. It is in response to this question, answered from within the framework of this alternative 'ontology of relation to Christ' that Barth gives the resounding and unequivocal response *simul iustus et peccator*, able to attribute reality to both the *totus iustus* and the *totus peccator*, and hence to take the *simul* absolutely seriously. Considered in ourselves we are still the sinful and guilty people that we were: considered in Christ we are the new creatures of God, faithful covenant partners, and set free, therefore, to live as such.

Our 'being' as the justified is to be discovered precisely in this paradoxical tension. While, therefore, there is a sense in which Jesus Christ and his history are 'objective' to us, they are objective to our experience, and not to the reality of our being. On the other hand, while the justification of God wrought in the history of Jesus Christ has altered our situation to the roots of our *being*, this reality is not locatable within our experience, nor is it something which we can master or control. It is a matter of the electing grace of God made concrete in Jesus.

---

[37] Dalferth, 'Karl Barth's Eschatological Realism', p. 29.
[38] John Webster, for example, has suggested that the same is true of Barth's treatment of human sinfulness. See, ' "The Firmest Grasp of the Real": Barth on Original Sin', *Toronto Journal of Theology* 4 (spring 1988), pp. 19–29.

4. Justification and the history of Jesus Christ

Once we have recognized this fundamental shift in Barth's ontology we can begin to make better sense of what he has to say concerning the existence of the justified. His insistence that justification is a 'history' and not a 'state', for example, has two foci. First, it refers to the 'history' of the man Jesus Christ in whom God has justified his creation by putting it to death and raising it up afresh in a new form. This has actually taken place in the sequence of events which form the dynamics of the incarnate ministry of the Son of God. Yet his history is, as such, also our history. Thus,

> it is our wrong and death which is behind us, our right and life which is before us. The transition from that past to this future is our present. We are the participants in this great drama. That history is, in fact, our history. We have to say that it is our *true* history, in an incomparably more direct and intimate way than anything which might present itself as our history in our own subjective experience . . . It is indeed a riddle. But in spite of the riddle of it, it is not a fairy-tale or a myth. Compared with it, measured by the reality of it all, the things which we think we know of ourselves . . . are a fairy-tale and a myth.[39]

In this history of Jesus Christ in which human nature is both judged and executed on the one hand, and raised and exalted and vindicated (*gerechtfertigt*) on the other, we can discover our own true history. This is the solution to the riddle. This is the good news which sets us free.[40]

---

[39] *CD* 4/1, p. 547.

[40] McGrath's account of Barth, in which he makes the charge that for Barth 'man's dilemma concerns his knowledge of God, *rather than* his bondage to sin or evil (unless these are understood in the epistemically reduced sense of "ignorance" or "confusion")' and 'the death of Christ does not in any sense change the soteriological situation, in that this has been determined from all eternity' (*Iustitia Dei* 2, pp. 138–134, my italics), is seemingly wide of the mark at this point, and apparently results from the gratuitous thrusting of Barth's doctrine of justification onto a predetermined Procrustean interpretative bed (see esp. p. 178), rather than listening to what he actually says. To be sure, the history of Jesus

Yet justification is also a history in another sense in relation to our own existence as *die Gerechtfertigten*. In discovering this truth about ourselves, in finding ourselves in Jesus Christ, we are thrown into a crisis and launched into a 'way' – the way of hope and of living in accordance with the object of our faith.[41] The justified are not simply in a 'state' of being justified, therefore, but are caught up in a transition, called to live life as those in relation to whom the supreme reality (*höchste Realität*) is shown to be that which has taken place in Jesus Christ.[42] The existence of the justified is determined by this particular history in which they discover both their past and their hope for the future. Our 'justification' is not, therefore, an ontological or forensic *status quo* in which we can rest content, or upon which we can presume. Rather it is an alien history, a 'story' which we discover to be our own, and which projects us into the crisis of eschatological transition, living out the Kingdom of God in the midst of the world, living by faith in that reality which lies beyond our experience, but which stands over against us as our reality nonetheless.

---

[40] *(continued)* Christ in which sinful and evil human nature is put to death and raised up anew sees the fulfilment of God's creative and covenantal purpose (and is in that sense 'determined from all eternity'), but this in no way robs it of its central soteriological significance as the very locus of the actualization of God's saving activity towards his creature. It is also true that Barth stresses repeatedly the human plight in terms of our ignorance of God and of his own true situation as the fallen and redeemed creature of God; but to see this as in some way an alternative to the language of bondage to sin and evil is to make nonsense of what Barth actually says on the matter. His model of knowing is rich with the connotation of personal acquaintance and relationship, rather than the more purely intellectual model which McGrath seems to presuppose. Thus sin and ignorance are closely linked indeed, and need not be polarized. Yet Barth does not substitute the language of *Erkenntnis* and its cognates for that of *Sünde and Böse*. The history of Jesus Christ is not described simply or even primarily in terms of man's coming to know the Father, but as a history in which the divine judgement upon human sin is executed, the old humanity put to death in the Cross, and the new humanity raised up in the power of the Spirit.

[41] *CD* 4/1, pp. 595, 602.

[42] Ibid. p. 633.

To describe justification as a history, however, does not entail the idea that it is a process which begins 'objectively' and is completed 'subjectively'. That we are *in via* does not mean for Barth, as it certainly does for Küng,[43] that we are on the way to 'being justified' or at least to the *completion* of our justification. On the contrary, it is precisely the fact that 'in Him our justification is a complete justification' that places us decisively in this way in which we are caught up between the Whence of the *totus peccator* and the Whither of the *totus iustus*.[44] We cannot, therefore, be more or less justified at any given stage along this way. It is the discovery which faith makes of our 'real being in Christ' (*unser reales Sein in Christus*),[45] in which we are totally justified, that is the very basis of Christian existence and the ground upon which we hope, awaiting the revelation of that which we are in him. 'He is the concrete event of the existence and reality of the justified man in whom every man can recognize himself and every other man — recognize himself as truly justified.'[46]

But if justification is a reality in relation to us insofar as it is a concrete actuality in the history of Jesus Christ, and insofar as all are inevitably and inescapably bound up with his particular human existence, of whom are we to predicate this reality? Are we not compelled to say that all are justified, not potentially or virtually, but *really* justified in the depths of their being, since their being is determined by their relatedness to Jesus Christ and his history? And if so, what are we to say of the role of faith in relation to justification?

5. Justification as reality and acknowledged reality: the *sola fide*

Barth takes faith absolutely seriously as the necessary response to what God has done in Jesus Christ for us. The response of faith is the only legitimate and genuine response to the unconditional Yes in

---

[43] Küng, *Justification*, pp. 222f.
[44] *CD* 4/1, pp. 558, 573.
[45] Ibid. p. 636.
[46] Ibid. p. 630.

which God pardons us;[47] and faith itself consists in a corresponding and equally unconditional yes, a submission to the divine verdict, a casting of self wholly and utterly upon divine grace. There can be no other proper response: no 'ifs and buts', no qualified or half-hearted response. For it is in faith that we find ourselves to be the justified,[48] and that, as such, we are caught up into the transition from death to life, from old to new, from *totus peccator* to *totus iustus*. Faith, then, is the unconditional response which the gospel of justification, in its unconditional freeness, demands of us. It marks a decisive new beginning, a new way of existence which issues not from our 'natural' capacities but from the Word of God which addresses us and calls us out from our existence as sinners.[49] As such Barth takes it fully seriously, and nowhere speaks as if we could benefit from justification without it. He acknowledges, therefore, that there is a sense in which justification remains 'objective', without our experience until, in what he calls the 'self-demonstration of the justified man' to faith,[50] its reality impinges on our existence. Barth, in other words, recognizes the difference between belief and unbelief in relation to justification.

What, then, is the role of faith in relation to justification? How does Barth understand the *sola fide* of Luther's interpretation of Romans 3:28? Negatively, of course, it means that the *ergōn nomou* are of no avail in relation to justification. Paul's view of the old covenant and its law is that of 'the order of life which is revealed and holy but of no value at all for the justification of man.'[51] While, therefore, works cannot be regarded by the Christian with contempt, and must indeed be done as 'the (in itself) inevitable and good actualization of the (in itself) good creaturely nature of man',[52] we must appreciate their proper context and recognize their utter bankruptcy as a currency with which to trade for our justification. We cannot justify our own existence: nor can we cooperate in the justification which God fashions for us. We are disqualified by

---

[47] Ibid. p. 570.
[48] Ibid. p. 612.
[49] Ibid. pp. 612f.
[50] Ibid. p. 629.
[51] Ibid. p. 623.
[52] Ibid. p. 627.

our sin from being in any sense a partner in this operation.[53] That is precisely why God himself must come and take our place in a supreme act of self-substitution.

So it is not by works of the law but by faith that we receive our justification. But Paul, Barth insists, having excluded justification by works, did not intend now to bring in at the eleventh hour an alternative 'work' in the performance of which we achieve the self-justification which has hitherto eluded us. Faith is not a self-justifying act: here, in our response to grace, we are just as much in need of justification as anywhere else.[54] *Dikaiosyne* is *tēs pisteōs* or *ek pisteōs* or *dia pisteōs* but never *dia tēn pistin*.[55] Faith, insofar as it can be referred to as a work at all (i.e. as something which we *do*) has no intrinsic self-justifying value whatever, but is simply that human action which God accepts as the realization and appropriation of his own justifying work. From the human side faith is 'wholly and utterly humility',[56] the desperate surrender of vainglorious humans to the grace in which God meets them. It is an act of obedience in relation to the Word of God which encounters us, and in which we discover ourselves to be justified in Jesus Christ.[57]

Thus faith has the character of acknowledgement; an acknowledgement which does not, indeed, issue naturally from our capacities or our existence, but is based rather on the self-demonstration of the justified man which cuts into our mundane existence as a crisis. Here Barth, perhaps in conscious opposition both to the Catholic view and its counterpart in Liberal Protestantism, draws a sharp contrast between any attempt on our part to demonstrate to ourselves (*sich . . . beweisen*) our existence as the justified (as if this were readily locatable within our empirical existence) and the 'self-demonstration' (*der Selbstbeweis*) of the justified man which encounters us and in spite of our experience proclaims to us that we are the justified, to which proclamation faith submits in obedient humility.[58] The true nature of the contrast emerges

---

[53] Ibid. pp. 550f.
[54] Ibid. pp. 615f.
[55] Ibid. pp. 614f.
[56] Ibid. p. 618.
[57] Ibid. p. 620.
[58] Ibid. p. 629.

when, towards the end of §61, Barth finally answers the questions 'What is this all-important self-demonstration? Where is it to be found?' The answer, of course, is that it is the self-revelation of Jesus Christ to the sinner, the incarnate Word of God, the 'most concrete reality' in whom our justification is a completed reality prior to and apart from our acknowledgement of it.[59] Thus justification by its very nature is *complete* for us as an act of God. It is not something which can be augmented or completed or set in motion in our lives.[60]

Faith, then, is our humble and obedient response to that which is revealed to us concerning ourselves in Jesus Christ, namely, that we are justified. This is God's decision concerning us, and this decision has been actualized in the history of the God-man. 'Whether man hears it,' says Barth, 'whether he accepts it and lives as one who is pardoned is another question.'[61] It is, of course, rather an important question! The justification wrought in Christ is, Barth affirms, a reality for all: this is what faith discovers and what it is called to proclaim. What, then, are we to say of those who have not, do not, or will not acknowledge it? Are they justified? If Barth insists on uttering a carefully qualified 'yes' in response to this question, the reason

---

[59] *Loc. cit.*

[60] 'If (man) looks to Jesus Christ, to the event of his own redemptive history as it has taken place in Him, how can he also look to himself and his works? what interest can he have in them? how can he expect and claim that in them and therefore in himself there is, as it were, a little redemptive history, the completion, the continuation, the real fulfilment of the great history which has taken place in Jesus Christ? If he believes in Him, he knows and grasps his own righteousness as one which is alien to him, as the righteousness of this other, who is justified man in his place, for him' (*CD* 4/1, p. 631). 'What is the *sola fide* but a faint yet necessary echo of the *solus Christus*? He alone is the One in whom man is justified and revealed to be justified. He alone has fulfilled the penitence in which the conversion of man to God is actually and definitively accomplished. He alone has prayed in Gethsemane: "Thy will be done." He alone has shown Himself the One who in our place has destroyed the old and brought in the new. He alone was the One who was able to do this, who was sent into the world to do it, who was ordained to do it from all eternity as the Son of the Father' (ibid. p. 632).

[61] Ibid. p. 568.

is to be sought once again in his ontology. All are justified because God has justified human existence in Jesus Christ, and all are bound up with him whether they know it or like it or not.[62] Justification is the truth, the *reality* of their situation since their being is determined by his. If they do not choose to live in accordance with this truth, if they resist grace, then this does not and cannot revoke what he has decided and established as reality in the history of Jesus Christ for them. Their lives constitute a denial of this reality, but they do not undo it. Even if they persist in their denial and embrace hell as the outcome, they can never be those whom they seek to be; namely those who are unjustified, unloved, and separated from Jesus Christ.

All this means that Barth sees faith not as a human activity in which something virtual is actualized, but rather as that action in which we joyfully embrace something which is already real and already has our name firmly stamped upon it. He will not allow it to be spoken of as that which establishes the reality of justification for the individual. Justification is already real for me; it belongs to me prior to and apart from my acknowledgement of it because of my being in Jesus Christ. This in no way lessens the existential significance of that faith in which we begin to live the life of the justified and without which our existence constitutes a lie. Indeed it makes the response of faith all the more urgent and necessary. If in fact we have been justified by God in Christ (if this is the *reality* of our situation before God), how can we then continue to live as if we had not? For Barth the imperatives of the gospel flow inevitably and naturally out of the indicatives which proclaim to us that which God has established in his Son, and in which we are enveloped by virtue of his universal saving significance. Again, the focus of reality and truth is shifted by Barth away from the empirical experience of the individual to the reality established by God in Jesus Christ, the Justified One.

---

[62] 'As the One who has done that, in whom God Himself has done that, who lives as the doer of that deed, He is our man, we are in Him, our present is His, the history of man is His history. He is the concrete event of the existence and reality of the justified man in whom every man can recognise himself and every other man – recognise himself as truly justified' (ibid. p. 630).

Very briefly we may note two obvious points of difference between Barth and Küng over the *sola fide*. (1) For Küng justification is to be split into two parts: the objective (redemption) which is achieved for us in Christ, and the subjective (justification) which is worked out in us as we are made righteous by God's gracious activity.[63] While faith is certainly not a condition of the objective aspect (how could it be?), we may and must speak of it as properly a condition of the subjective.[64] Without our response of faith this 'making holy' cannot take place. Faith does not earn or deserve it, but is necessary in order for it to take place in us. For Barth, faith is not a condition of the subjective aspect of justification: faith *is* the subjective aspect of justification; it is the response of human beings in encounter with Jesus Christ (and hence with the truth concerning their own being), the point at which the completed reality of their justification impinges upon their existence and throws them into transition. (2) Precisely as such faith is a response to a reality and not merely to a possibility. Whereas for Küng the subjective aspect (the intrinsic *dikaiosyne*) is that in which virtual justification becomes a reality for man,[65] Barth sees justification as the reality to which faith responds. Again, the respective loci of reality are for Küng in us and our being as individuals and for Barth in Christ, and therefore in us and our 'being'. For Küng there is no sense in which we can refer to the unbeliever as justified in anything but a virtual sense. There is no real justification without faith.[66] Whatever may have been achieved objectively in Christ, something 'ontological' remains to be done in each of us before justification can be a reality for us.[67]

6. Justification and sanctification

It may be helpful to begin this final section by analysing the views of Küng, since it is in the relation between these two concepts that he

---

[63] See, e.g., Küng, *Justification*, p. 223.

[64] Ibid. p. 259.

[65] 'Only he who believes is *actually* (subjectively) justified' (ibid. p. 231; my italics).

[66] Ibid. p. 259.

[67] Ibid. p. 260.

sees a major source of terminological and conceptual confusion, and some opportunities for large-scale *rapprochement*.

We have noted already the fact that Küng himself (and, he argues, the Catholic tradition in general) distinguishes between 'redemption' in which God justifies his creation objectively in the death and resurrection of Christ, and 'justification', in which this objective deed is applied subjectively to the individual, and made 'real' or 'meaningful' for his or her existence. Barth, he argues, misunderstands the Catholic tradition (especially Trent) due to a rather different use of terminology whereby for Küng's 'redemption' we must read 'justification', and for Küng's 'justification', 'sanctification'.[68] Had Barth realized this, he would have seen immediately that the '*co-operari*' of Trent refers not to the objective sphere, but rather to the subjective ('sanctification' for Barth) and refers, therefore, not to self-justification or self-redemptive acts, but rather to 'getting oneself involved in what God alone has put into execution'.[69] God accomplishes everything: but he does not accomplish it *alone*: he accomplishes something precisely in us, and that means our involvement *on the basis of the grace of redemption objectively wrought*.[70] Through grace, God preserves the sinner in such a way that he or she is able to choose and to respond and to grow in 'justification/sanctification'.[71]

It is surprising that Küng could ever have seen this as the basis of any *rapprochement* between his own position and that of Barth, as if all that needs to be done is a little clarification or tweaking of terms and concepts. Doubtless such clarification is invaluable. But Barth is crystal clear throughout *CD* IV/1 and *CD* IV/2 that what *he* means by 'justification' must *not* be seen as the beginning or the 'first phase' of 'sanctification', as if the two terms can be seen as co-extensive, just as long as we distinguish carefully between the 'objective' elements and the 'subjective' elements. This is *not* a point of view which Barth can tolerate, and he says so quite explicitly. However closely we are to think 'justification' and

---

[68] Ibid. pp. 222f.
[69] Ibid. pp. 264f.
[70] Ibid. p. 265.
[71] Ibid. p. 264.

'sanctification' together, we must also see them as utterly distinct movements which must not be confused: and above all there can be no speaking of a human '*co-operari*' in justification, except in one very specific and unrepeatable instance.

In fact for Barth, as we have been seeing, justification does not have a 'subjective' aspect in the way that it does for Küng. As a reality it impacts us, leading to faith: but we do not share in that which 'justifies'. *Iustificare* is wholly and utterly God's *facere*,[72] a *fait accompli* wrought in the history of Jesus Christ, and 'objective' to us in that sense. It is a non-participable movement. Thus the application of the word 'justification' to that which takes place in Christian men and women is wholly erroneous. This is indeed their 'sanctification' in which they *are* involved, in which they *do* share.[73] But the terminological distinction is all-important to Barth. The two different aspects of the divine work *must not* be confused in any way: each must be accorded its own integrity.[74]

How then does Barth understand the difference? It is not, as with Küng, simply on the basis of an 'objective'/'subjective' demarcation. There are perhaps two other aspects to be taken into consideration: on the one hand, *orientation*, and on the other, *agency*.

Both justification and sanctification are elements in the one atoning and reconciling activity of God in Jesus Christ. But justification is that distinct aspect of this reconciling work in which God vindicates and exonerates his creation in the very face of its sinfulness and guilt and disease. Hence it is an activity which (eschatologically rather than chronologically) looks backwards to the old order, and cancels it out, establishing us as new creatures, faithful covenant partners of God. As such, in this retrospective orientation, it takes place and is completed wholly in the history of Jesus Christ, and is the activity of God. We have no part in it. Precisely insofar as what happens is *justificatory*, in other words, it is *God's* work, and not ours.

---

[72] *CD* 4/1, p. 500.
[73] See ibid. pp. 627f.
[74] *CD* 4/2, p. 504.

Sanctification, on the other hand, is orientated not retrospectively, but prospectively: it does not look back to our sinful past, but forward to our eschatological future. It is the saving work of God considered, not in relation to what we are saved *from*, but rather that which we are saved *for*: namely, sonship, covenant existence, fellowship with our Creator and so on. It consists positively in 'the creation of (man's) new form of existence as the faithful covenant partner of God',[75] his existence as the 'royal man'. In this movement God claims us for himself and converts us from our sinfulness to his holiness. Thus sanctification is man's 'reconciliation with God from the standpoint of his conversion to Him as willed and accomplished by God'.[76] It is the 'Ye *shall* be my people' which corresponds to the 'I will be your God' of justification.[77] It is the movement of humankind towards God within reconciliation, as distinct from the (logically prior) movement of God towards humankind. As such it is something which we share in, in which we are and must be involved, and is in that sense 'subjective'. But notice at once that for Barth *it* too is achieved first and foremost in the history of the man Jesus Christ. 'The God who in His humiliation justifies us is also the man who in His exaltation sanctifies us.'[78] Thus our sharing in sanctification is a sharing in that covenanted existence which God himself has established for us, as he pours out the Spirit upon the church. Again we find that the covenant partner whom God provides for himself is (in the final analysis) Jesus Christ, not to the exclusion of others, but as *the very ontic basis of their adoption* into covenant and filial existence.

The implication of all this is that in distinguishing 'justification' from 'sanctification' we are not distinguishing between two distinct sets of events, nor between two consecutive stages of a common series of events. Rather, both justification and sanctification are achieved in the one history of the incarnate Son in which reconciliation between God and humanity is wrought. 'Corresponding to the one historical being of Jesus Christ as true Son of God and true Son of Man, we can see (it) only as the movement from above to below,

---

75 Ibid. p. 499.
76 Ibid. p. 500.
77 Ibid. p. 499.
78 Ibid. p. 502.

or the movement from below to above, as justification or sanctification'.[79] The differentiation between the two, therefore, rests for Barth on this prior ontological differentiation within the inner dynamics of the incarnate Son. Viewed as the condescension of God in his movement towards humanity in Jesus Christ, and in relation to human sin, the history of the incarnation is seen as God's vindication of his creation. Viewed as the movement of this man towards God, and in relation to the eschatological future of humankind, the history of the incarnation is seen as the exaltation, the sanctification of our humanity in the Spirit, a movement which extends beyond this particular history into the history of the church. We may distinguish between the thing itself (the incarnate economy of the Son of God) on the one hand, and the particular aspect under which it is considered (either as justificatory or sanctificatory/glorificatory) on the other. As always, in relation to matters christological, Barth insists that these two aspects must neither be separated nor confused; the *achōristos* and the *asugkutos* of Chalcedon must provide the framework for their interpretation and exposition.

In particular Barth insists upon the distinctness of the two. Justification, he argues, must not merge into the process of sanctification, lest faith and works of love (both of which are a necessary part of Christian existence) come to be viewed as possessing justificatory worth.[80] They possess none, and to use even the term 'justification' in relation to them is to misunderstand or to risk losing the significance of the crucial distinctiveness of God's justifying activity, and thereby to undermine the very basis of the good news and of Christian assurance and joy. It is not at all clear that Küng sees this, or that the *rapprochement* which he attempts actually brings him any closer to Barth at all.

7. Conclusion

Our account has suggested the continuing existence of some very basic differences between Barth and his Catholic interpreter,

---

[79] Ibid.
[80] Ibid. p. 504.

which, if we are correct, pose some considerable problems for Küng's contention that the path to reconciliation between Catholic and Protestant lies through the relatively easy territory of the clarification of terms and meanings, and the redressing of balances and emphases. The map which we have charted shows some rather more daunting obstacles than this at the level of ontology, and suggests, consequently, that some fundamental divisions remain between Catholicism as represented by Küng and Protestantism as represented by Barth.[81] In conclusion it remains simply to reiterate that the significance of all this for the larger ecumenical debate over the doctrine of justification may prove to be relatively slight. Whether or not Küng may be taken as typical of the Catholic tradition, it must surely be admitted that Barth's approach to the subject would be as alien to many Protestant minds as it is to Catholicism. Here, as is so often the case, Barth occupies the uncomfortable territory set over against both camps: he remains, in many ways, an enigmatic figure, whose voice has still to be heard and whose message to be reckoned with seriously by those who, like himself, would consider themselves to be heirs of the Reformation. In this sense his theology stands as a clarion call to western theology in its entirety to look again at the metaphysical presuppositions which it brings to bear on the doctrine of reconciliation, and to consider whether they actually provide the most congenial framework for the proclamation of the gospel message that God has saved us, and has done so 'in his Son'.

---

[81] The question as to why Barth was able warmly to approve Küng's account of his own point of view is an interesting one. Part of the answer must lie in the fact that what Küng says about Barth's position is usually accurate. It is what he does not go on to say in addition that is significant. Furthermore, there is little doubt that Küng's presentation of the Catholic position on Justification represents a major shift from the way in which Barth himself had formerly understood it, and does indeed bring it much closer to Barth's own point of view. That much cannot be denied. What must be asked is whether or not, even after this task of reinterpretation has been completed, there remain significant points of difference which ought not to be glossed over in an enthusiasm for ecumenical progress. I have sought to demonstrate that this is indeed so.

4

Mapping the Moral Field and Mediating the Promise: A Study in Barth's Ethics

1. Mapping the moral field

In §74 of *CD* Barth defines the ethical endeavour briefly for us as 'an attempt to answer theoretically the question of what may be called good human action'.[1] This is not, of course, a question which arises solely or primarily within the context of Christian or even religious forms of life and thought. The question 'What ought I or we to do?', attempts to discern what it is that ascribes moral value to some modes of action rather than others in certain circumstances. To answer 'the supremely critical question concerning the good in and over every so-called good in human action'[2] is, as Barth notes elsewhere, one which haunts every age and culture.[3] Deep down it is the question which gnaws away in the soul of every man and woman who has ever lived. It is as if we are unable or unwilling, in the final analysis, to rest content with the deliverances of tradition and convention, and are troubled by the question of truth and ultimate goodness, eager and yet afraid to know how our own lives will be measured in relation to whatever answers lie out there beyond us. The question of the

---

[1] *CD* 4/4 (§74 published as *The Christian Life*, Grand Rapids: Eerdmans, 1981), p. 3.
[2] *CD* 2/2, p. 515.
[3] Ibid. p. 535. NB Barth insists that this ubiquitous moral questing is evidence not of a 'natural' propensity to seek and to do the good, but rather of the situation of fallen humans as those who have arrogated to themselves the responsibility for defining it. See ibid. pp. 522f.

goodness of our actions is, in other words, basic to our self-understanding and sense of self-worth as human beings. 'For it is as he *acts*', Barth writes, 'that man exists as a person. Therefore the question of the goodness and value and rightness . . . of his activity, the ethical question, is no more and no less than the question about the goodness, value (and) rightness . . . of his existence, of himself. It is his life-question by whose answer he stands or falls.'[4] But if the ethical question thus transcends the Christian church, being in some sense a universal and fundamental human concern, for Barth it is certainly not to be construed as a universal constant in anything other than this most basic sense. When we turn to consider the precise form and content of ethical reflection, he insists, then it is immediately apparent (and vital to recognize) that the question both arises and must be resolved in a quite distinctive manner within Christian theology.

John Webster reminds us that 'all ethical reflection has implicit within it an anthropology and an ontology of history – a construal of the moral agent and of the field in which the moral agent acts'.[5] If Christian ethics has a distinctive approach and answer to the ethical question, then for Barth it is undoubtedly largely to do with the particular way in which Christianity, so to speak, maps the moral space within which human action occurs. The gospel which the church proclaims, and the 'moral ontology'[6] which unfolds from within its logic, provides a quite distinct context and purpose for ethical reflection. This is precisely why, for Barth, dogmatics and ethics stand and fall together.[7] As he is always eager to remind us, 'Not God alone, but God and man together constitute the content of the Word of God attested in Scripture.'[8] Given that this is so, and that to be human is to act, there can clearly be no dogmatic reflection upon the

---

[4] Ibid. p. 516.

[5] J.B. Webster, *Barth's Ethics of Reconciliation* (Cambridge: CUP, 1995), p. 98.

[6] A phrase helpfully borrowed by Webster from Charles Taylor. See Webster, *Barth's Ethics of Reconciliation*, p. 215.

[7] See, e.g., *CD* 3/4, p. 3: 'As dogmatics enquires concerning the action of God and its goodness, it must necessarily make thorough enquiry concerning active man and the goodness of his action. It has the problem of ethics in view from the very first, and it cannot legitimately lose sight of it.'

[8] *CD* 1/2, p. 207.

gospel which does not have immediate implications for the question of the constitution of good human action, so that a Christian theological ethics can only be 'an integral element of dogmatics'.[9] The explication of this gospel, and the actual situation of God and humankind in their mutual relatedness which it describes, must therefore furnish the horizons for any serious discussion of human action.[10]

Furthermore, since 'the question of good and evil has been decided and settled once and for all in the decree of God, by the cross and resurrection of Jesus Christ . . . theological ethics . . . can only accept it as a decision that has been made actually and effectively'.[11] The task of theological ethics, therefore, is not and can never be that of the *investigation* of what (in ultimate terms) constitutes good and evil, or the attempt to justify the answer to this question which it has received in Jesus Christ by setting it within some wider and more ultimate court of appeal. To do this would in fact be to abandon the way of obedience, and to rehearse the history of the Fall over again, arrogating to humankind itself the responsibility for making final judgement on such matters.[12] Thus the characteristic mode of theological ethics must be that of witness, 'witness to the foundation which all things actually have, and which has actually been revealed as such'.[13] Such witness involves the claim 'that good human action is action which is most in accord with the way the world is constituted in Jesus Christ'.[14] This is the reality of the human situation, according

---

[9] *CD* 4/4 (§74), p. 3.

[10] Cf. Webster who draws our attention to Barth's own perception of *CD* as essentially an ethical dogmatics, and suggests that in this sense *CD* as a whole may be viewed precisely as 'a moral ontology – an extensive account of the situation within which human agents act . . . primarily devoted to the task of describing the "space" which agents occupy' *Barth's Ethics of Reconciliation*, pp. 1–2.

[11] *CD* 2/2, p. 535.

[12] Cf. *CD* 4/1, p. 448, where Barth suggests that 'What the serpent has in mind' in the temptation of Eve in Gen. 3 'is the establishment of ethics'! Ethics, in the generally accepted sense, in other words, is closely linked to the essence of the original sin.

[13] *CD* 2/2, p. 536.

[14] Webster, *Barth's Ethics of Reconciliation*, p. 219.

to the Christian gospel; we are who and what we are precisely and only in relation to Jesus Christ. Apart from him we have nothing but the most shadowy and wraithlike of existences, and any ethics which fails to consider human action in this its proper context, or which substitutes for it some abstract and fictitious account in which (for example) the essence of human moral agency is bound up with indeterminacy and freedom from transcendent or objective moral referents and boundaries, is doomed to disastrous failure. Hence the task of carefully mapping the moral space within the parameters of which human action occurs is fundamental to the ethico-theological endeavour.

2. The kingdom in our midst: an objective matrix for responsible action

What, then, is the substance of this description? Webster offers us a summary statement which may serve as a point of departure. What Barth presents, he suggests, is 'a depiction of the world of human action as it is enclosed and governed by the creative, redemptive and sanctifying work of God in Christ, present in the power of the Holy Spirit'.[15] We might develop this by saying at once that for Barth humans exist (and therefore act) as those concerning whom a decision has been made; namely, as objects of divine election. It is no coincidence that Barth's explicit discussion of ethics in *CD* first arises within the context of the discussion of the doctrine of God, and in the immediate wake of Chapter VII on election. Election is, after all, 'the sum of the Gospel, because of all words that can be said or heard it is the best'.[16] That God has elected himself to be the God who is for us, and elected us to be with him, is the best of all possible news. But it leads necessarily and directly into a consideration of the problem of human behaviour. That God is for us, that he does not will to be God without us, that he elects himself to be gracious to us and at the same time elects us to bear witness to his glory, all of this has the most direct consequences for ethics. Barth asks:

---

[15] Ibid. p. 2.
[16] *CD* 2/2, p. 3.

> For who can possibly see what is meant by the knowledge of God,
> His divine being, His divine perfections, the election of His grace,
> without an awareness at every point of the demand which is put to
> man by the fact that this God is his God, the God of man? How can
> God be understood as the Lord if that does not involve the problem
> of human obedience.[17]

In other words, to take seriously the character of the God who is
revealed to us in Jesus Christ as Lord, to take seriously his election of
us to participate as his partner in the covenant of grace, is to be faced
at once with the ethical problem in the proper sense. The problem
here is not, of course, the discernment of the good. That is manifest
to us; it confronts us in the character of God himself (who is its
objective source and guarantor) and of his incarnate Word. The real
problem for the theological ethicist is that of the discrepancy
between the good thus revealed and the behaviour of those who
have been elected by God, and to whom the demand of grace is
clearly stated: 'Ye shall be perfect, even as your Father which is in
heaven is perfect' (Mt. 5:48, AV). That God is for us, in other
words, bears with it the realization that he can only also be against
us; or, rather, against the sinners we have become, inasmuch as our
sin and its destructive consequences constitute a denial of what God
himself has decreed for us, a denial which he will neither tolerate
nor allow to prevail. Thus the election of humans as God's covenant
partners can only involve their judgement and the execution of
God's wrath upon them. The gospel is inseparable from law, a law
which stands over against us as demand and judges us.

Yet the relationship between grace and law, mercy and wrath
must be perceived aright. To get it wrong (as Christian theology too
often has) is to risk subverting the logic of the gospel altogether and
substituting for it 'another gospel which is no gospel at all'. The law
arises precisely within the context of grace, and for the sake of the
triumph of grace. The law expresses not the conditions of grace, but
the obligations of a gracious covenant which God has established
and within which he has placed us for our benefit. 'The law would
not be the law, if it were not contained and locked up in the ark of

---

[17] Ibid. p. 512.

the covenant.'[18] Similarly, God judges his creature 'by rushing pow-
erfully to his aid to create right for him, that is, to put him in the
right against all forces, and not least of all, but decisively, himself, to
acquit him, and to save him from corruption . . . He thus judges him
to his salvation.'[19] Furthermore, Barth reminds us that Matthew
5:48 reads both as imperative and indicative, as demand and as
promise. 'Ye *shall* be perfect!' And according to the logic of the gospel, it is the indicative which must be accorded the prior force.[20]
The demands follow on from the promise and not vice versa. In
electing himself to be our God and us to be his people God takes
responsibility for us and for our well-being upon himself. Thus he
establishes the covenant of grace and upholds it and bears it forward
to its goal, justifying us and sanctifying us for his service.[21]

At this point, however, we need to remind ourselves of the most
characteristic feature of Barth's treatment of the doctrine of election, namely, his insistence that the man Jesus Christ 'is the election
of God before which and without which and beside which God
cannot make any other choices'.[22] For our purposes what is significant about this statement is its stark and uncompromising assertion
that the man whom God is with and who is with God is, in the first
and decisive instance, not me or you or the Christian community or
the human race as a whole, but this one particular historical
instantiation of *humanitas*, Jesus of Nazareth. We do not have time
to go into the christological underpinnings of this claim in detail
save to indicate that for Barth, following the christological orthodoxy of the tradition, Jesus Christ is none other than God himself
present among us in person as a human agent, experiencing to the
full what it means to be human, and in the process transforming
what it means to be human. He is God with us. But he is also, as it
were, us with God, as the dynamics of hypostatic union and those of

---

[18] K. Barth, 'Gospel and Law', in *God, Grace and Gospel* (Edinburgh:
Oliver & Boyd, 1959), p. 3.

[19] *CD* 4/4 (§74), p. 15.

[20] Cf. *CD* 2/2, p. 512: 'The truth of the evangelical indicative means that
the full stop with which it concludes becomes an exclamation mark. It
becomes itself an imperative.'

[21] Cf. *CD* 4/4 (§74), p. 16.

[22] *CD* 2/2, p. 94.

atonement are fused together and become coterminous. In his very person God and humankind are united, not in some crude 'physical' sense, but morally, spiritually, in a meeting and concurrence of wills and purposes and desires. God becomes a human person in order to fulfil the determination of humanity within the covenant from the human side as well as the divine side. The dynamics of the covenant relation are swallowed up and healed and secured at this point within the dynamics of Jesus' own divine–human life.

Thus in Jesus we see,

> the one faithful and obedient Israelite in whom Israel's justification, sanctification, and vocation are unproblematically enacted by its God . . . the man in whom the whole human race is set in the light of God's grace and in relation to whom the whole human race is to be told that God's name is already hallowed in its midst, God's kingdom has already come, and God's will in and with it is already done. The history of completed fellowship between God and man, not merely commencing on one side but established on both.[23]

This, then, is the high point of the gospel as Barth understands it from his reading of the New Testament; the kingdom, the covenant, and with them creation itself have been realized in our midst in this one man's history. Here, as Webster observes, 'so much hangs on so little; an entire ontology of created being rests upon a mere fragment'.[24] What needs to be said immediately, however, is that far from tending towards exclusivity, Barth's vision is *inclusive*. The one who acts here is the very same one in whom all that is lives and moves and has its being. Hence all reality is bound up with this reality; the truth about all other humans is a function of the relationship which they have to this one man and his history which has become their history. God, in other words, has realized his election of humankind in this one man not to the exclusion of others, but precisely for them, securing the covenant and the kingdom for their participation in it. Barth writes:

> The man to whom the Word of God is directed and for whom the work of God was done – it is all one whether we are thinking of the Christian who has grasped it in faith and related it to himself, or the man in the

---

[23] *CD* 4/4 (§74), p. 11.

[24] Webster, *Barth's Ethics of Reconciliation*, p. 86.

cosmos who has not yet done so – this man, in virtue of this Word and work, does not exist by himself. He is not an independent subject to be considered independently . . . whether he knows and believes it or not – it is simply not true that he belongs to himself and is left to himself, that he is thrown back upon himself. He belongs to . . . Jesus Christ . . . He exists because Jesus Christ exists. He exists as a predicate of this Subject, i.e., that which has been decided and is real for man in this Subject is true for him. Therefore the divine command as it is directed to him, as it applies to him, consists in his relationship to this Subject.[25]

This, then, is, in the most precisely defined sense, the moral space within which human action is permitted and demanded. Believers and non-believers alike are situated (have their true being) within the dynamics of this one man's fulfilment of the covenant on their behalf.[26] Consequently we are called to live in God's world as constituted thus, a world in which good human action is defined and realized on our behalf by Jesus Christ, in whose life, death and resurrection God has fulfilled the covenant and thereby established the kingdom in our midst, bringing our humanity (and with it creation itself) to its proper *telos*. Our action is thereby bounded and determined by our identification (not identity) with the one who stands before and among us as 'the elect of God'. It is characterized as obedience or disobedience accordingly as it confirms or contradicts our being as those who exist only in relation to him and his history. The good news of our election and justification in and with him bears inexorably in its wake the command to live as those of whom this is true. Yet the command of grace is paradoxical; for it no longer stands over against us as an unfulfilled demand but (*post Christum*) as a divine promise kept. The 'ye shall be' has become also 'ye are' inasmuch as our identity is bound up with Christ; but for that very reason the 'ye shall be' itself is all the more pressing. The logic of Barth's ethics at this point mirrors that of the apostle Paul. The text

---

[25] *CD* 2/2, p. 539.

[26] The metaphysical implications of and background to this claim in Barth have caused some commentators considerable difficulties since, like so much else in this theology, they are counter-intuitive in the modern context. For an invaluable discussion of the matter see Ingolf Dalferth's essay 'Karl Barth's Eschatological Realism', in S.W. Sykes (ed.), *Karl Barth: Centenary Essays* (Cambridge: CUP, 1989), pp. 14–45.

in which its orientation is best summed up is Romans 6:2, 'how can
we live in it any longer?' The law arises within the context of grace,
and by grace its fulfilment is secured and the covenant placed on the
securest possible footing, being underwritten on both sides by
the God who is for us.

3. Divine command as creative event

We turn next to consider the way in which, according to Barth,
God's command cuts into the here and now of our human existence. In so doing we move from the sphere of 'general ethics' to
'special ethics' in his terminology.[27] Barth's obvious preference for
the language of command rather than that of law is instructive at this
point. The problem with the language of law is that it may be interpreted in accordance with what Barth sees as a complete misreading
of the ethical circumstance of human beings. We are not, he insists,
engaged as moral agents in the task of handling some prescribed
text, whether that 'text' be the dictates of a supposed universal rational principle, the accumulated moral wisdom of human experience,
or even a set of universally binding divine ordinances derived from
Scripture. In his discussion of the matter in *CD* III/4 Barth develops
a careful critique of moral casuistry, an approach in which the ethical task is deemed precisely to be one first of expounding a general

---

[27] According to Barth general ethics has to do with 'the claim, decision
and judgment of God which in his Word become evident as the command confronting human action' (*CD* 4/4 (§74), p. 4), and is as such part
and parcel of the doctrine of God and his election of humankind in Christ.
It is 'general' inasmuch as it has to do with the moral ontology, the dimensions and contours of the moral space within which *all* human action
occurs, and which we have been discussing thus far. In special ethics, on
the other hand, we move to the sphere of the particular, 'following the
command of God with particular reference to the man to whom he turns
in it . . . with its significance and outworking in the life of the man to
whom it comes . . . (looking) at this particular man at this particular time
and place, who yesterday selected and acted on the basis of the possibilities
available, who does the same today in different circumstances, and who
will do the same tomorrow in different circumstances again' (ibid. p. 4).
See further *CD* 3/4, pp. 4f.

'law', and then applying it creatively to particular cases which present themselves.[28] Such an approach is unacceptable for Barth because it misconstrues (and consequently denies) the actual circumstances in which moral judgements are to be made.

The command of God, Barth insists, is not some objective entity to be codified, expounded and applied by human beings. It is something particular which occurs, an event in which God commands and we hear and are summoned to respond. Responsible action, therefore, can never consist in human beings manipulating and applying some general moral deposit in accordance with the dictates of their own moral reason (conscience). Such a scenario is unthinkable, since it places the human agent in ultimate control of the procedure and thereby limits the freedom of God to command what he wills in particular circumstances, usurping the prerogative of judgement which is God's alone. As we have seen, it is this very displacement which constitutes the essence of human sinfulness for Barth. Rather, responsible action consists in the obedient response to a command which encounters us in the particularities of our circumstance and addresses us directly. It is God speaking to us, telling us what we ought to do today. There can be no question of human beings having any control over or decisive independent contribution to make to this event. In this respect the command of God is simply a particular instance of the revelation of God which always has an event character, which is dynamic rather than static, and which involves the drawing of the recipient into a personal and transforming relationship with the divine subject. Barth states:

> The command is that of the living God. Thus the concept speaks of God's action to the extent that this is also a specific Word directed to man . . . It is a specific command of God in each specific form of his dealings with man, in each specific time, in relation to the presuppositions and consequences of each specific existence of each man. It . . . is not a principle of action revealed to man and imposed upon him. It is not a collection of such principles which man . . . must expound and apply to the best of his knowledge and conscience.[29]

---

[28] See ibid. pp. 6f.

[29] CD 4/4 (§74), p. 33.

The command of God, then, is a particular, dynamic, uncontrollable event in which God speaks and summons forth response-ability from us, presenting us immediately with the crisis of obedience or disobedience. In such circumstances there can be no place for detached deliberation, or weighing of the legitimacy of the command. We have simply to hear it, and then either to obey or disobey.

This central aspect of Barth's ethics has attracted vehement criticism from Christian ethicists more content with some version or other of the casuistic method. The analogies with responses to Barth's rejection of natural theology are easily drawn; indeed to a large extent the two are instances of one and the same issue. Nigel Biggar, in his largely sympathetic reading of Barth's ethics, surveys the criticisms of Gustafson, Hauerwas, Lehman, Niebuhr, Willis, Yoder and others in a helpful manner.[30] Most of the criticisms listed centre around the uncompromising heteronomy of the divine command in Barth's account: it short-circuits rational processes and transcends rational assessment and public warrant; it tends (in the name of divine freedom) towards a voluntaristic occasionalism which erodes the predictablility and universality upon which moral reflection depends; it manifests wholly unwarranted optimism with regard to the hearing by moral agents of an unambiguous command of God; it fails to take seriously the moral complexity of many issues, and ignores empirical data relevant to the consideration of particular cases, and so forth. Much of this criticism reveals simply how little the critics have actually grasped Barth's intention.

Biggar himself, sympathetic though he is to much of what Barth says, demurs from the latter's complete rejection of 'systematic ethics'. The problem with such a wholesale rejection, he argues, is that it goes too far, and in any case is unnecessary in order to secure what Barth wishes to secure.[31] Thus, Barth's concern in his polemical identification of the establishment of 'ethics' with original sin is

---

[30] See Biggar, *The Hastening that Waits: Karl Barth's Ethics* (Oxford: 1995), pp. 19f.

[31] Readers experiencing a sense of *déja vu* at this point are encouraged to consult the early paragraphs of Emil Brunner's 1934 essay 'Nature and Grace' (Tübingen: JCB Mohr, 1934).

laudable enough. It is decisively to exclude 'the autarkic refusal to acknowledge any moral authority external to the human self' on the one hand, and 'the autonomous pretension of the human subject to a kind of jurisprudential mastery over the objective moral law' on the other.[32] In order to achieve this, however, Barth uses a sledgehammer to crack a nut, rejecting ethical systematizing as a whole (rather than identifying deviant forms of it) and thereby leaving no ground whatever for the legitimate exercise of moral reasoning. This, Biggar suggests, is both unnecessary and inconsistent, since Barth himself clearly engages in a form of systematic ethics in his own writings. The resolution of the apparent conundrum, he proposes, lies in a differentiation between closed systems (knowledge of the basic principles of which would render the good in a given circumstance in principle deducible) and an open system. Characteristic of the latter is that on the one hand it will be structured a posteriori in accordance with 'knowledge in faith' (namely, 'knowledge whose subject accepts and respects what is given her with humility and gratitude, repentance and obedience')[33] and on the other it is open to new and exceptional cases of divine commanding, and therefore 'does not claim the power to identify conclusively what God is commanding in a given situation'.[34]

One wonders, however, whether Biggar has really seen what it is that Barth is concerned to avoid and to affirm, and whether, therefore, his proposal really helps much at all. What Barth *does* in his ethics may resemble in some respects what Biggar intends by an 'open system'; but there is an entire dimension which Biggar's description (crucially) appears to overlook. The language of system still resonates with the suggestion of an *independent* human ethical activity, even if such activity be deemed a posteriori with respect to God's previous commanding, and essentially open with respect to his commanding in the future. When Biggar examines the language of 'command' he notes that, 'unlike "law", it does not denote a natural or conventional institution but rather a momentary utterance

---

[32] See Biggar, *The Hastening that Waits*, p. 8.
[33] Ibid. p. 11.
[34] Ibid. p. 32.

issued directly by one person to another.'[35] This is true, but it appears to lose sight of what is so vital in Barth's conception, namely, that the command renews and is part of an ongoing relationship between two subjects, a 'history' as Barth calls it in which the human agent is enabled through encounter with something other than itself 'to transcend itself in response and in relation to this new factor'.[36] To speak instead, as Biggar prefers to do, of having an open system of known principles and laws derived from 'revelation' but open to modification would seem in effect to be a two-dimensional way of expressing a three-dimensional truth; but the missing dimension is vital, and its absence opens the model up to all the mistakes of natural theology which Barth so consistently fears and opposes.

Significantly, the ways in which Barth describes the ethical context could more readily be allied to an account of personal formation in terms of the inculcation of virtue than to Biggar's preferred model of systematic reflection. Through a history of encounter with a God who has a particular character, whose character is known, and association with whom shapes our own character in particular ways, that is to say, we come to be the sort of people who know God's command when we hear it, and when we hear it respond in obedience. Bank clerks are trained to recognize forged currency by becoming utterly familiar with the 'feel' of the genuine article, handling thousands of legitimate banknotes until, when a fake is deliberately fed into the pile before them, they are able to identify it (without necessarily being able to say precisely why). A mixture of habit and the known character of the real thing suffices to identify the dud instinctively and without deliberation. So for Barth, while God's command is always particular and free and can never be predicted, nonetheless:

> this free and particular disposing always takes place in the context and order which are laid down by the fact that he is not a dark and formless numen but the almighty Lord who wills the best for the man who is responsible to him . . . We can and should count on it that in all cases, always and everywhere, his free commanding is characterized by his being this and no other God.[37]

---

[35] Ibid. p. 14.
[36] See *CD* 3/2, p. 158.
[37] *CD* 4/4 (§74), pp. 34–35.

On such an account, discernment of what is and is not a genuine command of God begins to look less like reflection or deliberation, and more like intuition or connoisseurship, a judgement founded on a mixture of familiarity with the God who commands and personal habit. This will not do as an account of the *whole* story about God's commanding and our hearing of and responding to it, but insofar as it tells any significant part of that story it goes some way towards eliminating the impressions of arbitrariness and occasionalism which are sometimes assumed to attach to Barth's model. There is not just the punctiliar command of God to be taken into consideration for Barth, but the history of the God who commands with the one whom he commands; and what feeds into the particular ethical moment from that history must not be overlooked.

Nonetheless, Barth, we should insist, does not deride, exclude or belittle moral reflection as such (any more than reason in general), but only *independent* moral reflection – that is, moral reflection in which there is at the time only the activity of a human subject to be taken into account. The command of God is not, for Barth, an utterance which, once uttered, leaves behind it a deposit to be handled and dissected by human beings, like archaeologists poring over the remains of some earlier civilization. The command of God encounters us and in doing so *creates and sustains* human moral subjects capable of making sense of themselves, transcending their own (fallen) capacities and incapacities, and becoming what they can never be apart from the continuing of this divine address, namely, responsible human agents. Another way of putting this would be to insist that the *analogia fidei* applies just as surely in the ethical sphere as anywhere else. *Homo peccator* becomes *capax verbi Dei* here as elsewhere only as the *Verbum Dei* speaks and is heard. The only moral reflection which has a place in Barth's ethics, therefore, is moral reflection in which God is involved both objectively as the source of the command and subjectively in enabling and undergirding our free response to the same. Hence the command of God, like revelation in general, is act of God from first to last. God stands on both the divine and the human side of the covenant relation not only in the incarnation of the Word in Jesus Christ but in his continuing address to humankind in the Spirit. Insofar as Biggar's attempt to rehabilitate the language of system misses or fails to account for this fact, it must be deemed misguided. The words are those of Biggar, but the voice has unmistakeable (and unfortunate) resonances with that of Brunner.

4. Moral space as limited space

We turn now to the fact, as Barth sees it, that moral space is limited space. As we have already seen, the human agent is situated decisively in relation both to God's action in Jesus Christ at a particular point in the past and God's continuing action in the present moment in the dynamic command which lays hold of and sanctifies us. It takes little familiarity with the alternative depictions of our moral space offered by modern and postmodern accounts of human action to realize just how far such a picture lies both in its broad outlines and its detail from the most cherished dogmas of the late (as indeed the early and mid) twentieth century. The most obvious of these dogmas centre around the idea of freedom defined as freedom from all limitations, the freedom to determine oneself and one's own destiny and identity without interference, the notion that authentically responsible behaviour is behaviour rooted in self-reflection and a natural human capacity both to discern the good and to act in accordance with that discernment, and so on. As Barth's discussion of the relationship between theological and 'general' ethics in *CD* 2/2 reveals, Christian theology has often sought some level of accommodation of such ideas. If Barth refuses to do so then it is precisely because his understanding of the gospel and the grace manifest in it forbids any such procedure. 'Grace which has from the start to share its power with a force of nature', he writes, 'is no longer grace';[38] not, at least, the sort of grace of which the gospel speaks.

Not surprisingly, this emphasis in Barth's theology and ethics has provoked strong responses among those who can only see in it either an outright denial or tacit erosion of authentic human freedom, and thus moral responsibility. If human persons are the objects of God's sovereign choosing and deciding, and if God's decision about them has already been realized in some inclusive manner in

---

[38] *CD* 2/2, p. 531.

Jesus Christ, if the command of God is essentially heteronomous and comes to us ready-made with no need for serious moral deliberation on our part, how then can we think of human action as responsible? If Christ has already sealed and secured the covenant, fulfilling the command on our behalf, do we even need to respond? And (assuming that we do) if our response can never be *purely* our response, but only ever part of that revelatory event in which God is involved as Subject from first to last, does grace not overwhelm and thereby render morally nugatory any such response we might make? Are we not simply 'acting under the influence'?

Clearly, a substantial part of a full response to questions such as these would have to consist in a critique of the essentially libertarian notion of freedom which they presuppose, a critique which I do not have time to develop here. All I can do is to note the concerns, and try briefly to indicate how Barth counters them.

First we should note that Barth construes the relationship between God and humans as a genuine encounter between two distinct subjects who (and whose actions therefore) remain distinct in the midst of the encounter: 'God and Man do in fact confront one another: two partners of different kinds, acting differently, so that they cannot be exchanged or equated.'[39] Here the logic of hypostatic union (and in particular the assumption of full humanity by the Logos) informs the logic of theological ethics. As there is no overwhelming or short-circuiting of the genuine human willing of Jesus (which yet remains the human willing of the Logos) so nor can there ever be any confusing, mixing or separating of the divine and human agency in the ethical moment. The suggestion that where grace is at work 'God is everything and man nothing' Barth rejects as a complete misconstrual of the divine-human relation as revealed in the person of Christ.[40] Even in the context of the gracious determining of human existence by divine election, Barth is clear that there is and can be no overwhelming of the creature's

---

[39] *CD* 4/4 (§74), p. 27.
[40] See *CD* 4/1, p. 6. See further ibid. p. 89: 'God is indeed everything but only in order that man may not be nothing, in order that he may be His man . . . This creating and grounding of a human subject which is now in relation to God and therefore in itself is, in fact, the event of the atonement made in Jesus Christ.'

self-determining response. It is persons whom God elects into covenant partnership, and their election would be empty of meaning 'if to the divine decision there did not correspond a human one in which the partner in the covenant has to give his answer to what is said to him by the fact that God has concluded it'.[41] Indeed, personhood as such is inexorably tied to action: the human person 'exists and lives as he deliberately posits himself in some way in relation to God, to his fellow-men, and to his environment. His actions are this deliberate positing of himself'.[42] His life consists in a history of such action, and anything which threatens to transform it into a mere process would be a denial of his essential humanity, and of that which God most seeks in his creature, namely, 'that out of man's life there should come a repetition, an analogy, a parallel to His own being'.[43]

'What characterizes the creatureliness, nature, existence and life of man, and therefore man as such . . . is that . . . he exists and lives in freedom.'[44] If God would seriously have *man* as covenant partner, therefore, then it must certainly be in and with the freedom which characterizes his existence. Yet the sort of freedom which Barth has in view is not of the sort envisaged by libertarianism. The space within which it is exercised is limited space. God limits the existence of his creature. But this is not to be construed as a problem for or denigration of the creature, but rather as a blessing and opportunity.

> When God . . . limits, there can be no talk of a curtailment or impoverishment or deprivation of the one thus limited. His very limiting is His special, exalted, rich and glorious giving. His limiting is His definite, concrete and specific affirmation. The man who is limited by Him is the man who is loved by Him. Rather than tolerating our limitation with a sigh, we have every reason to take it seriously, to affirm it, to accept it, and to praise God for the fact that in it we are what we are and not something else.[45]

---

[41] *CD* 2/2, p. 510.
[42] *CD* 3/4, p. 470.
[43] *CD* 1/2, p. 276.
[44] *CD* 3/4, p. 470.
[45] Ibid. p. 568.

The limitation of human freedom, in other words, is the establishment of the proper boundaries of creaturely existence, the bestowal upon the creature of its particular nature and end, an end towards the fulfilment of which God determines and enables it to move. 'The individual thing receives its particular dignity and value on the basis of a formative economy which assigns to all things a place and time and function.'[46] Hence the limitation of the moral agent is its preservation as the good creature of God, and as such the prevention of its movement towards final hellish self-destruction.

The true freedom of the creature, therefore, far from being at odds with the determination of God's election, is in reality utterly contingent upon this gracious determination. The paradox of grace is precisely that it both liberates and binds us in the very same moment. Or, as Barth characteristically expresses the matter, 'it is as He makes Himself responsible for man that God makes man, too, responsible'.[47] So, the fact that, objectively in Christ, God has secured the fulfilment of the covenant and thereby of his own promise to the creature that 'ye shall be perfect', far from displacing other human subjects from a position of moral responsibility, stands over against them as a fact of their very being which lays claim to their allegiance and demands a response. Yet, on the other hand, it is a liberating fact, for this is a scenario in which the reality of the covenant between God and humans is neither established nor perpetuated by our performance as moral agents, but envelops our moral agency in an objectively actual matrix founded upon Christ's self-substitution for us, within the security of which we are now both commanded and set free (from the fear of failure) to act in accordance with what and who we are in him.[48] Thus the

---

[46] *CD* 3/3, pp. 192–193.

[47] *CD* 2/2, p. 511.

[48] See ibid. p. 540: 'What we have to investigate is (man's) participation in the righteousness of this Subject . . . When we say: what ought we to do? we are asking about Him, for it is in Him that this question of ours is answered. In Him the obedience demanded of us men has already been rendered . . . so completely that we, for our part, have actually nothing to add, but have only to endorse this event by our action.'

determination of grace *makes us* responsible rather than *robbing us* of responsibility.

Similarly, the dynamic command of God, as it encounters us in the midst of our history with him, places us under the particular determination of his willing in the present moment and thereby demands of us responsibility. It binds us as a sovereign Word about our action here and now. And yet, as we have already seen, for Barth it is precisely as this occurs that God calls into being a correspondence in the creaturely realm to his own being and activity. In the ethical moment (as in the revelatory moment in general) God 'does not find an existing partner in man, but creates a partner',[49] setting us free from the forces of evil which enslave us, and enabling us to respond in accordance with our true nature in Christ. Again, therefore, the determination of grace both binds and liberates. The moral space within which we live and move and have our being is limited; but it is limited precisely in order to set us free to become what God intends us to be, namely, responsible covenant partners in fellowship with him.

5. Mediating the Promise

If the most important dimension of the moral space which we occupy as responsible human agents is our relatedness to God through Jesus Christ, another vital aspect of it, for Barth, is our given relatedness to other human persons, again, through our relation to Jesus Christ who is the Head of the human covenant community, and the one in whom we live and move and have our being. The vertical and horizontal dimensions of our existence meet in him, in relation to whom alone we are who and what we are. We are, to coin a more contemporary expression, persons only in relation. Our relatedness to God and to other persons is not something subsequent to our existence as such, something contingent upon our willing and acting; it is part of the very objective moral fabric of our personal existence. We are bonded objectively to others (a bonding which bears with it all manner of responsibilities which we may or may not

---

[49] *CD* 2/2, p. 531.

be aware of or choose to acknowledge) by what Scots theologian T.F. Torrance calls 'onto-relations'; relations, that is to say, which are irreducibly basic to our being. Thus our self-realization and self-interest as persons can only be furthered as we direct our attention and concern not to ourselves alone, but to others. Humanity is, in Barth's phrase, co-humanity or fellow humanity. 'Humanity which is not fellow humanity', he writes, 'is inhumanity. For it cannot reflect but only contradict the determination of man to be God's covenant partner, nor can the God who is no *Deus solitarius but Deus triunus*, God in relationship, be mirrored in a *homo solitarius*.'[50] Here, then, the structure of human personal being, the structure of the covenant, and the structure of the divine life are in some respects superimposed and intertwined.

But if, as human persons, we exist within a complex network of onto-relations, it is also true that our relatedness to others is of a differentiated sort. We are not, in other words, related to all equally closely or deeply. Both in synchronic and diachronic terms there are degrees and intensities of relatedness to be taken into consideration.

It is to consideration of one of the closest and most fundamental of these relations that Barth turns in the second part of §54 in *CD*. It is part of our limitation as creatures, he observes, that we exist within a sequence of generations. Each of us is conceived and born if we exist at all. Thus the relationship between parent and child is the most basic of human relationships. It is also one which exemplifies the given objectivity of our location within the onto-relational web. It may not be obvious that we have our being in relation to our disadvantaged neighbour, to a refugee in war-torn Bosnia, or even to Jesus Christ. But the fact of our biological relatedness to at least two human persons (whether we know their identities or not) is something which we accept as a fact of our condition: historical accident maybe; not what we might have chosen given the choice of gene pool and social situation perhaps; but a fact nonetheless. We cannot change it. We are necessarily related to our parents, and they to us. A relationship arises (and in most cases we indwell it) which is particular, exclusive and permanent. We don't choose our parents and they

---

[50] *CD* 3/4, p. 117.

(mostly still even in this day of sophisticated gene technology) don't in any obvious sense choose us.

Barth does not have and does not seek to develop a theology or theological account of the family, a fact which may be striking to us given the current constant appeals within a decaying western culture to traditional 'family values' as if they were an undeniable part of God's blueprint for human life. The 'family' as such, Barth suggests, has relatively little place in biblical patterns of thought where other sorts of relationships are equally or more important than those loose clannish ties we have with siblings, grandparents, aunts and uncles, cousins, etc. 'It was', he writes, 'the habits of thought and actual customs of the Christianised heathen which later gave to the idea of the family the splendour of a fundamental concept of Christian ethics. We have no occasion to adopt this view.'[51] It is to the parent–child relation in particular that he directs us as theologically significant.

The first thing to note about this relationship is that Barth sees it as tied to physical and biological 'parenthood' only in an incidental manner. The essence of the relation, in other words, is not genetic, even though in actual fact those who perform the parental role may most often be those whose physical union has resulted in the birth of the child concerned. And perhaps in some ways it is appropriate that it be so. But for Barth it is certainly not *necessary* that it be so. Rather, the role of parent with respect to child is that of transmitting a tradition of life and faith and practice from one generation to the next, inculcating and nurturing a hope and vision in those who are entering the earliest stages of life, that they may grow and develop not just physically, but in this hope, learning to live their lives within the world as construed by it.

Thus, the particular form of the command of God that children should honour and respect their father and mother (Exod. 20:12; Deut. 5:16), while it certainly has to do with a relationship of subordination, has little to do with what has all too often been extracted from it. Specifically, it 'does not mean the outward and formal subjection of the will of the younger to that of the older generation' in general terms, 'but the respecting of the latter as the bearer and

---

[51] Ibid. p. 242.

mediator of the promise given to the people with regard to its existence'.[52] The 'people' concerned initially, of course, was Israel; but the church as inheritor of this promise and its fulfilment in Christ also inherits the basic form of life intended of the covenant community at this point. For it, too, the oversight and responsibility pertaining to parenthood:

> does not belong to the physical but . . . to the historical order. It consists in the fact that the parents are really the elders in relation to the children, and that they are their particular elders, those who have lived before and longer than they, and are therefore wiser and more experienced. And in relation to their children they do not merely represent their own knowledge and experience but that conveyed to them by their own predecessors.[53]

Parents, then (who are inevitably themselves also children) are links in a chain of transmission. Their responsibility is to pass on faithfully what they themselves have received, and they are, therefore, a vital part of the missionary activity of the church. Children 'are not by nature their property, subjects, servants or even pupils, but their apprentices who are entrusted and subordinated to them in order that they might lead them into this way of life'.[54]

Barth illustrates this point by referring the reader to all those places in the Old Testament where children are shown asking their parents what is meant by certain rites and practices, and thereby generating the opportunity for the telling of the story of God's mighty acts. The promise is transmitted as the story is told, heard and interpreted, and the covenant community extended through time. Put differently, we might say that what is passed on in this way is precisely a map of the moral space for human action in God's world. The command to honour those who mediate this tradition is thus to the end 'that thy days may be long in the land which the Lord thy God giveth thee'. In other words, what is required is 'that the parents convey to the children that knowledge and wisdom in the conduct of life without the observance of which the dwelling of

---

[52] Ibid.
[53] Ibid. p. 243.
[54] Ibid.

the people . . . in the land would be pointless and could have no permanence'.[55]

In all this, Barth notes, it is perfectly legitimate to speak of human parents as representative in a certain sense of God himself to the child, although no human parent should ever explicitly *seek* to be this by their actions. Indeed it is one of the characteristic features of the New as opposed to the Old Testament context that God's fatherhood (from which human parenthood derives) is explicitly known and made concrete in the life of Jesus, and so exercises a qualificatory and controlling function with regard to human parenthood. Our children are related to God as Father through Christ *alongside* (and not through) their relation to us as parents. Christ is the sole mediator of the covenant: we can only mediate the promise in the sense of transmitting it. The fifth commandment is therefore always to be qualified by the first. The duty to honour one's parents must be subordinate to the prior duty to be subject to God alone. The task of mediating the promise is, after all, essentially that of inculcating a faith and hope and trust in this same God, an understanding of human life as the sphere into which he has entered in the person of Christ, and over which he rules in the power of his Spirit. It is, in other words, not for the sake of the parent-child relation itself, but of the Father-child relation of which it is a mere shadow and pale copy, that the parental role exists. Even as parents we are strictly *in loco parentis*, and nothing that we are or do or say must detract from that more ultimate and important relationship.

The raising of children 'will be wholesome and effective only when it consists in training up the children to a point at which all parental disciplines fall away, and God Himself takes over the work.'[56] 'It is the parents' responsibility to give their children the opportunity to encounter the God who is present, operative and revealed in Jesus Christ, to know Him and to learn to love and fear Him.'[57] Parents must take their responsibilities in this regard seriously, especially in formative years:

> [They] have to remember that it is a time which does not last. They themselves may be present only for a restricted period. Similarly the

---

[55] Ibid. p. 244.
[56] Ibid. p. 280.
[57] Ibid. p. 283.

life of their children may come to a sudden end. In any case, their youth will end . . . The special relationship will sooner or later come to an end. What will its content then have been? This is the question to which parents must seriously address themselves before it is too late.[58]

Yet, Barth reminds us, we are raising our children within the tradition of a covenant of grace, and within this context we can do no more than offer opportunities for the assimilation and extension of this tradition. Parents,

> while themselves doing everything which they can and must do within the compass of their responsibility . . . can only commit (their child) to the hand of the God from whom they have received him, to the Holy Spirit of God who alone is able to make their weak testimony efficacious to him and to ward off the influence of evil spirits, some of which may be parental in origin.[59]

In all this, then, what we are talking about is the formation of responsible moral agents through a process of apprenticeship. As with most types of apprenticeship, learning is best achieved not through the communication of abstract theory but through gradual and supervised imitation of the skilled (if in this case far from perfect!) practitioner. Thus, according to Barth, the parental authority of which Scripture speaks and submission to which the command of God compels 'is exercised as the children realize that the parents, like themselves, stand under an authority, i.e. that they live under an immediate and unconditional majesty and power . . . Attention, respect and obedience are aroused in children by the fact that the parents themselves live out this attitude as their own characteristic way of life.'[60] For those of us charged with the responsibility of mediating the promise of grace by this particular means, mapping the moral space by indwelling it responsibly ourselves and thereby helping the next generation of the community of faith to do so for itself, there can be few thoughts more sobering or challenging.

The chief significance of the vision expressed in *CD* §54 for our purposes is the way in which it points to something otherwise easily

---

[58] Ibid. pp. 283–284.
[59] Ibid. p. 284.
[60] Ibid. pp. 279–280.

missed in Barth's discussion of ethics. His disavowal of systematic ethical reflection and his consistent preference for the model of personal encounter makes him vulnerable at first sight to the charges of arbitrariness and ethical subjectivism. How is anyone else to know that I have heard God commanding me to do a particular thing? How, for that matter, am I myself to know? How is my knowing any different to that of the serial killer who also claims to have heard God's command, and is merely 'obeying orders'? These are serious questions. But there are good answers to them inherent in Barth's theology, even if they don't always leap out at a first reading.

I have referred already to the theme of that constancy of character – God's and ours – which issues from the ongoing history of the individual with God, and which directly informs and shapes his or her hearing of and response to the command of God when it comes. We have, as Barth puts it, always to do not just with a vertical but equally with a horizontal dimension of the ethical event. The punctiliar aspect of God's commanding is nonetheless a point in a linear pattern which may be traced. 'Only as the vertical intersects a horizontal can it be called vertical.'[61] Only as the command of God can be located clearly within the pattern of *this* God's history with us (his known character) can it be recognized and responded to as the command of *God*.[62]

But we can now see that there is another vital aspect to this horizontal plane which must not be missed. For in truth, while the command is certainly an event in which particular persons are addressed and summoned to response by God, it is anything but a *private* event from which other persons are excluded by definition. On the contrary, if humanity is essentially co-humanity, then there can in fact be no such thing as a purely individual or private relationship with God. In the church our particular identity is given to us by our relatedness to God and to others through our relatedness to Christ. Our history together with God is thus precisely a shared history, the history of a community of which we are part and within which we have been nurtured and have served as apprentices; a

---

[61] Ibid. p. 17.

[62] This is significantly distinct from the claim that what God commands in the present cannot conflict with *what he has commanded* in the past, let alone with ethical precepts to be found in Scripture.

community defined above all by the fact that God's kingdom has already come in its midst in the obedient history of the one man, Jesus of Nazareth. The existence of this community and its history lies at the heart of that horizontal pattern with which the vertical command intersects, and in terms of which its identity is determined. Within this community the promise of God is transmitted from one generation to the next. It is precisely in and through the forms of this community's life under God and our participation in them that God's character is mediated and known, our expectations and experience of God shaped, and our moral vision and character formed. It is through the same community, indeed, that the command of God is mediated to us and our response to it enabled and undergirded.[63] We are part of a community of verifiers within which our moral bearings are constantly checked and reorientated, not by the imposition of a moral magisterium, but by an objective social context of shared life, faith, hope and understanding. Belonging to this social reality (in which God is abroad in his Spirit) makes us who we are, inculcates virtue, and thereby forms us for receptivity to the command. This is the form which God's creating and sustaining of human moral subjects takes. It is not, that is to say, something which occurs in isolation, but in fellowship.

While hearing and responding to the command of God within the church remains a thoroughly personal thing, therefore, it is nonetheless for Barth never a solo effort, but an event for which we are prepared and in which we are supported and guided by the God who commands us, by the Son whose own human obedience to God's commanding furnishes the objective ground for ours, and by the community of character which his Spirit has called into being in the world. It is within the complex dynamics of this divine-human, trinitarian triangulation that we hear and obey in a responsible manner, and not otherwise.

---

[63] See *CD* 3/4, p. 9: 'The individual with his actions is not an atom in empty space, but a man among his fellows, not left to himself in his cases of conscience nor in a position to leave others to themselves . . . It can please the Holy Spirit – and it continually pleases Him – that not merely ethical advice and direction but the very command of God should be given in a very concrete form immediately from one man to another or to many others.'

5

Person and Prerogative in Perichoretic Perspective: The Triunity of God

It seems fitting to open this chapter with a quotation from Gregory Nazianzus, the aptness of which as a procedural guideline or control for all trinitarian thinking and speaking has struck me more than once in the course of writing it. Gregory writes as follows:

> No sooner do I conceive of the One than I am illumined by the splendour of the Three; no sooner do I distinguish them than I am carried back to the One. When I think of any One of the Three, I think of him as the whole . . . I cannot grasp the greatness of that One so as to attribute a greater greatness to the rest. When I contemplate the Three together, I see but one torch, and cannot divide or measure out the undivided light.[1]

By way of comment on this the Orthodox theologian Vladimir Lossky writes: 'Our thought must be in continuous motion, pursuing now the one, now the three, and returning again to the unity; it must swing ceaselessly between the two poles of the antinomy.'[2]

It would certainly seem to be the case that for a theology rooted consciously in that self-revealing economy of God witnessed to in the narrative and interpretative tradition of the church (rather than in some prior metaphysical or religious set of commitments) some such constant fluctuation between two distinct levels of thinking and speaking about God is requisite. In the gospel tradition we are

---

[1] Oration XL, 412; Migne, PG XXXVI, 417 BC. Cited in V. Lossky, *The Mystical Theology of the Eastern Church* (London: J. Clarke, 1957), p. 46.
[2] Ibid.

confronted with the same God three times and in three quite distinct ways.[3] Yet this threefold aspect pertains properly not simply to our perception of and relationship to God, but equally to God's relationship to himself, or, we might say, to the relationship of Father, Son and Holy Spirit (as distinct *hypostases* or *personae*) to one another. The God revealed to us in Jesus Christ is thus a God properly spoken of in terms of the second- and third-persons singular: thou, thee, thine; him, he, his. Yet if we are to be faithful to the economy then we must say that without in any way compromising or abandoning this way of thinking and speaking, we are also and equally forced to use the third-person plural in worship, prayer and theology as we invoke, adore and refer to the Father, Son and Holy Spirit together. Such is the paradoxical truth to which the ecclesiastical dogma of the trinity and the age-old structure of catholic liturgy bear witness. It is in the attempt to accord equal recognition to both sides of this mysterious paradox, rather than seeking some intellectually satisfying but theologically dangerous resolution of the tension in which either threeness is (in practice) reduced to oneness or else oneness to threeness, that the problematic nature of trinitarian thinking and speaking consists. It is this problem that trinitarian theology addresses.

In particular the alternate use of singular and plural pronouns in relation to God directs us to what must be admitted to be among the most vexed and vexing issues in trinitarian theology through the ages: namely, the question of how precisely to understand the respective terms rendered variously into English as 'being', 'essence' and 'substance' on the one hand, and 'persons', 'modes of being', 'distinct subsistences' and 'manners of subsisting' on the other. What, in other words, is it that we confess as threefold and one in God respectively? Two very different answers to this question can be identified in modern trinitarian theologies, answers which are in part determined by and in part determinative of two quite distinct trinitarian ontologies. Barth is located firmly on one side of this divide, together with others such as the Catholic theologian Karl Rahner. As representative of the other side we shall consider the

---

[3] See T. Smail, *The Forgotten Father* (London: Hodder & Stoughton, 1987), pp. 22–23.

views of Jürgen Moltmann whose theology has in several key
respects been formulated in direct response to the influence of
Barth.

1. Barth (and Rahner): persons as ways or modes of being

According to Barth, 'The God who reveals himself according to
Scripture is One in three distinctive modes of being subsisting in
their mutual relations: Father, Son and Holy Spirit.'[4] At first sight
this formulation seems to achieve the desired balance between oneness and threeness in God. Yet the rendering of *persona* as 'mode of
being' carries a dangerous sting in its tail. Barth's concern is admira-
ble enough. From what is at root an epistemological concern he is
determined to avoid the danger of incipient Arianism which he sees
as inherent in the very nature of all so-called social analogies for the
trinity. To suggest that there are in God three persons in the sense
that we think of three human persons is to slide inevitably into
Arianism, since 'a juxtaposition of human persons denotes a separateness of being which is completely excluded in God'.[5] It is the
integrity of God's self-revelation which is at stake here. 'If revelation is to be taken seriously as God's presence,' Barth writes, 'then in
no sense can Christ and the Spirit be subordinate hypostases.'[6] What
must be stressed, therefore, is in the first instance the unity of
essence between Father, Son and Spirit, that which the church
fathers confessed via the *homoousion*. In Jesus Christ and the Holy
Spirit the church has to do with God himself, not with some other
(and by implication lesser) 'selves'.

In fact, Barth argues, social analogies are misguided in any case.
The rendering of *hypostasis*, *prosopon* or *persona* in terms proper to
modern concepts of human personhood or personality commits a
fundamental category mistake. This is not at all what the fathers
intended in their formula 'one *ousia* and three *hypostases* (*personae*)'.

---

[4] *CD* 1/1, p. 348.
[5] Ibid. p. 355.
[6] *CD* 1/1, p. 353.

The term 'person', if it is to be used in this context, should therefore be shorn of any suggestion it may bear today of 'distinct self-consciousness' or 'subject'. It is better avoided altogether, and can helpfully be replaced by 'mode of being', which is closer to its original and proper sense as it emerged in the fourth and fifth centuries. If the modern concepts 'person' and 'personal' are legitimately to be applied to God at all, then it is precisely at the level of that which in God is one, and not that which is three. Barth is insistent that we do not have to do with three distinct selves in God, or three separate self-conscious agents.[7] Rather we have to do with one divine subject who exists in three distinct ways or 'modes' both in relation to the created other, and in relation to himself. Barth cites Diekamp approvingly at this point: 'In God, as there is one nature, so there is one knowledge, one self-consciousness.'[8] Rahner concurs with all this in his treatment of the matter: 'There exists in God only one power, one will, only one self-presence, a unique activity, a unique beatitude, and so forth.'[9] That which is threefold in God, therefore, is the ways[10] or modes in which this one subject (one 'person' in the modern sense of the word) is God. He is so as Father, Son and Holy Spirit.

Thus God is one personal substance subsisting in three distinct internal self-relations. The trinitarian 'persons' or *Seinsweisen* do not have their own distinct subjects of inherence. Rather they are modes of existence of one common divine subject. They are thus not just 'of one substance' with one another, but 'of one subject' as well, since it is precisely at the level of substance in God that what we call personality, self or subject is discerned by Barth. Essentially the same point is made by Rahner who writes: 'There are not three consciousnesses; rather the one consciousness subsists in a threefold way . . . The distinctness of the persons is not constituted by a distinctness of conscious subjectivities, nor does it include the latter.'[11]

---

[7] See ibid. p. 351.

[8] Diekamp, *Katholische Dogmatik* 1, p. 271.

[9] *The Trinity* (Tunbridge Wells: Burns & Oates, 1986), p. 75.

[10] According to Rahner the language of *hypostases* is to be understood in terms of 'three relative concrete ways of existing of the one and same God' (ibid. p. 74).

[11] Ibid. p. 107.

Barth again: 'We are not speaking of three divine "I's," but thrice of the one divine I.'[12]

Considering such statements it is perhaps unsurprising that both Barth and Rahner have been accused of lapsing into a tacit Sabellian modalism. Yet careful and sympathetic treatment of their respective writings shows both to be concerned to avoid this at all costs. Both are successful at least to the extent that they affirm three simultaneous and not consecutive modes or ways of subsisting in God, and in as much as they utterly refute the suggestion that God has any other existence than that perceived in these three simultaneous modes. Thus the one divine subject exists now and eternally as Father, Son and Holy Spirit in relation. Yet it is not clear that this provides us with an adequate or satisfactory model for trinitarian thinking and speaking, and the charges of Sabellianism are not altogether in vain.

While, for example, Barth plainly denies that we can or should seek after 'God' at some distinct and higher level of existence than that in which he is Father, Son and Spirit, thereby positing the existence of some fourth divine entity,[13] his language is not infrequently suggestive of the idea that we should in fact do precisely this. His relegation of divine threeness to the level of modes of being compels him repeatedly to refer us to a divine self or subject who is strictly speaking identical with none of the three named above, since these are relative ways in which this one divine 'I' is God. In defence of Barth it might be argued that this one subject is in no way hidden behind these three modes, but is precisely revealed in them, since (far from being identical with none of them) he is in a sense identical with all of them, and has no naked independent existence.

Notwithstanding this anticipated response, however, it should be observed that in practice much more is predicated of this one divine 'I' as such than is accorded to his three different ways of being God. Thus it is to the common divine *ousia* (and therefore to the one personal subject of this *ousia*) that all divine prerogatives are properly to be ascribed for Barth. This principle is rigorously applied in his discussion of the *Filioque*, for example, where Barth is adamant that the spiration of the Holy Spirit is the prerogative not

---

[12] *CD* 1/1, p. 351.
[13] Ibid. p. 382.

of the Father alone, but of Father and Son together as common and equal possessors of the one divine nature. Yet prerogatives (as opposed to attributes) are not properly ascribed to abstract natures, but to persons or ontological subjects inhering in natures; and when we scrutinize Barth at this point it becomes clear that the logic of the *Filioque* follows quite naturally from his conviction that there is only one such 'person' in God. Of course the Spirit proceeds from the Father and the Son. How could it possibly be otherwise? How could the Father and the Son be isolated from one another here or anywhere else, when in reality the subject inhering in both, the answer to the question 'who?' is precisely the same in both cases?[14]

Barth is perfectly correct in his assertion that the patristic use of *hypostasis* had little to do with what we today would call the personality. Without space to trace the development of the concepts in detail we must simply assert that that which Chalcedonian dogma refers to variously as *hypostasis* or *prosopon*, and which is referred to as one in the case of the incarnation and three in the case of the trinity, is strictly a metaphysical and not a psychological category.[15] In the

---

[14] Thus of 'God' Barth asks, 'How could He be less the origin of love in being the Son than in being the Father? . . . How, then, can the breathing of the Spirit belong less essentially, less properly and originally, to the Son than to the Father? . . . As the Son of the Father He, too, is thus *spirator Spiritus*. He is this, of course, as the Son of the Father . . . This Son of this Father is and has all that His Father is and has. He is and has it as the Son, But He is and has it. Thus He, too, is *spirator Spiritus*. He, too, has the possibility of being this' (ibid. p. 484). To be fair to Barth we must certainly note that his explicit motive for affirming the *Filioque* is one rooted in exegetical considerations taken together with his conviction that 'the reality of God which encounters us in His revelation is His reality in all the depths of eternity' (ibid. p. 479.). There is no reason whatever to doubt Barth's integrity here or elsewhere. My point is simply to observe that, quite apart from such exegetical considerations (which, incidentally, seem to acquire a different significance where the incarnate Son's evident dependence upon the Spirit is concerned), Barth's trinitarian ontology makes the confession of the *Filioque* virtually inevitable.

[15] For what follows see further, e.g., C.C.J. Webb, *God and Personality* (London: Allen & Unwin, 1919); J. Zizioulas, *Being as Communion* (London: Darton, Longman & Todd, 1985); R.D. Williams, 'Person and "Personality" in Christology', in *The Downside Review* 94 (1976).

philosophical tradition at the disposal of the fathers the term *hypostasis* had come to designate the incommunicable and unmultipliable aspect of a concrete particular (i.e. that which makes it *this* particular as opposed to *that* particular instance of a thing). *Prosopon*, meanwhile, lacking the ontological stability of *hypostasis*, carried with it the overtone of relationality: the face, or role, or outward aspect of a thing is that which looks outwards to others and is viewed by others. The fusion of these two in Christian theology (in which they came to behave as virtual synonyms) resulted in a concept which we might describe as that of 'the incommunicable ontological subject in relation'. The term 'subject', however, is used here strictly in the grammatical sense, and not in the sense of consciousness or mind. These psychological overtones entered in later, partly due, no doubt, to the Boethian definition of person as *naturae rationabilis individua substantia*. For the fathers rational agency, while closely linked to personhood, was not to be confused with it, and came under the heading of *ousia* rather than *hypostasis*. This much is clear in the christological context from their willingness in due course to ascribe two wills and two minds (one human and one divine) to the one person of the Son.

So Barth is correct to challenge an automatic shift from speaking of three persons to thinking in terms of three rational agents, or three centres of consciousness in trinitarian theology. In as much as metaphysical subject and psychological subject or self-consciousness are logically distinct this step is by no means a necessary one, and while we do not, generally speaking, encounter 'persons' in this metaphysical sense who lack such psychological faculties,[16] such a separability does not constitute logical nonsense. This may well be an important consideration where the distinct 'personhood' of the Holy Spirit is concerned, for example, where, as theologians on all sides are generally agreed, we are certainly dealing with a more anonymous mode of

---

[16] Unless human personhood is identified with or reduced to rational agency in an a priori manner, however, it might be argued that in the case of the human foetus in its early stages of development, or in the case of those humans who have effectively lost the capacity for thought or self-consciousness of any rational sort, we have precisely to do with this phenomenon.

personhood, and not a third divine 'personality' alongside those of Father and Son.[17]

Where Barth's formulation falls down, however, is in its separation of that which was fused together so decisively and significantly in the course of the fourth-century debates, namely, the incommunicable ontological subject on the one hand, and relationality on the other. While he is prepared to speak of three relations in God (Fatherhood, Sonship and Holy Spirit), precisely what Barth is not prepared to tolerate is that which the patristic confession of three *hypostases* entails, namely, the presence of three unique incommunicable ontological subjects in one *ousia*, one concrete reality. Yet this is in effect to go back behind the careful christological and trinitarian redefinition of terms, and to confess three *prosopa* and only one *hypostasis*. It may or may not be the case that trinitarian theology needs to work out a way of thinking and speaking of these three metaphysical subjects as somehow mysteriously sharing one mind, will, consciousness and so forth (all of which may be supposed to fall under the heading of *ousia* rather than *hypostasis*). That is a separate issue. Here it must simply be observed that Barth's denial of more than one subject in God makes the traditional language of, for example, interpersonal communion or love between Father and Son, or of the obedience of the Son to the Father, difficult to take altogether seriously. In the final analysis these reduce to self-love and self-obedience in God. Love for the other, and obedience to the other are, strictly speaking, absent except in the relations of the one divine subject *ad extra*.

---

[17] So Barth: 'The Holy Spirit in particular then, even were that possible in the case of Father and Son, could under no circumstances be regarded as a third "person" in the modern sense of the concept. The Holy Spirit in particular is in a specially clear way what Father and Son also are, not a third spiritual subject, a third Lord alongside two others, but a third mode of existence of the one divine subject or Lord' (cited by Baillie, *God Was in Christ*, p. 136). Cf. Moltmann, *God in Creation* (London: SCM Press, 1985): 'The Spirit always points away from himself towards the Son and the Father. To say this does not mean that we should give up the personal character of the Spirit, as that was . . . defined in the trinitarian doctrine of the patristic church. But it does mean that we cannot apply the concept of person to the Father, the Son and the Spirit in exactly the same way', p. 97.

The question which must constantly be put to Barth is, given that we encounter God in three distinct ways at once, does God encounter himself in these same ways? Does he meet, relate to and commune with 'internal others', others who (pushing language to its limits) are mysteriously himself, yet genuinely encounterable as other within the one reality of God? There is little doubt that Barth intends that we should be able to affirm that this is so. Yet pushed hard, the logic of his trinitarian ontology makes it exceedingly hard to do so. In denying that it is in any real sense legitimate to refer to the persons in God as 'they' Barth (and Rahner with him) effectively fails to hold onto both poles of the trinitarian antinomy, and allows threeness virtually to collapse into oneness. The weakness of the theological construct which results is its ultimate poverty for exegetical and liturgical purposes in which we have to speak properly, for example, of one divine person standing over against the other two in a mediatory relationship, or of our participation in the relationship which one divine person has with another via the ministrations of yet a third. According to one central strand of biblical soteriology, the Christian life is fundamentally a sharing in the Son's relationship with the Father in the power of the Spirit through the economic earthing of that same relationship in the particular flesh of Jesus of Nazareth. We do not share in the person of the Son, but precisely in the relationship which he has with the Father and the Spirit in the triune life of *koinonia*. This is the trinitarian shape of the kerygma and of the Christian experience of God. Yet if the incommunicability of the threeness in God is denied, and persons are defined as modes of subsistence of just one ontological divine subject, all this takes on a decidedly different and problematic hue. Then it is not difficult to see how a gap might begin to open up between the structure of Christian preaching and experience of God on the one hand, and his immanent being on the other.[18] Or else, since doctrine does not simply reflect Christian experience, but also informs and shapes the expectations which in part create that experience,[19] it

---

[18] This is ironic, of course, given the insistence of both Barth and Rahner that a relationship of identity is to be posited between the so-called economic and immanent trinities. Clearly neither intends any severing of this relationship, but the problem remains, given the way in which they each choose to define divine personhood.

[19] See A. McGrath, *The Genesis of Doctrine* (Oxford: Blackwell, 1990), p. 71.

might explain precisely why so much Western Christianity has in practice been reducible to an ethical unitarianism. Thus Jenson writes of the Western trinitarian tradition which both Barth and Rahner reflect at this point: 'it is likely to reflect negatively upon the fundamental liturgical and proclamatory levels of discourse . . . The doctrine in its Western form has not easily been seen as functional within religious life.'[20]

Perhaps Barth can even be hoist with his own petard to some extent over this matter. For while he is surely correct to proscribe any unqualified or crude application of the analogy of three human 'persons' to the *treis hypostases* of trinitarian confession, he himself commits a similar (equal and opposite) error in applying the analogy of one human 'person' to the *mia ousia*. If three persons characterized by separateness of being are excluded by the Christian understanding of God, then so too is one person characterized (as persons certainly are in our human experience) by lack of relation with 'internal others'. Neither model is adequate. The problem is precisely that, as Barth himself insists, human analogies fail us at this point; but this is no less true of personal oneness than it is of personal threeness. We must think and speak of God both as he, and as they, constantly shifting from one level of discourse to the other, not allowing the one to compromise the other, maintaining the mysterious and apparently paradoxical nature of trinitarian confession.

2. Moltmann: hypostatic diversity and perichoretic unity

In many ways Moltmann represents the opposite end of the scale to Barth, and has certainly worked his own trinitarian position out in

---

[20] R.W. Jenson, *The Triune Identity* (Philadelphia: Fortress Press, 1982), p. 131. See further on this theme J.M. Houston, 'Spirituality and the Doctrine of the Trinity', in Hart and Thimell (eds.), *Christ in Our Place*, pp. 48–69. We must be fair to Rahner at this point and note his own express concern with such failure to take the trinity seriously in life and in worship. See *The Trinity*, pp.12f. One must simply question whether his own trinitarian ontology allows a proper escape from this mentality to seeing worship and Christian discipleship as events in *God*, and not simply as directed to *God* by independent human agents.

polemical response to him. The logic of Barth's trinitarian ontology when pushed to its natural and logical conclusion, he contends, 'transfers the subjectivity of action to a deity concealed behind the three persons',[21] a criticism which we have already considered. Yet, Moltmann argues, to think thus in terms of a threefold 'holy tautology' is not to think in properly trinitarian terms. The ever-present danger is that of robbing both the Son and the Spirit of any genuine personhood, as 'God', the one divine 'I', is tacitly identified with the person of the Father.

According to Moltmann both Barth and Rahner err because the modern notion of person to which they refer us is unduly individualistic, 'an independent, free, self-disposing centre of action in knowledge and freedom, different from others.'[22] Quite properly they refuse to reckon with three such persons in God. Their mistake, however, is to leave the concept itself intact, and to proceed simply to transfer it from the level of that which in God is three to the level of that which is one instead. Thereby they posit a God who is one individual, independent, free subject in three distinct and simultaneous modes or ways.

Over against this, Moltmann, following Lossky and others within the eastern tradition, resists any reduction of the concept 'person' to the concept 'relation', and stresses the absolute hypostatic diversity of Father, Son and Spirit. Thus Lossky writes: 'the relations only serve to express the hypostatic diversity of the Three; they are not the basis of it. It is the absolute diversity of the Three *hypostases* which determines their differing relations to one another, not vice versa.'[23] 'Uniqueness', writes John Zizioulas, 'is something absolute for the person.'[24] Persons, then, are not relations but those who exist in relation; and in God there are three such, and not one only.

For Moltmann too there are three unique and irreducible subjects in God and not one. Correspondingly he emphasizes the

---

[21] J. Moltmann, *The Trinity and the Kingdom of God* (London: SCM Press, 1981), p. 135.

[22] K. Rahner, *The Trinity*, cited in Moltmann, *The Trinity and the Kingdom of God*, p. 145.

[23] V. Lossky, *In the Image and Likeness of God* (St. Vladimir's Seminary Press, 1974), p. 79.

[24] J. Zizioulas, *Being as Communion*, p. 47.

diversity of hypostatic prerogatives, rather than viewing all divine prerogatives (both immanent and economic) as ultimately predicated of one subject who exists as Father, Son and Holy Spirit. On the contrary, Father, Son and Spirit are ultimately distinct in their several activities, both in their relationship to the created other, and in relation to one another in the eternal life of God. In particular the uniqueness of the Father's prerogative as origin and cause of Godhead is to be acknowledged. He begets the Son. He breathes the Spirit. Notwithstanding Moltmann's willingness to concede a qualified version of the *Filioque* at the levels of economic activity and immanent personal relations (Moltmann's 'personal form'), he is clear that where the question of the Spirit's divine existence (relation of origin) is concerned the procession is *ek monou tou patros*. There is not space to pursue this important issue further here. We may simply note that whereas Barth's acknowledgement of only one divine 'I' in God renders all attribution of distinct personal prerogative within the trinity (whether at the level of the immanent or the economic) ultimately ambiguous and problematic,[25] Moltmann's recognition of three distinct and unique subjects provides a secure basis for it. The problem then, of course, becomes that of determining in what sense it is still possible to speak of a genuine unity between the three, such that we are properly able to refer to God as 'he' as well as 'they', and to predicate of the three together that which we wish first and foremost to attribute to one in his unique distinctness. This, Moltmann insists, is the trinitarian problem as raised by the economy itself. How are these who are three nonetheless truly one? How, then, is the question to be answered?

Moltmann rejects the answers rooted respectively in homogeneity of substance and sameness of subject. The unity of the trinity is rather a unity of *koinonia*, a unitedness or at-one-ment of the three distinct persons, a perichoretic unity in which the persons 'indwell' one another. 'We must dispense', he writes, 'with both the concept of the one substance and the concept of the identical subject.'[26] Perichoretic unity is a unity which presupposes rather than conflicts

---

[25] So, e.g., 'No attribute, no act of God is not *in the same way* the attribute or act of the Father, the Son and the Spirit' (*CD* 1/1, p. 362; my italics).

[26] *Op. cit.* p. 150.

with absolute hypostatic diversity, since it is only unique persons who can be at one or in fellowship with each other. Relations or modes of being cannot be. Furthermore perichoretic unity is a unity in which the distinct personal prerogatives, far from being compromised or relativized, are actually fulfilled: 'Precisely through the personal characteristics that distinguish them from one another, the Father, the Son and the Spirit dwell in one another and communicate eternal life to one another.'[27] Thus the unity of God is to be found in the triunity of the Father, the Son and the Spirit. It neither precedes this nor follows it.

In his 1928 article on '*Perichoreo* and *perichoresis* in the fathers'[28] Prestige observes two distinct senses of this concept. In the first and weaker sense the term *perichoresis* denotes what was later referred to in terms of the *communicatio idiomatum*, namely, the notion in christology that by virtue of the close association of natures through the *unio hypostatica*, things properly predicated of the divine nature might now legitimately be predicated of the human Jesus, and vice versa. The uniquely close involvement of two distinct realities (the humanity and divinity of the Son of God) and the fact that together they constituted a single concrete reality legitimized a degree of linguistic licence in which (since they shared a common grammatical subject) they might be treated as interchangeable for the purposes of predication. The metaphor involved in the use of the verb *perichoreo* is that of a rotation or revolution in which 'two opposites are revealed as complementary sides of a single concrete object' such that 'it no more matters by which nature Christ seems to operate than it does by which title he is called; since he is both divine and human, both natures are involved in his incarnate actions, and the human side rotating through a complete half-circuit reveals the divine side.'[29] Such a *perichoresis* is the result of a prior (hypostatic) union which it presupposes and upon which it depends. In the stronger use of the term, however, *perichoresis* comes to suggest an actual ontological interpenetration of two entities (not simply their close association and reciprocation) such that *it is itself*

---

[27] Ibid. p. 175.

[28] *Journal of Theological Studies* 29 (1928), pp. 242f.

[29] Ibid., p. 243.

the process whereby a union exists, and not the result of a distinct and prior union. As Prestige observes, in the christological context this concept led inevitably to the danger of monophysitism, but it provided trinitarian theology with an invaluable tool with which to secure the avoidance both of Sabellian modalism and tritheism, pointing to a genuine unity which yet presupposed an absolute hypostatic diversity.

Whereas in the trinitarian theology of Barth it would seem to be the case that *perichoresis* is posited only in the weaker of these two senses (being in effect a necessary implication of the prior ontological oneness of the divine subject), for Moltmann it is in the *perichoresis* itself, the interpenetration of the three distinct divine persons, that the unity of God consists. We must not think of this, however, as if we have to do with three individual persons who have some independent existence prior to their mutual relatedness and perichoretic interpenetration. The *perichoresis* is eternal. It is given in the very being of God. To be God is to be Father, Son and Holy Spirit in eternal perichoretic *koinonia*. But this surely means that we cannot abandon or dispense with the language of one substance or *ousia*. For precisely what the *homoousion* is intended to safeguard is the given eternal oneness of the three persons. As Zizioulas notes, the insistence of Athanasius that the Son is eternally from the substance of the Father, rather than a product of his will, carries within it the implication that the divine substance as such is inherently relational.[30] But if this entails a departure from the traditional Greek ontology in which being logically precedes relationality (which is an adjunct to being rather than constitutive of it), the *homoousion* nonetheless says rather more than that God's 'being is in relation'. It does indeed say this; but it says more specifically that God's being is constituted precisely in the relations pertaining between these three persons, Father, Son and Holy Spirit, who indwell one another in such a way as to be one reality and not three (relational) realities. In this sense for the Christian theologian to confess 'one *ousia*' of God, and to confess 'three persons in eternal perichoretic union' is to confess precisely the same thing, since the *ousia* is constituted by this very perichoretic

---

[30] See Zizioulas, *Being as Communion*, pp. 83f.

koinonia. Thus to speak of *perichoresis* is to predicate a level of onto-logical unity between these three persons (who inhere one substance numerically, and not just generically) which could never be predicated of human persons in relation.

It is here, perhaps, that Moltmann's presentation is at its weakest. Perichoretic unity, he argues, is a unity which is open, a unity in which the God of the gospel unites himself to others and others to himself.[31] But can we really speak in this way of the unity in which Father, Son and Spirit are one God, such that to encounter the one is genuinely to encounter the other two and to refer to the one is to refer to the others? Is the union with God in which men and women are drawn into the very life of God, being granted to share in the eternal relation of the Son to the Father in the Spirit, really of the same sort as that union in which Father, Son and Spirit perichoretically inhere in one another? Surely not. There is a dis-tinction to be drawn here between two distinct strata of trinitarian ontology; between that in God which is participable by humans and that which is not; between what it means to be Son of God *kata physin* on the one hand, and *kata charin* on the other; between *koinonia* as an ontological category and *perichoresis*. The concept *perichoresis* in its strong form says more than the concept *koinonia* (which it embraces). It is this crucial differentiation that the *homoousion* was intended to safeguard and we must do nothing to weaken it. If the divine unity is indeed a perichoretic unity of three distinct persons, and not the simple unity of a single divine subject, it is nonetheless a unity of a variety quite distinct from that pertain-ing among human 'persons in relation', of any two of whom we should not wish to say (even on the basis of the closest of fellowship) that they were *homoousios* with one another.

3. Concluding remarks

Deus, St. Thomas reliably informs us, *non est in genere*. But if he were, if 'God' were a class concept or universal, then the Christian doctrine of the trinity would wish to posit only one particular and not three.

---

[31] *Op. cit.* p. 150.

That is what the confession of *mia ousia* entails. Father, Son and Holy Spirit are one numerically where their 'being' is concerned. This is the great concern of Barth's trinitarian discussion, and where it is at its strongest. In so far as Moltmann's theology fails to account adequately for such identity of being it is correspondingly weak. Yet the *ousia* of God is constituted and inhered by three distinct, unique intrasubstantial hypostases in eternal perichoretic union and communion, each indwelling the others in such a way that to name any one is to name the others by implication. Here the shoe is on the other foot. It is Moltmann whose account safeguards this truth of genuine and ultimate hypostatic diversity, and Barth whose final inability to sustain it must be acknowledged as a weakness.

At the heart of the difficulty of trinitarian reflection lies the truth that there is no created *vestigium* with which to compare or illuminate this paradoxical *Dreieinigkeit*. Neither the three human persons of social analogies nor the one person in self-relation will suffice. We are dealing with a permanent antinomy rather than a dialectic to be resolved in a higher synthesis, and we must therefore continue to speak and think on two distinct levels; now referring to the mutual interpenetration in which Father, Son and Spirit can be named together as 'he'; and now of them severally in their unique hypostatic distinction in which they may legitimately be set alongside and even over against one another. Thus to say, 'The Son obeys the Father' and 'God obeys himself,' or 'The Father pours out his wrath on the Son' and 'God pours out his wrath upon himself,' are equally legitimate ways of expressing the same truth in its stratification. That we cannot, on the other hand, put the Father on the cross of Golgotha, or speak of the Son as the source of the Father and the Spirit, or of the Spirit as the one to whom the Son offers himself in obedience, these are matters every bit as significant as the fact that we can speak of God putting himself on the Cross, of God as self-originating, and of God as offering himself to himself in the economy of salvation.

It is in the constant toing and froing between these two levels of discourse that trinitarian theology is done. What we say at one level ought always to be translatable into terms proper to the other. Sometimes this will mean stretching our language to the limits of its semantic possibilities, or rather redefining those possibilities through a metaphorical shift in its sense as it is applied to this mysterious reality. Perhaps we might even employ a metaphor from trinitarian theology itself, and speak of a linguistic coinherence (in the weak sense, and by virtue of the ontological coinherence of the three persons in which they are one reality) of that which pertains to the divine threeness and that which pertains to the divine oneness, such that when we speak about the threeness the oneness is never far from view, and vice versa.

What I have tried to suggest in this chapter, through a comparison of Barth's approach to this problem with that of Moltmann, is that attempts to resolve this tension into a more logically satisfying equilibrium habitually run the danger of collapsing over onto one side of it. The man who walks a tightrope probably never achieves a perfectly balanced vertical stance; he is constantly casting his weight first in one direction, and then, by way of compensation, in the other. It may well be that if, in our wrestling with the triune mystery of God, we find ourselves no longer having to engage in precisely some such constant conceptual shifting of our position the real reason is that we have toppled off unawares and landed on some more secure, but theologically one-sided, surface.

6

Truth, the Trinity and Pluralism[1]

The title of this chapter draws together into creative interaction two major concerns for the Christian theologian. Of one, the trinity, Karl Barth had much to say, a fact more surprising in his generation than in ours, and one to which the current resurgence of interest in trinitarian theology owes no small amount. On the other topic (pluralism) however Barth is, unsurprisingly, less forthcoming. For while the roots of contemporary pluralism lie buried deep in the philosophical soils of a century or more, and while its implications were already beginning to be worked out in the writings of theologians such as Troeltsch at the turn of the century, the pluralistic spirit which holds our age firmly in its grip has manifested itself clearly only in the years since Barth's death. It was not an issue in his day to the same degree that it is in ours.

This fact presents us with something of a problem. How to proceed? Are there sufficient materials to make an excursus into Barth's theology a worthwhile one with this particular combination of themes in mind? I believe that there are, although it will be clear from what has been said already that I shall not be attempting an exposition of Barth's own critical engagement with pluralism. Nor shall I be speculating as to what Barth might have said if he had survived to his one-hundredth year and witnessed for himself the growing dominance of pluralistic views in the academy and other circles. What I hope to do instead is to approach his theology with the broad outlines of the contemporary discussion in view and to ask whether Barth

[1] This chapter was first published as 'Karl Barth, the Trinity and Pluralism' in K.J. Vanhoozer (ed) *The Trinity in Pluralistic Age* (Grand Rapids: Eerdmans, 1997) and has been reprinted in this revised form with the permission of the publisher, Wm. B. Eerdmans.

himself may be construed as a pluralist of any sort. Does the thrust of the overall scheme of his theology as it emerges in *CD* and elsewhere lend itself to a form of what might be called 'soft' pluralism? Or is Barth a theologian who, in a stalwart defence of the universal truth of the gospel of Jesus Christ, altogether eschews pluralism in all its forms?

This, I hope to suggest, is not so easy a question to resolve as might at first seem to be the case. To some it may seem outrageous even to entertain the hypothesis that one whose name is so closely allied to such phrases as 'the triumph of grace' and 'a positivism of revelation' (neither of them Barth's own) could be thought guilty of pluralism of any kind. One who concludes the views of many other Christians under the category of 'heresy' and classifies human religion outside the church as essentially a manifestation of 'unbelief', it might reasonably be argued, can hardly be taken seriously as a candidate for classification among the pluralists! This observation (while it is crudely and unfairly couched here) carries a significant amount of weight, and such considerations, even when qualified and more subtly and fairly presented, certainly rule Barth out as a pluralist of a certain sort. But, as I shall suggest shortly, we may differentiate between different sorts, and there are elements within the overall superstructure of Barth's theology which point strongly to the compatibility of his theological project with a certain understanding of what a feasible epistemological pluralism might consist in. It is not for nothing that George Lindbeck points to suggestive parallels between his own so-called cultural-linguistic model of doctrine and Barth's approach to dogmatics.[2] Just how far can these parallels be pushed before they topple?

1. Pluralism agnostic and committed

In order to pursue this discussion further I want at this point to borrow a careful and significant distinction drawn by Bishop Lesslie Newbigin.[3] The contemporary intellectual scene is often portrayed

---

[2] G. Lindbeck, *The Nature of Doctrine* (London: SPCK, 1984), p. 24.

[3] For what follows see, e.g., L. Newbigin, *Truth to Tell: The Gospel as Public Truth* (London: SPCK, 1991), pp. 56f. See also for a development of the position espoused here Trevor Hart, *Faith Thinking: The Dynamics of Christian Theology* (London: SPCK, 1995).

as if the decline of modernism and the ascent of postmodernist perspectives has left us with two basic options: on the one hand an optimistic objectivism of either an empiricist or rationalist variety and on the other hand a pluralism which is essentially relativistic and sceptical. We may either embrace the certainty afforded us by alleged universal truths of morality and reason, or by a hard-nosed concern with 'facts', or else, disillusioned with these, throw in our lot with those whose only absolute commitment is to the uncompromising belief that such certainty is a will-o'-the-wisp, and that truth, if there is such a thing, lies utterly beyond our epistemic capacities. Certainty or despair; these, many commentators would seem to want us to believe, are the only options. It must be said at once that neither of them is particularly attractive for the Christian theologian, although across the theological spectrum they seem to have seduced roughly equal numbers. Part of what Barth saw in his day remains true in ours; namely, that very often theological 'liberals' and 'conservatives' are united in their basic methodologies and in the tools which they brandish as weapons with which to destroy one another's fortified positions. That which each despises in the other's point of view is often simply a distorted mirror image of their own basic presuppositions and procedures. While they appear to be utterly different, therefore, in truth they are twins, separated at birth and raised in wholly different environments, unable to identify precisely what it is about the other which so angers them when they meet face to face.

Part of what Newbigin attempts in his publications is to draw our attention away from the particular alternatives of objectivism and relativism and to point to a third way. His choice is to describe this way as a variant of pluralism, although the semantic associations of the word are immediately ruptured by its use in a quite distinct epistemic framework.

There is, Newbigin tells us, on the one hand 'agnostic pluralism'. This is the point of view which celebrates plurality and diversity for its own sake, viewing it as part of the richness of our human situation, and preferring it in every respect to any alleged or attempted uniformity of outlook or understanding. Emerging from the gradual realization that the eighteenth-century quest for a certain, absolutely reliable and universally accessible basis for knowing has, over the course of two hundred years or more, failed time and again to render its promised results, this pluralism departs from the despairing assumption that truth (if there be such) is unknowable to

humans, and lies far beyond any of our several versions of it. This
being so, it stands to reason that every and any claim to truth in anything more than a coherentist sense (i.e. something is true because it
coheres with some overall paradigm or view of things) must be
denounced as a lapse into tribalism, an intolerance of the other for
which, in our postmodern age, there can no longer be any excuse or
any room. Above all, the attempt to convert, to change the mind of
the other until he or she sees things differently, is palpable violence
and can result only in the sort of partisan conflict which we have
now left behind as the by-product of a darker age. Openness, tolerance, humility before the great mystery of life; these are the
hallmarks of a truly pluralistic and liberal society. Hence necessity is
seized and turned eagerly into a virtue. We are, after all, all in the
same epistemological boat, so we might as well own up to and make
the best of our circumstances. No one has access to the way things
really are. All our perspectives are physically, socially, historically
and culturally determined. No one way of seeing things can be
deemed better or worse than another. The differences which divide
us from one another must not be categorized in evaluative terms,
since no criteria exist for making any such evaluation, or choosing
any one point of view over another. We can only ever compare our
own ways of thinking and seeing things with others; never with the
way things really are. The responsible mode of relation to others,
therefore, is to occupy the context granted us by historical and
social accident, and then to seek to supplement and enrich it by borrowing the insights of other traditions as and when we are able to
access them. Thereby we may become more rounded and fulfilled
human persons, better equipped in the quest for the great enigma of
truth. The quest itself, however, must continue, for it is in principle
and by definition endless.

Newbigin's second category is 'committed pluralism'. This, he
suggests, is a stance which concurs in certain basic respects with
agnostic pluralism but differs substantially at key junctures. Hence
the committed pluralist too has learned from the failure of univer-
salist objectivism, and concedes that there is no detached standpoint
from which to view the world, but only a diverse series of perspectives some of which are utterly incompatible with one another.
Such quantities as rationality and morality, far from being the

para-contextual bedrock of 'what every intelligent human person knows to be true' are themselves inseparable from the warp and woof of historically and socially particular frameworks of meaning. What counts as a rationally or morally compelling case for one person, therefore, may be deemed irrelevant or wholly irrational/immoral by another. Such clashes of framework demonstrate the futility of simple appeals to reason in apologetic exercises, and the verity of pluralism in its contention that the way we see things depends largely on where we happen to find ourselves. While, however, in rejecting objectivism agnostic pluralism risks rapid collapse into its logical opposite of subjectivism and ultimate solipsism, the committed pluralist remains what may be termed a 'critical realist'. He remains, that is to say, committed to the view that pluralism is a feature of human knowing rather than of the way things are beyond human knowing, and optimistic in the capacity of humans to establish genuine and reliable epistemic contact with reality. Truth is there to be known, and may be known if not absolutely or in any 'objective' or universally compelling manner then at least with sufficient certainty and in a mode which compels what Michael Polanyi refers to as knowledge claims bearing 'universal intent'.[4] Reality can be known by placing oneself in the places where it makes itself known, by viewing it from certain standpoints rather than others, by employing certain physical and conceptual tools rather than others, and so on. The knowledge obtained thereby is not of the absolutely certain variety craved by Descartes and those who followed in his wake, but is rather built on the precise foundations which he eschewed: namely, personal trust and faith. Polanyi presents this as the basic *modus operandi* of scientific knowing, notwithstanding the objectivist myths perpetrated and exalted even in our day concerning scientific procedure as a public enterprise.

The rub with all this, of course, is that it still breaches the code of tolerance as defined by modern liberal sympathies. To suggest that truth makes itself known or is in some (even partial) way knowable

---

[4] M. Polanyi, *Personal Knowledge* (London: Routledge & Kegan Paul, 1958).

from one particular perspective with its assumptions and tools is thereby inevitably to claim for this perspective some superiority over others, and hence to assert their relative falsity. This, as I have suggested, is the one great unforgivable sin, if we could be certain that there is such a thing as sin which, of course, we can't! But in fact, as Newbigin and those upon whose thought he draws at this point (notably Polanyi and Alasdair MacIntyre) suggest, the attitude which this committed stance fosters is not one of arrogance or dismissive intolerance, but precisely one of humility and openness. Since such truth claims are non-demonstrable in the sense usually intended by that term, and since the knower knows only on the basis of a personal commitment to certain fundamental assumptions, she has no universally recognised or intellectually superior case with which to bludgeon those who do not stand where she does, or on the basis of which to call into question their intelligence or common sense. As one who believes that truth is indeed to be known in one way rather than another, but who must submit in her knowing to reality itself in its willingness to be known, she can only enjoin those who see things radically differently to 'come and stand where I am standing, view the world from this place and using these tools, and see whether what you find here doesn't make more sense'. Thus if the mode of certainty is that of faith, then the mode of proclamation is that of witness. (The resonances with the situation of the Christian believer, and the Christian theologian, are apparent even at this level.) There is a moral component to the committedness of committed pluralism. For the person who believes sincerely that reality grants itself to be known in one way and one place rather than in others, albeit not in any absolute or exhaustive or controllable manner, there is on the one hand an obligation to seek it there and not elsewhere (Martin Luther's 'Here I stand; I can do no other'), and on the other hand a charge to proclaim this 'good news' that the despair of scepticism is not the only alternative to Descartes' project. Universal intent demands that we do so.

The thesis of the rest of this chapter will be that it is possible to read Karl Barth, and his treatments of the doctrine of the trinity and human religion in particular, as operating within the boundaries of a committed pluralism of this sort. Let us return briefly, then, to the suggested parallel with Lindbeck in order to discern its limits.

2. Dogmatics as grammar?

The church, according to Barth, is constituted as the church by its faithful hearing of the divine Word, the address of God himself, and its obedience in the task of handling this same Word and handing it on to others. In this way the central act of the church is one in which, even in its essential humanness, it becomes the vehicle of divine self-giving to the world. But the church is very much a human entity. And for this reason the question of its faithful acquital of this responsibility must be faced. 'When the church receives the Word', Barth writes, 'the question has to arise: To what extent is the address that takes place in Christian preaching identical with the address that took place through the prophets and apostles . . . To what extent is it the *Word of God*?'[5] What is God's Word? What, that is to say, is God saying? And how is what is being said in the preaching of the church related to this Word? It is with this question that Barth sees the dogmatician as primarily concerned. Dogmatics is the scientific or reflective self-examination of the church with respect to its talk about God. It listens to what is said, and offers judgements. It acts in a normative, regulative and corrective role, seeking to ensure (so far as is humanly possible) that what is said humanly from the pulpit coincides in some sense with what God has said and is saying to his church. Thus 'what dogmatics has to give' to the preacher 'does not consist of contents but of guidelines, directions, insights, principles and limits for correct speech by human estimate'.[6] Dogmatics, as it were, articulates the grammar of Christian speech about God, lays down the rules for speaking Christianly about him. It tells us 'what will do and what will not do, what we may say and what we may not say if what we are to say is to be Christian preaching'.[7] This essentially diagnostic and prophylactic role is necessary precisely because of the full humanity of the church. 'Dogmatics is required', says Barth 'because proclamation is a fallible work.'[8] 'In every age', he notes, 'the church's preaching has been sick.'[9]

---

[5] *GD* p. 24.
[6] *CD* 1/1, p. 87.
[7] *GD*, p. 18.
[8] *CD* 1/1, p. 82.
[9] *GD* p.16.

This account of the essential activity of dogmatics certainly bears more than a passing resemblance to the 'cultural-linguistic' model espoused in Lindbeck's *The Nature of Doctrine*. Precisely the same regulative task is ascribed to the dogmatician. Thus, for Lindbeck, doctrines may be seen to be functioning 'as communally authoritative rules of discourse, attitude and action'.[10] They lay down rules of speech precisely similar to those found in the literal grammars of human speech. They regulate truth claims by excluding some and allowing others, tolerating certain forms of speech as appropriate to and coherent with the reality and value system of the believing community (the 'language'), and proscribing others as inappropriate and incoherent, as breaking the grammatical rules. Thus far this is utterly at one with Barth's understanding.

There is, however, a fundamental difference between the two. For while in Lindbeck's account the criteria with which doctrine adjudges communal discourse are essentially empirical (i.e. 'these are the rules' equals 'this is in fact the way the language has operated in the past') and the standards of truth and falsity purely coherentist (defined in terms of keeping the given rules), Barth will not rest content with this alone. The criteria with which dogmatics approaches its critical task are for him concerned not simply with the grammatical superstructure of a given language or system of beliefs, but with the reference of that same system beyond itself. They are not (to use Lindbeck's terms) simply intrasystemic, but radically extrasystemic. They concern a model of truth understood not in terms of coherence alone, but, in some sense at least, correspondence. In other words, the dogmatician does not simply ask, 'How does this preaching measure up to traditional and communally acceptable ways of speaking about God?' but 'How does this preaching measure up to the Word of God himself as he has given himself to be known?' There is, then, for Barth an objective criterion to be considered, a reality which gives itself to be known and to which he understands Christian preaching as referring. *Deus dixit*, God has spoken, and has been heard by the community of faith. That is the radical assumption of Christian proclamation, and therefore, indirectly, of church dogmatics.

---

[10] Op. cit. p. 18.

3. Revelation and the givenness of our knowledge of God

Theology begins and ends with the self-revelation or self-proclamation of God in his living Word, incarnate in Jesus Christ, and attested in Scripture and the preaching of the Christian community. The familiar statement 'God reveals Himself as the Lord'[11] is in a sense a recapitulation of the entirety of Christian dogmatics, referring us not only to the sole legitimate presupposition for theological activity, but also to the decisive shape to which that theologizing must conform if it is to be truly Christian. God has spoken, and that speaking alone furnishes a basis upon which the church may in turn speak about God, and thereby grants theology its *raison d'être*. God, Barth writes, 'makes Himself present, known and significant to (men) as God. In the historical life of men He takes up a place, and a very specific place at that, and makes Himself the object of human contemplation, human experience, human thought and human speech.'[12] This self-revealing, when it happens, does not allow itself to be understood as one option among many, or to be treated with indifference. It certainly cannot be set alongside human religion, or compared with the products of human religious endeavour as if it were something of the same sort. To view it thus is simply to misunderstand its true nature as revelation. 'Revelation is understood only where we expect from it, and from it alone, the first and the last word about religion . . . Revelation is God's sovereign action upon man or it is not revelation.'[13]

God has spoken concerning himself. It is on this basis and this basis alone that the church may speak about God. Every independent attempt by humans to know or speak about him is futile and doomed to failure. It is in this light that we must view human religion as an entity. However sincere it may or may not be, its fruit is, as Feuerbach rightly saw, essentially idolatrous, the projection of

---

[11] *CD* 1/1, p. 295.
[12] Ibid. p. 315.
[13] *CD* 1/2, p. 295.

human needs and desires onto the clouds. Its failure is the failure to
address itself to the proper place; the place where God has made
himself known, and continues to make himself known. It is in this
sense that Barth insists that human religion in and of itself is to be
characterized as unbelief or faithlessness (*Unglaube*) and as such
concluded under the condemnation of the cross. As we shall see,
however, there is a subtle irony here which is too often missed by
those who leap upon Barth's apparent intolerance of other religious
possibilities. Revelation is indeed the abolition of religion. But the
word *Aufhebung* also bears the ironic sense of lifting up or exaltation,
and, since Barth concedes that Christianity too can be viewed
humanly as a religion, what he seems to be suggesting here is that
revelation indeed judges and puts to death human religious
endeavour, but only in order that it may raise it up and set it upon a
new and more appropriate footing; just as in Christ our humanity in
its entirety has been assumed, judged, crucified and resurrected into
a glorious new existence.

Barth's concern in emphasizing the place of revelation as the
presupposition of theological activity is to insist that the logic of
theological statements refers beyond human experience to a reality
which provokes or creates that experience. The nineteenth
century, with its various attempts to root and validate theological
language in some aspect or other of human experience, had simply
indulged Feuerbach's damning reduction of theological statements
to anthropological statements. This, Barth insisted, is untrue to the
proper intention of theological language. Theology is not concerned to express or articulate the contents of experience, but rather
to respond obediently to the form of God's own self-giving and
self-revealing initiative, an initiative which is already couched in
verbal, cognitive and fleshly form: the humanity of Jesus Christ, the
text of Scripture, and the preaching of the church.

In all this there would seem to be little room for pluralism. In
the event of revelation the truth of God stands over against us
unconditionally. It will allow of no compromise, no bargaining,
no partial or half-hearted response. What it demands of us and
itself creates in us is obedience: an obedient hearing and speaking
on the part of the church. And what this hearing and speaking in
fact has to report is, as we shall see, triune in structure. God is made
known to us as Father, Son and Holy Spirit. Henceforth, Barth

insists, this trinitarian understanding must be heard whenever the term 'God' is used in the church. It must be placed at the head of all dogmatic endeavour as a determinative hermeneutical principle.[14] In answer to the all-determinative question 'Who is the God in Whom we believe?' the church must not fail to give this answer and this alone. To entertain belief in any other god, or to allow the term 'God' to be defined differently for the sake of some apologetic argument or in pursuit of some common denominator of shared understanding, is simply to capitulate once again to the very idolatry from which revelation seeks to deliver us. Thus the doctrine of the trinity, or rather the church's proclamation of the triune God who has made himself known in revelation, cannot be set alongside other alternative models or ways of understanding as 'one view among many', or one route to God among many. God has spoken and has been heard. That this is so rules out either agnosticism or the categorical substitutability of religious constructs as valid options for the church. It can only do what it is called to do, namely, to bear witness to the truth which it knows.

4. Revelation as a closed circle of knowing

And yet, Barth is in no way optimistic concerning the impact of such witness upon the world at large, at least in the short term. For this full-blooded affirmation of the possibility and actuality of true knowledge of God, while it certainly flies in the face of agnostic pluralism, does not embrace any form of universalistic objectivism as its alternative. (It should be noted that the term 'objectivism' here is used in the sense defined earlier in this chapter, rather than the specific sense given to it by George Hunsinger.)[15] There is no succumbing to the temptation to appeal to the self-evidently rational or moral, nor to some objectively given and self-authenticating universal revelation which the church may control and use at will.

For Barth revelation is to be understood not as some abstract historical quantity, or as a body of knowledge or data to which all

---

[14] See *CD* 1/1, p. 300.
[15] G. Husinger, *How to Read Karl Barth* (Oxford: OUP, 1991).

humans in principle have equal access. The church may and must direct people to the human Jesus, to the text of Scripture and to its own preaching, for these are the forms which the Word of God takes in the sphere of the human. But they are not to be confused with revelation itself which is the event (*Ereignis*) in which these various creaturely realities become pregnant with revelatory power for us in such a way that God speaks and is heard by particular people. The human and the divine aspects of God's Word are *inseparabiliter* in this event; but they are equally *inconfuser*. God remains free and mysterious even in the midst of his self-limiting in revelation. He gives himself to be known, but not in such a way that he may be laid hold of or treated as an 'object'. Revelation takes human form in history, but it is not confinable within these human forms. Not all who met Jesus found themselves encountered by him as the Son of God. Not all who open the Bible discover in its words the words of eternal life. Not all who sit under the preaching of the gospel hear the gospel preached. Revelation is not historical in this sense.

The presupposition which lies behind Barth's view of revelation as an event in which human realities become the Word of God is that of the radical unknowability of God. 'We have to admit', Barth writes, 'that we cannot hear, feel, touch or either inwardly or outwardly perceive the one who reveals himself, not because he is invisible or pure spirit, but because he is God, because he is wholly himself, "I am who I am," the subject that escapes our grasp, our attempt to *make* him an object.'[16] Again, 'God does not belong to the world. Therefore He does not belong to the series of objects for which we have categories and words by means of which we draw the attention of others to them, and bring them into relation with Him. Of God it is impossible to speak, because He is neither a natural nor a spiritual object.'[17] This, of course, would be the end of the story and the ultimate endorsement of the agnostic pluralist point of view were it not for one other thing, namely the fact that this same God has made himself known, has 'objectified' himself that we might lay hold of him. But he has done so and does so in such a way

---

[16] *GD*, p. 9.
[17] *CD* 1/2, p. 750.

that he becomes that which is not God, enters the realm of the creaturely, lays himself before us in a form which we are capable of receiving. But the form, as that which is not God, is not to be confused with revelation as such. It makes revelation possible. It furnishes the conditions under which it may take place. The creaturely form itself, however (whether we think of the human Jesus, the text of Scripture or the words of Christian preachers), serves as much to conceal the divine reality as to reveal it. In order for revelation to happen (and, as *Ereignis*, 'happen' is precisely what it does) there must be in, with and under this human form a specific self-giving of God to particular persons, an unveiling of himself, a granting of eyes to see and ears to hear. Revelation, in this sense, is always particular, something which happens to particular persons, and never an abstract quantity.

It is in his reflection upon the event of revelation that Barth discerns the logic of the doctrine of the trinity. God exists as the unknowable and unspeakable Lord. Yet this same God objectifies himself as other, in such a way that he is over against himself as revelation over against revealer. But, if human persons are to receive this revelation, then, since we possess no natural aptitude to do so, it is necessary for this self-objectification to be accompanied by another, this time one in which God indwells us directly and creates in us the subjective conditions for receiving the Word which he speaks; namely, the Holy Spirit who creates faith and obedience. As this event happens the veil is lifted and we perceive the Word of God in the flesh of Jesus, the words of Scripture and preaching. But even once this has happened there is no sense in which we are able to lay hold of these creaturely objects and wring from them God's Word. Precisely because revelation is an event, a relationship which 'straddles objectivity and subjectivity'[18] and in which we are effectively drawn into the triune life of God, knowing the Father through the Son in that *koinonia* which is created by the Spirit, it must be new every morning, or else it has petrified and is not revelation at all but merely the empty form from which life has passed. Revelation as such cannot be grasped, held on to, or controlled by the human

---

[18] Baxter, 'The Nature and Place of Scripture in the Church Dogmatics', p. 35.

knower. We know only as we are in turn known by a God who draws us into relationship with himself. This same God it is who determines to whom he will reveal himself.

What all this amounts to, then, is a claim by Barth that the truth of God is known only from within what he describes as 'a self-enclosed circle',[19] namely, the triune circle of God's self-knowing into which humans are drawn in the event of revelation. This revelation, therefore, is not universally known or knowable, and humans have no natural aptitude for it. It is an act of sovereign grace on the part of God himself when anyone finds themself drawn into it. Christian theology, if it is done at all, is done only within this same circle in obedient response to the self-giving of God. Thus the truth to which it refers us, the arguments which it deploys, the language which it chooses, are all radically contextual and the theologian certainly cannot look forward to any straight-forward endorsement or recognition of them by the intellectual community at large. Only for those who indwell the same frame-work of meaning, who view the world with the same eyes, will what is said here make any real sense. For Barth this in no way compromises the universal intent of theological statements. It sim-ply means that they are precisely church statements, statements of a faith shared by a community of knowing, a community which is both synchronic and diachronic in nature, but which is in many ways set over against the world as a scandal. Here, then, the doctrines of election and of the Holy Spirit serve to underwrite something very close to a committed pluralism of the sort which Newbigin describes. Those who are drawn into this circle, who are granted 'eyes to see', are thereby given to see what cannot oth-erwise, from other perspectives, be seen. Faith, as a moral relation to God in Jesus Christ, a participation in the very inner life of God, is thus precisely a relation which grants 'conviction of things not seen'. From this there follow some clear implications for the way in which the church may handle the truth claims which it is com-pelled to make over against those who indwell or espouse other worlds of meaning and discourse.

---

[19] See, e.g., *CD* 1/2, p. 280.

5. Apologetics and *vestigia trinitatis*

Brief mention must therefore be made of that aspect of Barth's
thought with which most students of theology will at least be familiar in broad terms; namely, his resolute opposition to all forms of
natural theology.

Barth defines natural theology as follows: 'every . . . formulation
of a system which claims to be theological, i.e. to interpret divine
revelation, whose *subject*, however, differs fundamentally from the
revelation in Jesus Christ and whose *method* therefore differs equally
from the exposition of Holy Scripture'.[20] Barth's rejection of all such
apologetic enterprises rests precisely on a conviction that the logic of
the gospel is not universally accessible, but can be grasped only in the
moral venture of faith as people indwell the Christian gospel itself as
their primary world of meaning. Apologetics, in most of its traditional forms at least, begins with the opposite assumption, that some
universal canon or index of rationality exists to which the gospel may
be brought for justification. This may be couched in terms of a 'general revelation' rather than suggesting any essentially autonomous
Promethean storming of the heavens by human reason, but the key
point for Barth is that it is posited as prior to and independent of the
specific self-giving of God in Jesus Christ and the Holy Spirit. There
is, he is adamant, no such *preparatio evangelica* to which the truths of
Christian faith may be brought for approval and recognition, or to
which apologetic appeal may be made, therefore, in the task of
proclaiming Christ to those who do not know him.

The truth of the gospel is self-authenticating and self-involving
for those to whom it manifests itself. They cannot deny it once they
have encountered it, but can only point others to it in the hope that
they too may see it. To see it, to hear and obey it, is to enter into the
community of faith in which life is lived in accordance with the gospel. But the harsh fact of the matter is that to those who do not yet
see it, to whom it has not revealed itself, it remains utterly hidden.
There can be no partial knowing, no preparing of the ground or
preparing the Way of the Lord here. The gospel cannot legitimately

---

[20] *Natural Theology* (trans. Peter Fraenkel; London: Geoffrey Bles,
Centenary Press, 1946), pp. 74–75.

be brought to some other, more ultimate, human court of appeal in an attempt to secure for it a hearing. In fact it seems that the opposite is true, that, far from commending itself to some inherent sense of truth and goodness in humans, the gospel is received as a scandal, a word which contradicts accepted norms and mores. What we must be ever mindful of, however, Barth insists, is the fact that we are not dealing here with a gospel which is scandalous to some supposed 'human reason', since such is an abstract fiction. Rather we are dealing with a clash between the faith commitments of the Christian community and those of other communities as they find articulation in contextually normative canons of rationality and credibility. It is unbelief to which the gospel is a scandal; a commitment to other truths, other gospels, other gods. Once this is seen then the reckless folly (perhaps blasphemy is not too strong a word?) of seeking to afford the gospel warrant by appealing to prior canons of acceptability is manifest. It is to seek to justify faith on the basis of terms laid down by sinful unbelief, to bring Yahweh to Baal for his blessing.

It is in this light that what Barth has to say about the so called *vestigia trinitatis* (in *CD* §8.3) makes sense. The doctrine of the trinity, he affirms, is given to the church in both the form and content of the divine Word spoken in her midst and which she is in turn commanded to speak. In terms of an understanding of the very word 'God' which the church shares with other religious traditions (a fact about which she has cause to be somewhat uneasy and which must lead her to be careful in her use of it) it is this doctrine which 'basically distinguishes the Christian doctrine of God as Christian'[21] and which must therefore be set forth clearly at the outset of all Christian speech about God in order both to avoid any possible confusion as to the meaning of 'God', and as unshamed testimony to this truth by which the church lives. At this point, therefore, Barth sets his face against the pluralist theologies of religion of the present day in which such distinctive awkwardnesses for interfaith dialogue as the trinity, the incarnation and the atonement are conveniently classified in such a way that they can be set aside as mere matters of language, and attention directed rather to what is considered to be really important, namely, some alleged pre-doctrinal ethical or experiential common

---

[21] *CD* 1/1, p. 30.

ground between Christianity and other religious traditions. There can be little doubt that Barth would view such procedures as lacking in integrity and as rendering genuine dialogue (i.e. an informed meeting of different viewpoints in which difference is both heard and respected as difference, rather than seeking to obliterate it or swallow it up into some amorphous experiential uniformity) impossible. An interesting account of just what such dialogue between genuinely different traditions and worlds of meaning might look like is given by Alasdair MacIntyre.[22] His account is one which Barth might well have found congenial.

To return, however, to the matter of the *vestigia trinitatis*: notwithstanding the origin of trinitarian understanding in the very mode and manner of God's self-revealing activity, the history of Christian theology is littered with attempts to commend this particular doctrine on other grounds than this revelation itself, grounds which might render it more believable or palatable to the non-Christian, or which might at least be adduced as a confirmation of or support for what God in his revelatory act shows us of himself. Thus, appeals have been made to aspects of God's creation to show that the notion of triunity, far from being an outrage to common sense or an enigma, finds echoes, parallels and virtual foretellings in human psychology, in the formal properties of water and other elements, in the energy produced by the sun and so forth. Popular apologetics as well as its theological counterpart is full of such. And, of course, there are the inevitable attempts to find hints towards or even alternate versions of the doctrine of the trinity in other religions, whether pre-Christian or non-Christian. And somehow all this is meant to make the doctrine of the trinity itself more worthy of our acceptance, and more commendable to others.

Barth's rejection of such apologetic devices does not begin with an outright denial that there may indeed be facets of our human experience which, viewed from a certain perspective, may seem to bear some sort of crude similarity to the church's confession of God who is one in three and three in one. Rather his concern is one of method, and concerns the inevitable suggestion that the doctrine

---

[22] A. MacIntyre, *Whose Justice? Which Rationality?* (London: Duckworth, 1988). See esp. Ch. 19.

of the trinity itself may have some other basis than that given it in
God's self-revealing manifestation in his Son, and might actually
either require or receive warrant from some other set of considerations or criteria than those provided by the gospel itself. This, he is
convinced, is to misunderstand the situation. On the one hand, the
one who has been encountered by the triune God does not need
such bolstering or confirming of the truth of God's triunity. It is
given in the very structure of the gospel, and of the way, therefore,
in which she makes sense of or experiences the world. On the other
hand, the person who has not had any such encounter will hardly be
brought closer to it (since it rests upon God's sovereign freedom and
grace alone) by having such fascinating parallels placed before him,
and may, indeed, lacking the eyes through which such analogies
may be viewed in the light of the analogate, be led into all sorts of
misunderstanding and error in their thinking about this matter. If
there are *vestigia*, then, for Barth, they could only be recognized by
faith from within the framework of understanding and believing
determined by the gospel. To direct those who stand elsewhere to
them in the search for faith, therefore, is like sending someone into
hazardous terrain on a quest to find the map and compass which
would guide them and enable them to navigate it safely. If they ever
arrive at the intended destination then it will be in spite of, and not
because of, the strategy.

6. Christianity the one true religion

Barth has no qualms about referring to Christianity as the only 'true'
religion; but his attitude towards religious alternatives, far from
being dismissive or arrogant, is one characterized by respect and
humility. It is not, however, a humility which would seek to
endorse or commend the existence of such alternatives and what
they do as good in themselves, but rather that of a sinner among sinners, who feels that his own glasshouse is rather too fragile for him to
be throwing any stones.

   Christianity itself, Barth reminds us, is in its human aspect
precisely a religion. Like all other religions it is in this respect not
some prior receptivity for God or some aptitude to receive him, but
potentially a self-assertiveness over against God, an attempt to lay

down the terms on which it will deal with him. It tends toward an a priori grasping after truth, rather than a willingness to have truth granted to it freely and unconditionally Barth writes:

> Because it is grasping, religion is the contradiction of revelation, the concentrated expression of human unbelief, i.e. an attitude and activity which is directly opposed to faith. It is a feeble but defiant, an arrogant but hopeless, attempt to create something which man could do, but now cannot do, or can do only because and if God himself creates it for him: the knowledge of the truth, the knowledge of God.[23]

That this truth is known, that faith is created among humans, is therefore a matter of pure grace, and Christianity *as a religion* is no more capable of it than any other religious manifestation. Indeed, that the church itself is quite capable of unbelief, of a religiosity which distances God rather than draws nearer to him, is clear enough from its history and from any phenomenological survey of its practices. Thus the abolition of religion by revelation applies just as surely to Christianity as to every other religious tradition. Time and time again God makes himself known to us in ways which cut through and call into judgement the conceptual idols with which we so quickly replace him when left to ourselves.

The outcome of all this, however, is not the despairing conclusion that all religious traditions are equally false (and therefore equally true). Barth is quick to confirm that in Christianity, notwithstanding its essential and sinful humanity, we may speak of the existence of a true religion; but only in precisely the same sense that we speak of a justified sinner.[24] In God's gracious election the church becomes the place, the community, where God makes himself known in spite of its religiosity. This gracious choice rests not upon any intrinsic or inherent religious or ethical qualities which the church possesses, but rather upon the sovereign grace of God alone. 'If we look at the Christian religion in itself and as such,' Barth writes, 'we can only say that apart from the clear testimony of the fact of God some other religion might equally well be the right

---

[23] *CD* 1/2, pp. 302–303.
[24] See ibid. p. 326.

and true one. But once the fact of God is there and its judgment passed, we cannot look at the Christian religion in itself and as such.'[25] We can only view it as it appears to the eyes of faith, namely as 'the sacramental area created by the Holy Spirit, in which the God whose Word became flesh continues to speak through the sign of His revelation.'[26] Thus the *Aufhebung der Religion* is, like the cross in John's gospel, paradoxically both the crucifixion and the 'lifting up' of humanity.

One more thing must be said. If it is election and forgiveness which bestow upon the church the status of being the place where the truth about God is made known, they equally bestow upon it a greater degree of responsibility than pertains to other communities, other traditions. If the sin of religion is committed in the church then it is committed 'with a high hand' and is at once more needful of the very grace which establishes and nourishes it.[27] Human religion, even in its finest manifestations, constitutes idolatry and self-righteousness. But it only appears as such from within the place where the one true God makes himself known. 'The man to whom the truth has really come will concede that he was not at all ready and resolved to let it speak to him.'[28] Those who do not stand here, who have not stood here, find themselves possessed of greater excuse, therefore, than those who have and do stand here, and yet still perpetuate the sin of idolatry and unbelief. It is in this sense that Barth finds himself forced to adopt a tolerant and respectful attitude to those whose standpoint does not afford them a view of the truth which has drawn him into its sphere of manifestation and influence. If his conviction of this truth and his refusal to compromise it leads Barth to be arrogant and harsh in his attitude, then it is not towards the occupants of other frameworks, but precisely towards those who see and live life out of the same truth as himself, but who take their relationship to it for granted and thereby presume upon grace.

[25] Ibid. p. 354.
[26] Ibid. p. 359.
[27] Ibid. p. 337.
[28] Ibid. p. 302.

7. By way of conclusion

We conclude, then, by reminding ourselves that for Barth the doctrine of the trinity (and the Christian gospel of which it may be taken as representative in this respect) constitutes a truth claim with aspirations to correspondence, rather than being of a merely coherentist variety. This does not suppose any crude or naive linguistic understanding in Barth (such as that caricatured by Lindbeck under the label of 'cognitive-propositional'), but rather indicates that *in some sense* the mode of theological statements is one in which they refer beyond themselves and beyond the particular framework of the belief structure of the Christian community (the 'language' in Lindbeck's sense) to the reality of God himself.[29] They can do this only because God himself has taken human language and drawn it into the service of his self-revealing and redemptive gospel. Nonetheless, this reference functions and this language makes sense only within the context of this particular faith community as the place where God has made and makes himself known. To those who indwell other frameworks, who speak other languages, it remains foreign, an enigma, or even a scandal to be mocked. This does not mean that the doctrine of the trinity is true only for those who belong here, but rather that 'here' is the only place where its truth may be grasped and truly articulated. Theological statements are therefore truth claims bearing universal intent, although they can claim no universal demonstrability, but rest on a series of ultimate faith commitments which, like all others, remain vulnerable to rejection and mockery.

In all these respects, I suggest, Barth's understanding of the status of doctrinal statements fits neatly together with what Newbigin has described as a 'committed pluralist' epistemology. Neither a despairing agnosticism nor a confident objectivism (and the imperialistic apologetics which is its logical corollary) is acceptable to Barth. The gospel is 'public truth' in Newbigin's sense, but not

---

[29] For a helpful discussion of Barth's understanding of theological language in this respect see G. Hunsinger, 'Beyond Literalism and Expressivism: Karl Barth's Hermeneutical Realism', in *Modern Theology* 3:3 (1987), pp. 209f.

truth which can be forced down the throats of unbelievers with the strong arm of rationally compelling argument. On the other hand Barth has no time whatever for the suggestion that at the end of the day we should simply allow unbelief to go unchallenged or content in its own alternative religious or irreligious outlook. God has revealed himself, and commands us to make his name known among the nations. The gospel is precisely for those who do not yet know its redeeming power and the charge to the church is to proclaim it boldly. It has 'universal intent'.

The mode of knowing in this 'pluralistic' circumstance is that which the church has always owned; namely, faith with all its attendant risks: and the mode of proclamation that which, when it has been faithful to its calling, the church has adopted, namely, witness. That Barth's theology is so evidently structured around an acceptance of this fact makes it a potentially fruitful working example of the sort of third way between objectivism and relativistic pluralism to which secular philosophers are increasingly pointing us as the epistemic reality of every human rational undertaking. A recognition of this claim, and an attempt to face up to its implications in other spheres of knowing, would seem to provide the only satisfactory way out of the postmodern malaise.

7

The Capacity for Ambiguity:
Revisiting the Barth-Brunner
Debate

In this chapter I shall consider the very public disagreement between Karl Barth and Emil Brunner which reached its zenith in 1934, although it had murmured on for some considerable time beforehand and was continued with no small amount of enthusiasm long afterwards. The focus of this fierce disagreement was a fundamental question concerning the relationship between nature and grace, creation and redemption, state and church. The disagreement was remarkable not due simply to the passion and vigour with which Barth, at least, engaged in it, but because it had erupted between two men who hitherto had been viewed as theologically at one. An angry exchange between Barth and Harnack was perhaps unsurprising. But Barth and Brunner? Were they not from the same stable, and engaged in essentially similar theological projects? So it had seemed to many. And so, viewed from one perspective at least, it would continue to appear, even to Brunner himself as we shall see. But Barth insisted that the relationship between them was rather like that between two adjacent points on the circumference of a circle: looked at from one perspective as close as they could ever be; but from another, as far apart as possible. In what follows I shall set the debate and the issues in their proper context, pay close attention to the form of the exchange between Barth and Brunner itself, and finally pose some questions concerning the final adequacy of Barth's formulation of his response in the hope of exposing more precisely the contours of his position. The texts to which our attention will be directed are Brunner's pamphlet *Natur und Gnade: Zum*

Gespräch mit Karl Barth[1] and Barth's response *Nein! Antwort an Emil Brunner.*[2]

1. *Status confessionis* or storm in a teacup?

In order to appreciate just what was at stake in 1934 we must set the dispute in its context. The issues in question were, of course, ones which both men had considered and discussed before; but events, both in the life of the German nation and in Barth's own personal life and theological development, now served to bring them to a head.

As we have seen in previous chapters, Barth's early reaction to the so-called *Kulturprotestantismus* which characterized the theology of many of his teachers was to insist upon the essential otherness of God with respect to the cosmos, and to posit a relation of fundamental discontinuity between them. Like those of whom the Apostle Paul had written in his epistle to the Romans, Barth believed, many in his own generation had lost sight of this vital differentiation and were suffering the theological cost. 'Thinking of ourselves what can only be thought of God, we are unable to think of Him more highly than we think of ourselves. Being to ourselves what God ought to be to us, He is no more to us than we are to ourselves. This secret identification of ourselves with God carries with it our isolation from Him.'[3] When he turned to the question of the relationship between nature and grace in his Göttingen lectures in dogmatics of 1924, therefore, Barth already characterized it as essentially a relation of contradiction rather than continuity, insisting that human response to God's Word in

---

[1] Tübingen: J.C.B. Mohr, 1934.

[2] Munich: Chr. Kaiser Verlag, 1934. Both pieces were subsequently bound together in an English translation by Peter Fraenkel in 1946 under the title *Natural Theology* (London: Geoffrey Bles: the Centenary Press, 1946). Brunner furnished a more developed and longer second edition of his pamphlet in 1935 in which he continued the dialogue; but since we are primarily interested in Barth we shall limit our consideration here to the original 1934 version to which Barth's response was directed.

[3] Barth, *Romans*, p. 45. Cf. *Der Römerbrief* (Munich: Chr. Kaiser Verlag, 1924), p. 20.

faith and obedience, where it arises, is to be construed precisely as miracle, a surprising activity of God's Holy Spirit in the life of fallen human beings the fruits of which, in and of themselves ('naturally'), they are utterly incapable of.[4] Similar sentiments are to be found scattered through his lectures on Schleiermacher delivered in the same year.[5] Barth's reflection on this theme had been stimulated and sharpened by his encounter in 1923 with the Jesuit theologian Erich Przywara.[6] In that year Przywara published an essay entitled 'Gott in uns oder über uns? (Immanenz und Transzendenz im heutigen Geistleben)'[7] in which Barth's theology received careful critical appraisal. Although he viewed Barth's work with considerable generosity compared to the liberal Protestant tradition, Przywara finally concluded that Barth's God (chiefly as described in the second edition of *The Epistle to the Romans*) was rather too much *über uns* and not sufficiently *in uns*. This, he concluded, left Barth finally incapable of affirming the doctrine of incarnation in any full-blooded and adequate sense. Przywara's critique is significant for at least two reasons: first, because it introduced Barth to the concept of an *analogia entis* (analogy of being) between God and humanity which, from 1929 onwards, became Barth's primary target in his discussion of this and related issues;[8] and second because Przywara's key criticism is one which has repeatedly been made[9] (not least, as we shall see below, by Brunner) and in order to refute it some clarification of Barth's position such as that attempted below would seem to be required.

---

[4] See, e.g., *GD*, p. 456.

[5] See, e.g., K. Barth, *The Theology of Schleiermacher* (Grand Rapids: Eerdmans, 1982), p. 242.

[6] See on this McCormack, *Karl Barth's Critically Realistic Dialectical Theology*, pp. 319f.

[7] The essay appeared in the Catholic journal *Stimmen der Zeit* (1923), p. 105.

[8] His first public treatment of the concept was in the 1929 lectures entitled 'Schicksal und Idee in der Theologie'; ET 'Fate and Idea in Theology', in H.M. Rumscheidt (ed.), *The Way of Theology in Karl Barth: Essays and Comments* (Allison Park, PA: Pickwick Publications, 1986).

[9] It is essentially similar to the charges made by Baillie and Roberts discussed above in Ch. 1.

In February 1929 Barth invited Przywara to speak in Münster. During Przywara's visit the two men immersed themselves in discussion, a process which served further to clarify Barth's thinking on just where the vital lines of theological demarcation between them lay. By the autumn of that year he had settled his mind sufficiently to deliver a stinging and sustained rejection of Przywara's account of the relation between God and humanity, and the roots of that account in the theology of Augustine. In a lecture on the theme 'Der Heilige Geist und das Christliche Leben'[10] Barth laid his newly whetted axe to the root of even the slightest suggestion of a settled continuity between God and humankind as the basic Creator-creature relation. Human beings are not, normally speaking, 'open upwards' as Przywara had maintained, not even when his careful qualification that they are open upwards only *von Gott her*, that is, 'from above', by virtue of God's opening activity, is taken into account. The danger with such a formulation, its closeness to Barth's own concerns and emphases notwithstanding, was its capacity to collapse quickly back into being a theological description of a 'natural' (i.e. a general and normal) human state of affairs rather than a circumstance which is intrinsically surprising when it arises and restricted in its scope to the objects of divine election who, by the Spirit, become the recipients of God's miraculous self-giving. Thus, in relation to human knowing of God, Barth writes:

> The discontinuity between God the Creator and man, when one considers the relation of Creator and creature, must mean that between being Lord and being lorded-over, there exists an irreversibility such as excludes the idea of God as an object of whom, in Platonic fashion, we have a reminiscence, as 'Ancient Beauty'. It denotes the knowledge of God, which man obtains as revelation, of what is really and utterly new, and which no innate awareness of beauty on man's part has ever seen objectively. If creature is to be strictly understood as a reality willed and placed by God in distinction from His own reality: that is to say, as the wonder of a reality, which, by the power of God's love, has a place and persistence alongside of His own reality, then the continuity

---

[10] K. Barth, *The Holy Ghost and the Christian Life* (trans. R. Birch Hoyle; London: Frederick Muller, 1938).

between Him and it (the true *analogia entis*, by virtue of which He, the uncreated Spirit, can be revealed to the created spirit) – this continuity cannot belong to the creature itself but only to the Creator *in His relation* to the creature. It cannot be taken to mean that the creature has an original endowment in his make-up, but only as a second marvel of God's love, as the inconceivable, undeserved, divine bestowal on His creature.[11]

Thus Barth insists upon a clear distinction being drawn between what is true of a person *as a creature*, by virtue of 'nature' on the one hand, and, on the other, as the object and recipient of God's self-giving in grace. 'But grace is ever and in all relations God's deed and act, taking place in this and that moment of time in which God wills to be gracious to us, and is gracious, and makes his grace manifest. It is never at all a quality of ours, inborn in us, such as would enable us to know of it in advance.'[12] Already here we can discern the emphasis on a dynamic relatedness to God (rather than a static possession of qualities or deployment of capacities) which later became so typical of Barth's portrayal of the relationship between God and his creatures. Insofar as there is any genuine continuity to be acknowledged between God and humanity, it is from moment to moment a matter of God's gracious action in the life of the particular creature, and never something which the creature possesses as such. Considered *as creature* there is only a relation of difference and, indeed, sinful alienation from God to be reckoned with.[13]

It was in 1929, then, and not 1934 that Barth's basic position on natural theology and the question of a created human disposition towards or capacity for God[14] was really settled and tightened up, even if events were to drive him to a sharper rhetoric in subsequent debates and publications. Barth himself traced his own decisive

---

[11] Ibid. p. 14.

[12] Ibid. pp. 17–18.

[13] See, e.g., ibid. p. 28.

[14] This is itself an important distinction to draw and, as we shall see, in many ways it was Barth's concern that the distinction might not hold, and that a passive 'capacity' might really amount to or be interpreted as an active disposition, however slight, which drove him to a vigorous rejection of the language even of a human *capacity* for God.

---

parting of the ways with Brunner back to 'roughly 1929'.[15] In his final contribution to the journal *Zwischen den Zeiten* in October 1933 ('Farewell'), reflecting on the emergence of the now manifest split, he noted: 'It came about that within our journal and outside it, I saw Emil Brunner . . . pursuing a theology that I increasingly came to view only as a return under new banners to the fleshpots of the land of Egypt, which I thought that he had left behind once and for all in our common exodus.'[16] Similarly strong comments are to be found in the first part volume of *KD*, published in 1932, especially with regard to Brunner's defence (in essays published in *Zwischen den Zeiten* between 1929–31) of a theological eristics and his cautious insistence upon the existence even in the unbeliever of a 'point of contact for the divine message'.[17] Clearly Barth attributed the split to a development in *Brunner's* position ('When . . . Brunner suddenly began to proclaim openly "the other task of theology", the "point of contact" etc.'),[18] but the clarification of his own position, his engagement with Przywara having been the chief catalyst, was probably the more significant factor. Now it was those, like Brunner, whose theology had seemed closest to his own who received the sharpest retorts, precisely because it was important for Barth to identify and to make manifest the serious differences which actually existed between them.

In 1933 Barth's already trenchant resistance to the idea of a natural theology was further bolstered by political developments in Germany. The election of Adolf Hitler as Reichs-Chancellor in January of that year and the subsequent domination of the political scene by the totalitarian claims of National Socialism produced a mixed reaction from the churches. The following proclamation of the so-called 'Committee of Three'[19] on 28 April furnishes an

---

[15] See *Natural Theology*, p. 71.

[16] Cited in E. Busch, *Karl Barth: His Life from Letters and Autobiographical Texts* (London: SCM Press, 1976), p. 195.

[17] See *CD* 1/1, pp. 27f.

[18] *Natural Theology*, p. 71.

[19] Three leading churchmen of the day: Dr Kapler, President of the Central Board of the German Evangelical Churches; Bishop Marahens (Lutheran) of Hanover; and Pastor Hesse of Elberfeld. Cited in K. Barth, *Theologische Existenz Heute* (Munich: Chr. Kaiser Verlag, 1933); ET

example of the sort of syncretistic attitude which provoked Barth's ire, and against which he duly thundered into print:

> A mighty National Movement has captured and exalted our German Nation. An all-embracing reorganisation of the State is taking place within the awakened German people. We give our hearty assent to this turning-point of history. God has given us this: to Him be the glory.
>
> Bound unitedly in God's Word, we recognise in the great events of our day a new commission of our Lord to His Churches.[20]

Barth saw such a deliberate accommodation of an ideology, the moral and political dubiety of which was already clearly apparent even if its worst excesses were still obscure, as directly facilitated by a theological appeal within the churches to any authorities ('natural' sources in human nature or culture) other than the Word of God. In June 1933, just six months into the so-called Third Reich, he wrote his pamphlet *Theologische Existenz Heute*, in which he utterly rejected the theology of the 'German Christians',[21] according to whom 'The Church has to prove herself to be the Church for the German people'.[22] Barth no doubt saw this as the, perhaps equally well-intentioned but certainly equally misguided, ecclesio-political equivalent of Brunner's suggestion that 'Eristic theology is distinguished from dogmatic by the fact that it has more regard to the one with whom it speaks about faith, that it addresses itself more . . . to his resistance, and that to this extent it speaks more *ad hominem*.'[23]

---

[19] *(continued)* *Theological Existence To-day!* (trans. R. Birch Hoyle; London: Hodder and Stoughton, 1933), p. 23.

[20] Cited in Barth, *Theological Existence To-day!*, p. 23.

[21] It is perhaps worth noting that the infamous Nein! of Barth's response to Brunner was but an echo of one already issued to the German Christians in this pamphlet. See *Theologische Existenz Heute*, p. 51: 'Was ich dazu zu sagen habe, ist einfach: ich sage unbedingt und vorbehaltlos Nein zum Geist und zum Buchstaben dieser Lehre.' Again, the similarity of Barth's formulated response reflects the generic connection which he detected between Brunner's approach and the teaching of the German Christians.

[22] Barth, *Theological Existence To-day!*, p. 48.

[23] Cited in *CD* 1/1, p. 29.

His response was vigorous and unequivocal as the following brief extracts indicate:

> The Church preaches the Gospel in all the kingdoms of this world. She preaches it also in the Third Reich, but not *under* it, nor in *its* spirit.
>
> If the Church's Confession of Faith is to be expanded it must be according to the standard of Holy Scripture, and not at all according to the examples, positive or negative, of a view of things existing at some one particular period of time, be it a political philosophy, or otherwise. Therefore she must not widen the Creed to include the National Socialists' 'world view' . . .
>
> The fellowship of those belonging to the Church is not determined by blood, therefore, not by race, but by the Holy Spirit and Baptism. If the German Evangelical Church excludes Jewish-Christians, or treats them as of a lower grade, she ceases to be a Christian Church.[24]

With typical directness Barth sent a copy of his text to Hitler. By the time the Nazi government got around to banning it in July 1934, however, some 37,000 copies were already in circulation and the text had been translated into English by virtue of a 'deep sense of the importance of Dr Barth's brochure for all sections of Christendom. This message is a solemn call to all the Churches to reflect upon the necessity for allowing the sovereign rule of God's Word in all the affairs of the Christian Church.'[25]

In later life Barth reflected on this document and its place in his development as follows:

> I did not have anything new to say in that first issue of *Theological Existence Today* apart from what I had always endeavoured to say: that we could have no other gods than God, that holy scripture was enough to forgive our sins and to order our life. The only thing was that now I suddenly had to say this in a different situation. It was no longer just an academic theory. Without any conscious intention or endeavour on my part, it took on the character of an appeal, a challenge, a battle-cry,

---

[24] Barth, *Theological Existence To–day!*, p. 52.

[25] From the foreword by R. Birch Hoyle and Carl Heath to Barth, *Theological Existence To–day!*.

a confession. It was not I who had changed: the room in which I had to speak had changed dramatically, and so had its resonance. As I repeated this doctrine consistently in this new room, at the same time it took on a new depth and became a practical matter, for decision and action.[26]

The apparent endorsement of some of the tenets of the German Christians by those who had been his close theological allies and colleagues soon served to confirm Barth in his view that with the question of natural theology, and of sources or authorities for faith independent of the Word of God, faithfulness to the gospel itself was finally at stake.[27] From now on the consequences of faithfulness to the gospel (determination not to confuse God's will with our human wishes as Barth put it in a lecture in Barmen in January 1934)[28] began to mean a willingness to stand out visibly from the crowd in ways which would attract unwelcome attention not just from the established ecclesiastical authorities, but equally from the state. In Barth's own case this would range from small but significant gestures (such as his refusal to submit to a university rule that every lecture be opened with the Hitler salute: Barth opened his lectures with a prayer instead!) to his involvement in the emergent Confessing Church and the drafting of its so-called Barmen Declaration in May 1934. This was provoked by an increasingly heretical rhetoric from the German Christians such as the following from March that year: 'Christ, as God the helper and saviour, has, through Hitler, become mighty among us . . . Hitler (National Socialism) is now the way of the Spirit and Will of God for the

---

[26] From Karl Barth, *How I Changed my Mind* (ed. J. Godsey; Richmond: John Knox Press, 1966), p. 46. Cited in Busch, *Karl Barth*, p. 227.

[27] In his 'Abschied' to *Zwischen den Zeiten* in October 1933 Barth makes some specific references; for example: 'Some time during this summer I read . . . in *Deutsche Volkstum* Gogarten's acceptance of Stapel's theological dictum that for us the law of God is identical with the law of the German people . . . I cannot see anything in German Christianity but the last, fullest and worst monstrosity of Neo-Protestantism . . . I regard Stapel's maxim about the Law of God as being an utter betrayal of the gospel.'

[28] Published as *Gottes Wille und unsere Wünsche* (Munich: Chr. Kaiser Verlag, 1934).

church of Christ among the German nation'.[29] Compare 'The Swastika is a sign of sacrifice which lets the cross of Christ shine out for us in a new light.'[30] In response to such statements the Declaration offers a blistering judgement upon any attempt to introduce any other standard or source for Christian faith, life and thought than 'Jesus Christ, as he is attested to us in Holy Scripture . . . We reject the false doctrine that the Church could and should recognise as a source of its proclamation, beyond and besides this one Word of God, yet other events, powers, historic figures, and truths as God's revelation.'[31] Hitler, the ideology of the *Volk* and of *Blut und Boden*, that is to say, were neither to be confused with the Gospel nor synthesised with it into some other gospel.

The questions of the relationship between church and state, grace and nature were thus thrust to the fore in a situation in which apparent compromises were being made between the gospel of Jesus Christ and that of Germany's other more recently adopted messianic movement. Barth was now utterly convinced that in such a context, in the face of all syncretistic blurring of boundaries, the Christian church and its theologians must return unequivocally to the one absolute authority for faith: the Revelation of God to humans in Jesus Christ and him crucified, a revelation the very substance of which spoke clearly of a judgement upon all purely human philosophies and ideologies, indeed upon human existence as such, considered apart from God's redeeming action in Jesus Christ. Christian theology, Christian ethics, therefore, could in no sense be held to derive their message from two distinct sources: revelation on the one hand, and nature or reason on the other. To suggest this in the Germany of 1934, when the most demonic fruits of human nature and culture were clearly manifest in the political and social sphere, was effectively to entertain the view that theology

---

[29] Cited in E. Jüngel, *Christ, Justice and Peace: Toward a Theology of the State in Dialogue with the Barmen Declaration* (trans. Hamill and Torrance; Edinburgh: T & T Clark, 1992), p. 22.

[30] W. Grundmann, *Die 28 Thesen der Deutschen Christen erläutert*, cited in Jüngel, *Christ, Justice and Peace*, p. 23.

[31] See the revised translation by Douglas S. Bax in Jüngel, *Christ, Justice and Peace*, p. xxiii.

must serve two masters: on the one hand the Lord of light, and on the other the lord of darkness.

It is easy to see how this specific context served to exaggerate the issues and present them in their starkest possible outline: but, as we have seen, the issues were already there to be exaggerated, and had now seriously to be wrestled with. Whether 'nature' be manifest in Nazism, or other, apparently less objectionable, secular philosophies and human disciplines, the methodological question remained essentially the same one. In terms of our knowing of God and his purposes and designs for his world, what part may 'nature' be expected to play? What is the proper relationship between 'nature' (the sphere of the human as given apart from any effective redemptive or revelatory activity on the part of God) and 'grace' (the impact of God's self-giving in Christ and the Spirit within this same sphere)?

This was the key question. It was, of course, an age-old question for Christian theology, and one to which Barth saw Roman Catholicism and Protestant liberalism alike as having given a similar answer, namely, *Gratia non tollit naturam sed perfecit*: 'Grace does not destroy nature, but perfects it.' In particular, this meant affording human reason some positive a priori role with respect to knowledge of God. Barth believed that in every age, and not just in the *status confessionis* of Nazi Germany, such an answer opened the floodgates to relativism, secularism and paganism, viewing the category of the 'natural' as standing in a relationship of fundamental continuity with that of 'grace', as a *preparatio evangelica*, and therefore as having a distinct and necessary role to play in the formulation of theology within the church.

In Nazi Germany such an approach was now leading and, Barth believed, could only lead effectively to free rein being granted to aspects of the same 'natural humanity' as was responsible for Nazi philosophies and policies as an authoritative source for Christian theology, to be set alongside that of the Word of God, and as a necessary context within which to interpret and make sense of that Word. Just as some of the early Greek fathers had insisted on referring to Plato as the Moses of the Greeks, so now Hitler was being alluded to openly as the Moses of the *Volk*.[32] To tolerate any such

---

[32] See ibid. p. xxiii, n. 9.

syncretism between nature and grace was thus effectively to rob the church of its capacity to resist Nazism at the very moment when it needed it most. It was, in short, to engage in a pact with the devil, and to place Christian theology under the servitude of false gods whose ends *did not simply fall short of but were diametrically opposed to* those of the one true God who brooks no rivals, and whose Word uttered in the crucified Jesus is one of judgement upon all human pretensions and achievements. Here, then, with this fundamental question of theological method, the very life and integrity of the Christian church was perceived to be at stake.

For Barth, therefore, the issue of natural theology was tangled up with the question of fidelity to the church's task of witness to Christ in a situation where his sole Lordship and sovereignty was being called into question, and the truth of the gospel sold down the river for the sake of compromise with an intrinsically evil regime. To give way at *this* point, to concede some other authority for faith than that of God's self-revealing act, to lay claim to some innate receptivity for knowledge of God on the part of humanity – albeit only the slightest concession – was, he believed, to have placed one foot on the slippery slope which led inevitably to a natural religion, a natural law and a Promethean challenge to the sole authority of God's Word. It was, in short, to have abandoned obedience to the form of God's self-revealing in exchange for an epistemic self-justification in theology which, however partial, posed a fundamental challenge to the doctrine of justification by faith. Humans, Barth insists, can no more contribute anything to that knowledge of God which alone saves than they can bring anything to the throne of grace in order to secure divine favour. On both counts they are effectively bankrupts, and must cast themselves on the mercy and grace of God poured out in his Son.

It was in the midst of all this that Emil Brunner presented his public complaint and defence *Natur und Gnade*, suggesting that Barth was making far more of any differences between the two of them than actually deserved to be made. It is important, when reading Barth's harsh and unrelenting response, to keep the context which we have sketched firmly in mind. Otherwise the passion and invective may seem to be unprovoked and inappropriate. Let us turn, then, to the Brunner-Barth dialogue itself as we are given to overhear part (and only part) of it in the book *Natural Theology*. We now know what the issue was: but in fact the main question posed in and by the book itself is not so much this issue as such, but where precisely Barth and Brunner stand in relation to it, and therefore to one another. Do they stand on the same side of the theological fence or not?

2. The case for the defence: Emil Brunner

Brunner's essay consists basically of an attempt to show that in fact there is very little substantial difference between their respective points of view. He commends Barth for what he desires and intends, which, Brunner argues, *he* too desires and intends. But Barth, he suggests, has gone too far in drawing some radical conclusions from his position: conclusions which are not necessary in order to achieve what both want to achieve, and conclusions which he (Brunner) is unable to endorse. Nonetheless, he argues, these are relatively minor matters, and he and Barth stand firmly in the same camp. 'We are concerned', says Brunner, 'with the fact that the proclamation of the Church has not two sources and norms, such as, e.g. revelation *and* reason or the Word of God *and* history, and that ecclesiastical or Christian action has not two norms, such as e.g. commandments *and* "Ordinances".'[33] 'In all this', he says, 'there is between me and Barth no difference of opinion, except the one on the side of Barth that there is a difference of opinion.'![34] Barth appears, he suggests, 'like a loyal soldier on sentry duty at night, who shoots every one who does not give him the password as he has been commanded, and who therefore from time to time also annihilates a good friend whose password he does not hear or misunderstands in his eagerness'.[35]

This metaphor is a telling one, for in it we find the basic thrust of Brunner's complaint. 'Barth', he says in effect, 'has either misheard or else misunderstood me – I *gave* the proper password, but find myself having been dispatched by the theological bullet all the

---

[33] *Natural Theology*, p. 18.
[34] Ibid.
[35] Ibid. p. 16.

same!' What, then, was the password? The following formulation captures the central issue: *Nature is not, in its historical state, predisposed towards grace, but resists it. The old creation is not capable of the new creation, i.e. there is nothing in the old Adam, the flesh, which could simply be developed or extrapolated to posit the new Adam. Redemption, therefore, is not a matter of evolution, or of development, or perfection: but of revolution, crisis and crucifixion.* A *prima facie* reading of their respective essays suggests that both Barth and Brunner would be able to offer broad agreement with this general statement so far as it goes. Brunner certainly supposed such basic agreement to exist. Yet the devil is ever hidden in the small print, and the formulations and expressions which each actually employed to unfold their understanding of such claims were in turn rejected by the other as utterly unacceptable. Interestingly, each denied meaning what the other insisted they *must* mean (a phenomenon with a respectable pedigree in the history of theology!). Let us, then, look more closely at these alternative expressions and claims.

Brunner lists a number of radical conclusions which he identifies in Barth, including the following:

> In the fall the image of God in humans was obliterated without remnant.
>
> Scripture is the sole source and norm of our knowledge of God, and we must thus reject any attempt to identify a 'natural' or 'general' revelation of God in nature, the conscience, or history.
>
> There are no grounds for speaking of a 'point of contact' for the saving action of God in human nature, since this would undermine *sola gratia*.
>
> The new creation is not a perfection of the old, but comes into being exclusively through the destruction of the old, and its replacement by something utterly new.

Brunner's response to these points centres around an emphatic denial of the third. We must, he argues, be able to speak meaningfully of a 'point of contact' (*Anknüpfungspunkt*)[36] for grace in nature in some sense, else we are left with a revelation and a redemption which are floating in mid-air never actually *making* contact, and never, therefore, actually revealing anything to or redeeming anybody. This is

---

[36] Brunner, *Natur und Gnade*, pp. 18f.

essentially the same criticism levelled by Przywara ten years earlier and echoed by various others over the subsequent decades. *The key claim of Christian faith is that God redeems humanity by himself becoming human. There must therefore be something with or on the basis of which such contact can in fact be made, even in sinful human nature.* Here we reach the core of the debate, and the source of much ambiguity and (possible) confusion. The key question is not whether Barth would or could concede such a statement (whatever he may have been he was not a self-confessed Deist) but rather how he might have understood it, and whether his account was coherent. These are questions to which I shall return later in the chapter. For now we may remain with an overview of Brunner's careful challenge to Barth.

First Brunner turns to Barth's (alleged) attitude to the *imago Dei*, and seeks to introduce a careful distinction. 'I agree', he writes, 'that the original image of God in man has been destroyed, that the *justitia originalis* has been lost and with it the possibility of doing or even of willing to do that which is good in the sight of God.'[37] But, he suggests, ought we not to differentiate between a 'formal' image of God, and a 'material' image of God? The 'formal' image is the *humanum*, that which distinguishes humankind from the beasts and the inanimate creation. This special status of the human creature is 'not only not abolished by sin; rather it is the presupposition of the ability to sin and continues within the state of sin.'[38] It is the status of human beings as subjects, possessed of a capacity for words (*Wörtfähigkeit*)[39] and therefore capable of being addressed by God. As we shall see, a good deal rests upon the translation of key terms such as *Wörtfähigkeit* and *Wortmächtigkeit* and the contexts within which they are used.[40] With this 'capacity', according to Brunner, is bound up the responsibility of humanity, and that which defines human sin as such. No animal can be guilty of sin – only human beings. And this is a reflection of the

---

[37] *Natural Theology*, p. 22.

[38] Ibid. p. 23.

[39] See Brunner, *Natur und Gnade*, p. 11.

[40] See ibid. p. 18: 'Der Anknüpfungspunkt ist eben: die auch dem Sünder nicht abhanden gekommene formale imago dei, das Menschsein des Menschen, die humanitas, nach ihren zwei vorhin bezeichneten Momenten: Wortmächtigkeit und Verantwortlichkeit.' It should perhaps be noted that the German *Verantwortlichkeit* is capable of a similar range of

retention of the formal image. But *materially* speaking, the image is utterly lost. That is to say, 'man is a sinner through and through and there is nothing in him which is not defiled by sin'. He is in no way predisposed towards grace, but hostile to it.

Humans, then, remain persons responsible before God, albeit sinful persons who have flouted and continually flout that responsibility, thereby incurring judgement. Thus,

> we must say that materially there is no point of contact, whereas formally it is a necessary presupposition (*unbedingte Voraussetzung*). The Word of God does not have to create man's capacity for words. He has never lost it, it is the presupposition of his ability to hear the Word of God. But the Word of God itself creates man's ability to believe the Word of God, i.e., the ability to hear it in *such a way* as is only possible in faith.[41]

Next Brunner turns to the theme of a so-called general revelation or 'perceptibility of God (*Erkennbarkeit Gottes*) in his works', an idea

---

[40] *(continued)* interpretation as its English counterpart 'responsibility'. It may simply mean 'accountable or answerable to or for', or it may imply the capacity to 'be the author of an action (a response) or state of affairs' for the presence or absence of which one subsequently 'bears responsibility'. The way in which Brunner ties these two particular concepts closely together in his definition of the *humanum* ('only a being that can be addressed is responsible, for it alone can make decisions', *Natural Theology*, p. 31) already begins to undercut his own simultaneous insistence: 'Nur darf dieses "empfänglich" nicht im materialen Sinne verstanden werden . . . Es ist die rein formale Ansprechbarkeit.' It is already clear at this early stage of his response that the distinction between formal and material is one which needs to be carefully monitored.

[41] *Natural Theology*, p. 32 (emphasis original). Cf. *Natur und Gnade*, p. 19: 'Das Wort Gottes schafft nicht erst die Wortmächtigkeit des Menschen . . . Das Wort Gottes schafft aber selbst die Fähigkeit des Menschen, Gottes Wort zu Glauben, also die Fähigkeit, es so zu hören, wie man es nur glaubend hören kann.' Brunner's following statement that 'It is evident that the doctrine of sola gratia is not in the least endangered by such a doctrine' invites the response that it is not at all obvious: it all depends on how such a doctrine is subsequently deployed and developed! In particular, in what sense is this capacity for words an *unbedingte Voraussetzung*, and for whom?

which he affirms on the grounds of the general premise that 'In every creation the spirit of the creator is in some way recognisable'[42] and by appeal to the testimony of Scripture. Here he introduces another careful distinction, although it is implicit rather than drawn out and developed. On the one hand, he insists, we can hardly attend carefully to the Bible and fail to recognize the fact that God's world is of such a sort that it 'speaks' of his workmanship. 'Wherever God does anything', Brunner writes, 'he leaves the imprint of his nature upon what he does. Therefore the creation of the world is at the same time a revelation, a self-communication of God.'[43] This fact does not alter due to the presence of human sin. The heavens do not cease to declare the glory of God after the Fall. In this sense, therefore, we can and must speak of a revelation of God (*Offenbarung Gottes*) in the natural world. But, on the other hand, Brunner affirms, what we must insist with equal vigour is that sin blinds human beings, and results in their failure to see or hear what is being shown or said. Hence 'The reason why men are without excuse is that they will not know (*nicht erkennen wollen*) the God who so clearly manifests himself to them.'[44]

Similarly with conscience; the consciousness of responsibility, of an 'ought' or categorical imperative which stands over us, no matter how imperfectly we perceive it, or how much we rebel against it, is present even in sinful humanity. Indeed again, Brunner insists, it is that which determines our humanity *as* sinful. 'Men have not only responsibility but also consciousness of it . . . Only because men somehow know the will of God are they able to sin.'[45] And this is, he argues, a knowledge of God through a level of knowledge of God's law;[46] although *again* we may reasonably say that it is not recognized as such, and that it serves no purpose whatever in terms of enabling us better to open ourselves to God or to receive further knowledge

---

[42] 'In jeder Schöpfung ist der Geist ihres Schöpfers irgendwie erkennbar,' *Natur und Gnade*, p. 11. Cf. *Natural Theology*, p. 24.

[43] *Natural Theology*, p. 25.

[44] Ibid. Cf. *Natur und Gnade*, p. 12.

[45] *Natural Theology*, p. 25.

[46] 'Dass Erkenntnis des Gesetzes Gottes irgendwie auch Gotteserkenntnis sei, ist das klare Zeugnis der Schrift' (*Natur und Gnade*, p. 13). We have already noted Barth's angry rejection of the suggestion that the law of God might in some direct way be linked with the law of the German people (see above n. 28). Here Brunner admits the potential dangers of his own

of him. The opposite may well be true; we may dig ourselves deeper into the trenches of our rebellion whenever such 'knowledge' manifests itself in a sense of guilt or obligation. Again, the distinction between a material and a formal *Anknüpfungspunkt* must be held on to.

Thus, Brunner concludes, the real question (asked and answered on a biblical basis) is not whether there are two kinds or levels of revelation (although we might note he never suggests anything other than one ultimate *source*), but rather how the two that *do* exist (in creation and in Jesus Christ) are related. He writes:

> taking our stand upon the revelation in Jesus Christ, we shall not be able to avoid speaking of a double-revelation: of one in creation which only he can recognise in all its magnitude, whose eyes have been opened by Christ; and of a second in Jesus Christ in whose bright light he can clearly perceive the former. This latter revelation far surpasses that which the former was able to show him.[47]

As we shall see, this way of stating the matter was totally unacceptable to Barth in 1934, although it is worth noting at least a formal (if not a material) link with something which the Barth of *CD* IV.3 was eventually prepared to acknowledge.[48]

---

[46] *(continued)* position 'im Blick auf unser jetziges Erkennen' (*Natur und Gnade*, p. 13) but falls back on the claim that, whatever its vulnerability to misuse, the linking of conscience to knowledge of God's law and hence to knowledge of God himself is utterly biblical.

[47] *Natural Theology*, pp. 26–27.

[48] See §69.2, 'The Light of Life', where Barth develops the view that those aspects of the cosmos which he refers to as the 'little lights' of creation, while they certainly do not reveal God to the unregenerate mind are, nonetheless, given to do so as and when they are viewed by the eyes of faith. The creation, he affirms in this context, is thus invested with 'a power of speech' which persists regardless of whether humans hear what it has to say or not. What is heard by those with ears to hear is altogether more full than that which is grasped by common sense alone; but there is a positive relation between the two! The key difference between Barth and Brunner remains, however, in as much as Barth refuses to think or speak of revelation as a commodity or thing (*Offenbarheit*) within the sphere of creaturely reality, let alone one for which either the natural world or

Brunner suggests that we should differentiate between an objective-divine and a subjective-human-sinful sense of the phrase 'natural revelation' (which he prefers to 'general' revelation). On the one hand it refers to an objective 'capacity for revelation' (*Offenbarungsmächtigkeit*)[49] with which God has invested his universe, or to the formal image of God which remains in humans despite their inability to benefit from it. On the other hand, 'nature' can refer to 'what sinful man makes of this in his ignorant knowledge' or 'what man himself makes of himself through sin'.[50] We might put this slightly differently and speak of a distinction between the ontic and the noetic: between what is there to be seen, and our ability to see it. Again, there are two distinct senses of *Wortmächtigkeit* or *Offenbarungsmächtigkeit* operative here. On the one hand the world possesses a God-given capacity for speech, or capacity for revelation, i.e. the ability to speak of God. On the other, the question arises of the capacity of human beings to see or to receive this 'speech' or 'revelation'. Both are rendered by the same ambiguous phrases 'capacity for revelation' or 'capacity for speech/language'. Brunner concludes: 'Only the Christian, i.e. the man who stands within the revelation in Christ, *has* the true *natural* knowledge of God.'[51] While these, it might be noted by way of anticipation, are words which Barth himself might have uttered, the sense borne by them within the contexts of Barth's and Brunner's theologies emerges as a locus of difference rather than agreement.

We turn, briefly, then, to the infamous phrase 'point of contact', a phrase which Brunner whispered in the shadows only to find himself on the receiving end of a salvo from Barth's barrel: it was not the password! Brunner's response is abrupt. 'No-one', he writes, 'who agrees that only human subjects but not stocks or stones can receive the Word of God and the Holy Spirit can deny that there is such a thing as a point of contact for the divine grace

---

[48] *(continued)* human beings have some created *Fähigkeit*. Revelation is, we have seen throughout this volume, a triangular relation in which God, created objects and human persons stand in the event by which God gives himself to be known.

[49] So, e.g., Brunner, *Natur und Gnade*, p. 15.

[50] *Natural Theology*, p. 27.

[51] Ibid.

of redemption.'[52] There is, in other words, *something* about humans which makes them suitable recipients of God's gracious initiative, as opposed to other creatures. Brunner goes further, identifying this 'something' with the formal image of which he has already spoken. It is in the capacity for language (i.e. the ability to be addressed) and the formal responsibility before God which this entails that the point of contact is to be located. Only because humans can hear and understand the divine address is God able to speak to them. 'This receptivity', Brunner stresses, 'says nothing as to [their] acceptance or rejection of the Word of God. It is the purely formal possibility of [their] being addressed.'[53]

Such 'receptivity' is not, therefore, Brunner claims, a predisposition for or an innate questing after the divine address. It is simply the ability to hear this address when it arises, however alien its substance may be, and even as it is a word of judgement which breeds resentment and rejection. Another way of putting this is to employ the now familiar distinction between a material and a formal point of contact. Brunner seems to trespass beyond this careful distinction, however, when he urges that in fact this capacity, this point of contact, the 'sphere of the possibility of being addressed', embraces not just the possession of grammar, but 'everything connected with the "natural" knowledge of God',[54] a vague phrase which threatens at once to open up a much more deregulated scenario.

Finally, Brunner argues that the metaphor of renewal or restoration (*reparatio*) is a wholly legitimate one, whereas the idea of the total replacement of something old by something essentially *novel* in redemption is unbiblical, and denies continuity of personhood. A person is not replaced; she is redeemed and healed and restored; something for which, as a sinner, she has no 'natural' potential or predisposition, but for which she has a *capacity*. The remainder of Brunner's essay is taken up mostly with a consideration of the teaching of the Reformers (claiming their support for his position), but it closes with a resounding defence of the category of *analogia entis*:

---

[52] Ibid. p. 31.
[53] Ibid.
[54] Ibid. p. 32.

The *analogia entis* is not specifically Roman Catholic. Rather is it the basis of every theology, of Christian theology as much as of pagan. The characteristic of Christian theology, and somehow also the difference between Roman Catholic and Protestant theology, is not the issue *whether* the method of analogy may be used, but *how* this is to be done and *what* analogies are to be employed.[55]

Perhaps the most telling phrase in Brunner's pamphlet, and one which finally makes manifest the yawning chasm of understanding which gaped between his position and that of Barth, arises in his discussion of the sense in which the retention by the creature of a natural but purely 'formal' capacity for words is a necessary or absolute presupposition (*unbedingte Voraussetzung*) for God's gracious self-revealing: 'The Word of God', he writes, 'could not reach a man who had lost his consciousness of God entirely.'[56] Quite apart from the question of how the idea of a remaining 'partial' consciousness of God might be squared with the distinction between a purely formal and a material point of contact for revelation (which is in itself an important inquiry), it is the words 'the Word of God could not'[57] which stand out so starkly. These are words which Barth could never have written, and which direct us neatly to the real heart of the dispute between their theologies. We turn, then, at last, to Barth's emphatic response to all this, the content of which is neatly encapsulated in its abrupt title, '*Nein!*'.

3. The case for the prosecution: Karl Barth

The heart of Barth's rejoinder lies in the bold question mark which he places alongside Brunner's appeal to the distinction between a formal and material image, or a formal and material capacity for words/revelation or point of contact. In short, Barth suspects from first to last that in, with and under the purely 'formal' Brunner slips

---

[55] Ibid. p. 55.
[56] Ibid. p. 32. Cf. Brunner, *Natur und Gnade*, p. 19.
[57] 'Einen Menschen, der nichts mehr von Gottesbewusstsein hätte, könnte das Wort Gottes nicht mehr erreichen' (Brunner, *Natur und Gnade*, p. 19).

in a degree of 'material', however slight. And to do this is to affirm
the possibility, no, the actuality, of a knowledge of 'the one true
God, the triune creator of heaven and earth, who justifies us
through Christ and sanctifies us through the Holy Spirit'[58] obtained
prior to and independently of the activity of Christ and the Holy
Spirit, and which serves, as it were, as a theological foundation for
receiving, making sense of and expanding this 'other' and fuller
knowledge. For all the reasons indicated in the first section of this
chapter, Barth will have nothing to do with any of this, and Brunner
quickly denies that this is his intention. Having heard the defence,
however, Barth remains convinced that, while there are many ways
in which their theologies appear to be at one, 'it seems clear to me
that at the decisive point (Brunner) takes part in the false movement
of thought by which the Church to-day is threatened'.[59]

Barth defines 'natural theology' as follows: 'every . . . formulation of a system which claims to be theological, i.e. to interpret
divine revelation, whose *subject*, however, differs fundamentally
from the revelation in Jesus Christ and whose *method* therefore differs equally from the exposition of Holy Scripture'.[60] In Brunner's
claim that there is in humans a 'capacity' for revelation, or a natural
'point of contact', Barth discerns something which, he believes, falls
into this category and must therefore be condemned 'as something
which endangers the ultimate truth that must be guarded and
defended in the Evangelical Church'.[61] He turns at once to consider
the all-important distinction upon which Brunner's exposition
hinges.

There is, of course, Barth concedes, a purely formal 'image of
God' remaining in humanity which is not destroyed by sin, if what
we intend by this is simply that 'Even as a sinner man is man and
not a tortoise.'[62] But what, he asks, has *this* to do with any supposed
capacity on the part of human beings for revelation or any natural
receptivity for the divine word, while it remains purely *formal*, and
does not trespass into the sphere of the material? He employs the

---

[58] *Natural Theology*, p. 81.
[59] Ibid. p. 67.
[60] Ibid. pp. 74–75.
[61] Ibid. p. 69.
[62] Ibid. p. 79.

following metaphor to make his point: 'If a man had just been saved from drowning by a competent swimmer, would it not be very unsuitable if he proclaimed the fact that he was a man and not a lump of lead as his "capacity for being saved"? Unless he could claim to have helped the man who saved him by a few strokes or the like!'[63]

Barth's point is that the ability to swim a few strokes (however few) constitutes a *material capacity* to participate in the rescue. If, as Brunner repeatedly insists, humans are utterly unable to contribute in this manner, then what possible sense or meaning is there in referring to a 'capacity' for revelation at all, or for speaking of an 'absolute presupposition' for it in human nature apart from which revelation cannot occur? Is this not a perverse way of speaking? Would it not be more natural to focus on the capacities of the rescuer rather than the rescued, unless in reality both are deemed to have contributed (albeit unequally) to the happy outcome? Barth's use of this particular metaphor highlights a problem of meaning and interpretation which lies at the very heart of the debate and to which we must return in due course.

Barth turns next to Brunner's insistence that the world, as created by God, is 'somehow recognizable' to humans as God's world. At one moment, Barth notes, Brunner wants to suggest that such recognition is only a formal possibility, concluded under the term 'objective-divine'; so far as the 'subjective-human-sinful' circumstance is concerned it is rendered of no practical benefit, knowledge of God being effectively obscured.[64] Yet in the next breath Brunner infers that the 'blindness' is not total; as if, albeit blurred and hazy, some partial recognition, and thereby some partial 'knowledge of God', remains in spite of sin[65] and by virtue of God's gracious preservation of the creature which 'does not abolish sin but abolishes the worst consequences of sin'.[66] Thus, Barth writes, 'I think that I understand Brunner rightly when I assume

---

[63] Ibid.

[64] See, e.g., ibid. p. 27.

[65] This would seem to be the clear inference of Brunner's insistence that the loss of God-consciousness cannot be and is not complete. See Brunner, *Natur und Gnade*, p. 19; *Natural Theology*, p. 32.

[66] *Natural Theology*, p. 28.

that the affection of the eyes, of which he speaks, is, according to his opinion, very acute, but not to the extent of resulting in total blindness. Hence real knowledge of God through creation does take place without revelation, though only "somehow" and "not in all its magnitude".[67] But in this case, Barth notes quite correctly, the carefully maintained distinction between formal and material effectively disintegrates, and we are back on the road to an alleged general and natural knowledge of God to be had apart from God's self-revealing activity, and with an account of the 'idolatry' which is the practical effect of such 'partial' knowledge as 'but a somewhat imperfect preparatory stage of the service of the true God',[68] rather than that which must be banished from within the borders of Israel. Such a weak assessment, we may remind ourselves, threatened to be incapable of a robust rejection of the German Christians' attempts to baptize the sort of ideology which clearly came 'naturally' to the Nazis.

What, then, of the infamous phrase 'point of contact'? Is there some formal anterior basis in human nature which provides a necessary precondition for the coming to humans of God's gracious Word? Again, says Barth, 'If we are prepared to call the fact that man is man and not a cat the "point of contact", "the objective possibility of divine revelation," then all objection to these concepts is nonsensical. For this truth is incontrovertable.'[69] This ready concession to Brunner's *terminology* at least must not be overlooked, precisely because it serves to highlight the differences of *substance* which easily agreed formulae may prove to conceal. Thus, Barth insists at once, there nonetheless can and must be no suggestion of any remainder of some original righteousness, or openness to God, or readiness to hear what he has to say. The Word of God does *not* rely in *any* way upon *such* a capacity on the part of humans. To suggest such would be to posit a meeting of God by humans, if not halfway, then some distance at least across the gap which separates them. Rather, the biblical view, worked out in the doctrines of *sola gratia* and justification by faith, is that God bridges the whole gap

---

[67] Ibid. p. 81. Cf. *Nein!*, p. 18.
[68] *Natural Theology*, p. 82.
[69] Ibid. p. 88.

himself, and far from finding humans to be ready recipients of His gracious offer of forgiveness (via some Roman *potentia oboedientialis*), meets only with opposition and recalcitrance. When the Word becomes incarnate, the human response is to crucify him in an act of supreme defiance which epitomizes the general truth about man's so-called capacity for God. It is precisely because God can *rely* upon this response that he is able to turn the tables on man and transform his typical act of rebellion and hate into the very fulcrum of his own redemption. Thus, according to Barth, what is required is no mere rejigging or repolishing or repairing of human nature: but rather the crucifixion of the flesh, and the raising up of a new creature. Regeneration is expressed not under the figure of repair or restoration, but of new birth, a completely new start.

Here Barth draws on what for him is the chief significance of the doctrine of the virgin conception of Christ's human life: the words of Mary 'How shall this be, seeing I know not a man?' is the question of all humanity in the face of that work of redemption and regeneration wrought in them by Christ.[70] The virgin conception at the beginning of God's entry into human flesh, just as surely as the resurrection at the end of it, speaks decisively of God's capacity to achieve his purposes in that which, by nature, has no capacity to realize the same ends. Mary, being a virgin (i.e. precisely *as* a virgin, rather than considered more generally as a woman), is utterly unable to conceive a child apart from the creative act of God in her womb. The crushed and lifeless body of the man Jesus has no capacity to live again, apart from the activity of the Spirit of God poured out in power. Human beings, sinful and fallen, have no 'capacity' in and of themselves for God, no natural predisposition to hear and receive his Word. Again, the Spirit of God must come and create (*ex nihilo* in this respect) precisely such a capacity. Faith is a gift of the very God towards whom it is directed. In this respect, it might be suggested, the attempt to secure some 'point of contact' in humanity for God is parallel to the doctrine of the immaculate conception: it assumes that wherever God and humanity come into close contact there must be some prepared ground, some fertile soil, some openness to and aptitude for God's purposes: as if Mary's obedient

---

[70] See ibid. pp. 93–94, 123f.

response were the result of some inherent immunity to the sin which blights the rest of us, rather than a result of the working of God's Spirit.

Brunner, Barth insists, in what he has to say about the matter, and notwithstanding his protestations to the contrary, indicates clearly that it is thus in his view also. There is, for him, at the very least a sense in man of his own sinfulness, a sense of need, a God-shaped gap in his life which provides the necessary keying point for God's word of forgiveness. But, while this is indeed quite different in scope from the 'natural theology' of those who wish to arrive at some decisive content for the category 'Knowledge of God' apart from God's own way of self-revelation, it is essentially similar in kind. It must posit something which even sinful humans can, and indeed *must*, bring with them as their portion or fragment of the map which, when placed together with God's, will reveal the location of the buried treasure! It is a long way, Barth admits, but a clear and logical way, he insists, from this to the *theologica naturalis* of the Enlightenment and its fruit in Neo-Protestantism, or the fatal joint endeavour between Christianity and the 'natural' knowledge of 'God and his will' which manifests itself in Fascism and other equally despicable manifestations of the unbridled human spirit: and for this reason he absolutely refuses to join Brunner in placing his foot on that particular slippery slope. Regretfully, but very definitely and with no small amount of fuss, he parts company with him.

4. Some questions concerning capacity

Having considered the background to and the nature and substance of the debate between Barth and Brunner, the final section of this chapter will address some questions about the adequacy and helpfulness of the terms in which the debate was cast, and the ambiguity attaching to the concept of 'capacity' in particular. My hope is that this may serve to clarify more precisely the nature and scope of the disagreement between them and the senses in which Barth's theology is and is not interested in or able to accommodate the idea of a 'capacity' for the event of revelation or a point of contact for it in the creature. Specifically I want to exclude certain ways of reading

Barth's fierce rebuttal of these closely related ideas as Brunner deploys them, and thereby to prevent certain inferences being drawn from this rebuttal about the wider coherence of his own theology.

In his introduction to the 1946 English translation *Natural Theology*, John Baillie observes that Barth seems to have confused two distinct words in Brunner's essay and thereby misdirected his fire. Barth's polemic, he suggests, is uniformly directed against the assertion of a 'capacity for revelation' (*Offenbarungsmächtigkeit*) in humans, whereas Brunner speaks rather of a 'capacity for words' or 'capacity for speech/language' (*Wortmächtigkeit*), a confusion likely to have arisen due to the prominence of the theme of God's Word in their respective theologies of revelation.[72] Even if this were true (which, strictly, it is not: Brunner uses a range of words to make his point including *Offenbarungsmächtigkeit*,[73] and Barth equally clearly considers and rejects the whole range including *Wortmächtigkeit, Wortempfänglichkeit* and others)[74] it is not clear that the dispute could ever have been resolved at the level of terminological agreement. It is the ways and contexts in which this whole range of words is actually used, and the consequent meanings attaching to it, which is at issue. What is clear is that what Brunner asserts by insisting that humans are *Wortmächtigkeit* is directly tied to the idea that in revealing Himself God *speaks*, and that in order to hear or receive this *speech* humans must be able to comprehend it. Were we mute creatures lacking the power of articulation, in other words, and were God limited to this mode of revealing Himself, we should lack the 'capacity for revelation' which Brunner certainly asserts that we in fact *possess*. Thus it would seem that Barth is quite correct to treat the various terms used by Brunner as virtual synonyms at this level and to respond to them in essentially the same manner.

We should perhaps note in passing the fundamentally different senses which the two men attach to the word 'revelation'. The idea that hearing in the purely natural sense (a physiological and grammatical appropriation of speech at the human level) may be

---

[72] Ibid. p. 9.

[73] So, e.g., Brunner, *Natur und Gnade*, p. 15.

[74] See, e.g., *Nein!*, pp. 15–16.

identified with 'hearing the Word of God' is quite alien to Barth, and constitutes a failure on Brunner's part to differentiate between the human and divine elements in the event of revelation. Thus, unlike Brunner, Barth does not hold that a merely natural hearing could ever render us responsible before God: such responsibility is created in the event whereby this physical locution and reception is drawn into the dynamic triangulation between hearer, speaker/ text, and God's living Word. Belief and unbelief are, for Barth, both products of God's electing activity, and not, as Brunner suggests, to be allocated to the categories 'outcomes of grace' and 'natural outcomes' respectively.[75] To 'hear' the Word of God in such a way as to respond to it as such, therefore, could never be within the range of natural human possibilities, but always depends upon the miracle of God's approach and his creation in us of the capacity to hear and respond.

In fact the more significant question and source of ambiguity lurks not so much in the relationship between *Offenbarung* and *Wort* as in the meaning attaching to the various suffixes *Mächtigkeit*, *Fähigkeit* and *Empfänglichkeit*, the former two generally translated as 'capacity for' in the Fraenkel text. This, if anything, is that upon which the whole debate hinges. What sort of 'capacity' is actually intended in Brunner's embrace and Barth's vigorous disowning of these terms?

The English word 'capacity', we may observe, may bear either a passive or an active sense, and it may help to clarify matters if, for our purposes, we choose the word 'aptitude' instead to indicate the *active* sense.[76] Thus, to cite Barth's own carefully chosen example again, Mary, as a virgin, had no aptitude for childbearing. Her

---

[75] So, e.g., *Natural Theology*, pp. 31–32.

[76] In German *Mächtigkeit*, according to Langenscheidt's *New Concise German Dictionary* (London: Hodder and Stoughton, 1987, p. 359), would seem typically to bear a strong and active sense, denoting 'power to achieve', *Fähigkeit* more usually denoting 'capacity to or for' (*Langenscheidt*, p. 184). That both words may bear a range of meanings, however, is indicated by their use in the Barth-Brunner debate, and by Barth's single-minded rejection of Brunner's use of both. In what follows we shall assume the semantic ranges of these words to be similar (and similarly ambiguous to) the English 'capacity'.

womb did not, that is to say, apart from the conditions furnished by extrinsic factors – either coming together with a man, or else the direct creative action of the Holy Spirit – have the *active capacity* (let us call this capacity1) to produce a fertile ovum. But passively, insofar as she was a woman and not a slab of granite, she might properly be said to have had a passive capacity (capacity2) for what happened to her to happen. We must clarify this more precisely, for there is a further distinction to be drawn within this capacity2.

To speak of a passive capacity may simply be an instance of circumlocution. Hence when we say 'x is capable of y' we mean at least (and may only mean) 'it is possible for y to happen to x'. Hence to say that Mary has a capacity2 for the virginal conception is to say in a roundabout manner that, although while she remains a virgin she has no intrinsic aptitude for conception, it is nonetheless possible for her to conceive (through the action of God's Spirit in her womb). Or (developing Barth's other metaphor) we might say (rather oddly, as Barth points out, but without lapsing into complete loss of meaning or equivocation) that a drowning man is capable of being (able to be) rescued from the water. To say 'x is capable of y' may mean more than this, however. It may be intended to indicate the relative judgement that 'y is more directly fitted to the circumstances of x than those of A, B or C'. To assert this is certainly not to shift into the sphere of capacity1 and to suggest that x possesses an aptitude for or natural disposition to y or can contribute anything positive to the achievement of y. Nor is it to suggest that y could not happen to A, B or C. (Thus it may have to be admitted that in some sense A, B and C also have a capacity for y, albeit a less apparent one.) Nor is it to suggest that y *must* happen to x, or that y happens *naturally* to x as an extrapolation from x's current range of possibilities. It may well be that y constitutes precisely a reversal or interruption of the pattern of what otherwise comes naturally to x (a drowning man for example). All that is being said is that in fact y is more directly addressed to x's circumstances than it is to the circumstances of A, B or C. Thus, returning to Barth's favourite biblical example, notwithstanding the truth that 'God can raise up children for Abraham out of these stones,' the fact is that, in becoming human and seeking a suitable matrix for his origin as a human person, God chose a *woman* and not a convenient slab of granite. Mary's *womanhood*, therefore, may be deemed significant in this choice, and it is perfectly meaningful to say that she possessed a capacity2 for what was to happen to her which other possible objects of divine action do not possess, or at least not in the same sense or to the same extent. That what happens to her happens is, to be sure, still an act of pure grace: Mary does not deserve it (whatever that means), and is not able to meet God halfway, or to contribute anything other than an empty womb with no intrinsic fertility. As one who 'knows not yet a man' she is, for all practical purposes, barren. Yet the fact that she is a woman and not a rock or a Number 16 bus is still related to God's decision to act in this particular way in her life to achieve his particular purposes.

Let us briefly take the other related example which Barth sometimes employs in this context.[77] Jesus' body in the tomb has, naturally, no capacity1 or aptitude for life, apart from the power of God's Spirit at work in resurrection. Yet Jesus' body has what may be termed a capacity2 to *become* a resurrected human body which the stone rolled over the entrance to the tomb does *not* obviously have to the same extent. Again, to say this is to say no more and no less than that (since in fact he has been raised from death) it is possible for resurrection to happen to him, and resurrection is more directly fitted to his circumstance on Easter Saturday than it is to the circumstances of other possible objects of divine action. Or, putting the matter into more straightforward terms Jesus, being a dead human person, is able to be taken by God and raised up into a newly alive human person. The advantage which this second example has over the first is that it highlights more clearly the relationship of discontinuity between nature and grace as Barth understands it. Thus, he insists, if we speak of contact between grace and nature, God and creation, we must be clear that 'The contact is made, not with something positive or neutral but with something negative.'[78] Nature, in other words, tends to struggle against rather than participate with (even by passivity) the purposes of grace. Before God can do anything positive with what he has made, therefore, he must first

---

[77] The parallel between these two 'signs' which are located at the beginning and end of Jesus' life, and serve to indicate the status of his life as a Novum with respect to the orders and possibilities of nature, is picked up and developed in *CD* 1/2, pp. 179f.
[78] *Natural Theology*, p. 113.

undo its natural propensities rather than being able to rely on their cooperation or non-resistance. Drowning men often struggle and must sometimes be rendered unconscious before the rescue can be completed successfully. Dead bodies, left to themselves, decompose. Yet it is possible for a dead body, acted upon by the God of the resurrection, to become a newly risen human person. If this is all that is meant by 'Jesus' body has the capacity for resurrection', then such a statement is relatively unproblematic, albeit a strikingly obscure and unnatural way of putting things.

Similarly, we might say, sinful humans have no *capacity* for revelation – if by that we intend an *aptitude*, or a predisposition in favour of that revelation, or even a neutrality with respect to it. Yet God actually *reveals* himself to human beings in a redemptive manner. When Barth writes, 'there can be no question of a capacity for repair on the part of man',[79] therefore we must inquire in what senses this can actually be held to be true. Is there not at least one sense in which it is manifestly false? In what sense does/can anything which *has been* repaired not in fact have had a capacity to *be* repaired? In what sense, that is to say, can it be possible for something which has happened simultaneously to be impossible? Well of course Barth does not mean that it was *absolutely* impossible for God's redemptive Word to reach his creatures; only that such an event did and does not lie within the 'natural' range of creaturely possibilities. But, as we have seen already in earlier chapters, in discussing the occurrence of this event Barth is much more concerned to ask and speak of what is possible for God, and to allow this to set the parameters and the shape of theological understanding and expectation. Thus, he insists that any capacity (capacity1) which the creature may be said to possess is one which God Himself creates and holds in being in his actual dynamic relatedness to the creature.[80] What is impossible considered from the perspective of humanity is not impossible for God. Hence, there can be no in-principle or absolute incapacity of the creature to become the object and beneficiary of such divine action. Unlike Brunner Barth is not tolerant of the phrase 'God's Word could not . . .' But if this is truly so, then we may revert to our

---

[79] Ibid. p. 94.
[80] Ibid. p. 89.

obscure and indirect way of speaking and insist that for every statement 'God can do y' a corresponding 'x is capable of y' is a perfectly
meaningful deduction in the precise sense which we have clarified.
Again, all that is being insisted upon by making such a statement is
that it is possible (in terms of God's possibilities rather than those
natural to the creature as such) for some x to be acted upon by God
in a particular manner y (an a posteriori judgement derived from the
fact that some x has been acted upon in this way). This claim may be
accompanied by the judgement that there is an identifiable sense in
which the particular form of this divine activity is fitted better to the
chosen object of this activity than to some other possible objects of
it, and reflects the content of God's purposes. God may be *able* to
raise up children from the stones of the Palestinian countryside, but
that does not render the distinction between rocks and human
beings wholly insignificant in considering the actual form which his
action takes. It does not indicate limits or constraints upon God's
activity, but rather the chosen mode of God's activity in relation to
humankind. Given that God has chosen to become incarnate, and
to do so precisely by laying hold of our humanity from within rather
than starting again *ex nihilo*, this is the way which his choice makes
necessary.[81] All of this is utterly consistent with Barth's thought.
Thus, to reflect Barth's own words back to him at this point, the fact
that 'man is man and not a cat'[82] may be all that is intended by the
phrase 'capacity for revelation', or, dare we use it, 'capacity for
salvation'. But that does not render the phrase entirely empty of
meaning or importance.

But this leads us back to what is surely the most obvious question; namely, given that one *may* speak of a 'capacity' in this way,
and mean by it something purely passive rather than active (or, in
Brunner's terms, purely formal rather than material), why choose to
do so? Is this not really rather odd language to use, and altogether a
peculiar way of approaching the matter, if there really is no 'material' capacity intended? Ought we not to suspect that, despite such
careful and painstaking definition, the continued use of the

---

[81] I am grateful to John Yates who, during the course of our long
discussions on the theme of this chapter, helped me to see this.
[82] See, e.g., *Natural Theology*, p. 88.

language points inevitably to the smuggling in of a material sense? Why insist on speaking about the 'capacities' of humanity in a circumstance characterized above all by miracle, surprise and discontinuity? This, as we have seen, was precisely Barth's question to Brunner, and the corresponding charge which he laid at his door. As has already been indicated it seems likely that he was correct to suspect Brunner of trespassing from the purely formal into the ascription of a material capacity to humanity. But this does not mean that such a distinction cannot be made and maintained, however contrived and unnatural it may seem to be. For our purposes I suggest that it is vitally important to insist that, in the careful sense which we have delineated, Barth is perfectly able to affirm a capacity2 for God's presence and action on the part of the creature. What is impossible for humanity as such is rendered possible by the God who calls new life into being out of nothing. God is capable of uniting us to himself. God is capable of revealing himself to us. This is the only content which Barth is prepared to allow to the statement 'humans are capable of being-revealed-to'. But it is content which must be taken notice of ! It is possible, in other words, within God's range of possibilities rather than ours, for our deaf ears to be unstopped and our blind eyes opened. Likewise, Barth *does not deny* the existence of a 'point of contact' between God and creation. He denies that such a point of contact exists *naturally* within the creature, and therefore that it preexists the event of revelation or is the 'absolute presupposition' for that event; but he is utterly emphatic that God creates a point of contact wherever and whenever he comes to the creature in grace and transforms creaturely life. The fact that the miracle of grace interrupts and is discontinuous with the normal pattern of nature does not make it any less a point of contact – it simply characterizes its shape.

Why should any of this matter? Why insist on twisting language in this unnatural and graceless manner? The only justification for doing so here is that Barth's denial of any *Offenbarungsmächtigkeit* and his eschewal of the idea of an *Anknüpfungspunkt* in his debate with Brunner have led so many commentators to misunderstand or misread him. Time and again one is forced to read how for Barth any serious contact between God and humanity is finally impossible; or how in Barth's christology God and humanity draw close but never actually touch one another, rendering incarnation an empty term; as if all that Barth says about God's presence to and action in the world, in Jesus Christ, and in the lives of men and women, is qualified dramatically at the eleventh hour by a metaphysical principle which renders his statements either inconsistent, incoherent or equivocal: *finitum non capax infiniti*. Of course Barth does say precisely this, and believes it. But this is not his starting point. Not even the incarnation is his true starting point. To the claim that if God has become human it must be true that there exists something within humanity with which contact can be made by God, Barth's consistent response is essentially as follows: Of course there *is* contact between God and humanity, and supremely in the man Jesus Christ who is God with us. But this does not mean that there is some thing, some component or aspect of our humanity naturally suited to divine approach. Rather it is us in our entirety which constitutes the locus of contact; and, more precisely, us in our sinful and rebellious entirety. The real claim of Christianity, therefore, made in the light of the contact between God and humanity in Jesus Christ, is not *finitum capax infiniti*, but rather *infinitum capax finiti*: God is capable of establishing and maintaining contact with us in all our alienation from and rejection of him, laying hold of us precisely in our sin and lifting us up out of the mire to become faithful respondents and correspondents to his Word. Only such a way of thinking about the 'point of contact' between God and the creature can be accommodated by a theology which begins not with creation, not even with the incarnate one, but with him crucified.

8

Speaking of God's Love: Analogy, Reference and Revelation

Theology is a wordy business. Words provide the theologian with both raw materials and tools. Yet for a theologian such as Barth Christian theology, while it may be inextricably tied up in the complexities of language, is certainly no mere matter of linguistic play. It is not *about* language and the relationships between words. It is *about* God. It seeks to bring to expression truths concerning God and God's relatedness to the world through the media of speech and text. Yet such a claim does not deliver the theologian from the problems attaching to language and its use. On the contrary, it raises those problems with an acute sharpness, and invests theological endeavour with a particular responsibility to address them. If human speech is problematic, then human speech about God, it is generally assumed, is all the more so. In this closing chapter I want to consider how Barth tackles some of these issues, and to do so by addressing a particular question which will draw in other dialogue partners from the theological community. How do we define the nature of God's love? When we echo the central apostolic affirmation that 'God is love', what are we saying, and what do we mean?

1. The problem of definition in horizontal and vertical perspective

Love, the words of the song remind us, is a many splendoured thing. This, of course, is offered to us by the songwriter as a virtue. But for the Christian theologian the multifaceted and diverse nature of human experiences of love has its distinct drawbacks. 'God is love' 1 John 4:8, 16 tell us. But what seems at first sight, perhaps, to offer a refreshingly straightforward intellectual handhold on the otherwise sheer, slippery and apparently inaccessible rock face of the divine nature proves upon closer inspection to do nothing of the sort. The very familiarity with love in the human context which draws us to it also serves to convince us of its potential risks and dangers as a point from which to begin the climb towards a description of the one in whom we live and move and have our being.

There are, after all, so many different human loves to choose from: the love of lover for his or her beloved; the love of husband for wife and wife for husband; the love of parent for child; the love of child for parent; the love of brother for sister and sister for brother; the love of grandparent for grandchild; the love between close friends; the love we have for our pets, for nature, for art, for good food and drink, and so the list might easily be extended. In none of these cases are we speaking of precisely the same thing, even if we prune the list of some of the more evidently metaphorical and strained uses of the verb. And in any one instance, the love of which we speak is a highly complex and elusive quantity. So simply to repeat the biblical assertion that 'God is love' is certainly not to answer any significant theological questions. It is, in fact, where the hard work of theology begins rather than ends. Given the complexity and diversity of that which the word love evokes, which, if any, we must ask, of the strands presenting themselves to us for consideration are relevant or appropriate to the interpretation of this statement? And on what grounds are we actually able to make a valid selection? That, it seems, is the first problem we face.

But it is far from being either the only or indeed the major problem. Alongside it we must set the more general problem of knowing what precisely is entailed in speaking of God at all, and of the meaning of any resultant statements. This is a problem which any religious or philosophical tradition which entertains belief in a genuinely transcendent God must necessarily face. Theology is a craft in which the chief tools are words and the ideas to which they are related. But these words and ideas are inevitably finite: drawn from the available pool of human language and experience, and handled by human thinkers and wordsmiths who can make no claim to have transcended their own finitude and sinfulness in the process, any more than can their readers in receiving the results. How, then, is it that these creaturely linguistic and conceptual tools, fashioned in order to bring to expression finite realities, are applied to the infinite Creator of all things? That they *are* so applied is not in doubt. Theology has no other language, no other conceptuality, no other experience to draw upon in its task than those of this world. What remains to be answered is the question of how or on what basis this dual application of terms across the boundary between finite and infinite, created and uncreated proceeds; and, crucially, what are its implications for the respective meanings of the terms which theology deploys in this linguistic joining of heaven and earth.

Barth delineates the precise contours of the question for us:

> Does there exist a simple parity of content and meaning when we apply the same word to the creature on the one hand and to . . . God on the other?' We are aware, or we think we are aware, of what being, spirit, sovereignty, creation, redemption, righteousness, wisdom, goodness, etc. mean when we use these terms to describe creatures. We are also aware, or think we are aware, what we are saying when in the sphere of the creature we say eye, ear, mouth, arm or hand, or love, wrath, mercy, patience and suchlike. Does all this mean the same thing when we also say it about God?[1]

Barth goes on to remind us what Christian theologians have always known; namely, that if we assume a univocal use of terms as applied to creatures and to God, we effectively deny God's transcendence, or else deify the creature, subsuming both God and the creaturely under common categories of description. If, on the other hand, we suppose that human terms assume a wholly new and different meaning when they are predicated of God, then our theology rapidly collapses into nonsense, and we effectively rob ourselves of any consequent knowledge of God at all, since, being finite, we are not in any position to know what these different meanings might be.

Returning, then, to our particular piece of theological construction, we must now face the fact that an intelligent account of the claim that God is love must cope not only with the inherent slipperiness of the word love itself in general discourse, but also with

---

[1] *CD* 2/1, p. 224.

the complications introduced by tacking these other words 'God is' in front of it. There is, as it were, a vertical as well as a horizontal dimension to the problem of definition with which we are concerned. To develop our rock-climbing image, we are not faced simply with a choice of numerous possible alternative routes across the rock face, some of which may prove fruitless or even lead us into danger, but also with the apparent risk that even the *best* of those routes may lead us ultimately only to the edge of a semantic crevasse which cannot be bridged, leaving us facing a gap of unknown proportions between our words and any meanings they might or might not have as applied to God. The problem of defining the love of God (or any other aspect of his being and activity) lies chiefly here, in discerning how, if at all, this gap may be closed, and our words terminate on the reality of God himself, rather than falling short or bouncing back, leaving us forever trapped in one form or another of agnosticism. I say 'if at all' advisedly, because, to anticipate briefly, it seems to me that the terms in which our question is phrased are presumptuous. Perhaps we should be asking '*Do* we define the nature of God's love?', and preparing ourselves for the possibility of a negative answer. There is, I think, a sense in which such an answer must be allowed.

It may be at this point, however, that someone will finally wish to unmask the rather obvious weakness in the metaphor I have used. Surely, it might be objected, attempts to liken the theological task to a rock climb, scaling unknown heights, choosing routes, facing insurmountable obstacles, are poorly conceived. It suggests that our task is one of climbing up to God, rather than grappling seriously with the claim implicit within most Christian theology in some form or another that God has come down to us and made himself known. This is a vital methodological point, and one with which we shall certainly have to reckon. And it probably does highlight the main weakness of my chosen image. But appeals to revelation, and neat and tidy distinctions between approaches to theology 'from above' and 'from below' can be introduced too quickly and in ways that finally fail to recognize the problems I have outlined rather than resolving them.

To begin with, immediate resort to the category of revelation does not resolve the 'vertical' problem of the ontological and noetic gap between transcendent and immanent, created and uncreated,

God and the world. This gap, it might be claimed, while it is unbridgeable from our side, is not unbridgeable from God's, and he has in fact bridged it, making himself known on our side of the gap: supremely in flesh-and-blood terms in the incarnation, but with a vital associated cognitive and hermeneutical matrix which we find in its raw form in the biblical writings. God has spoken. And on the basis of this speech we too now may speak of him, repeating after him, as it were, the words in which he speaks of himself.

But the claim that the Word of God has assumed *flesh*, far from resolving the linguistic, epistemological and ontological problem of the relationship between God and the world simply serves to raise it in a particularly acute form, as the history of christology bears adequate witness. On the one hand the fact of God's self-accommodation to human forms, in a human life, in human text, in human proclamation, robs us of the possibility of remaining silent. It demands an obedient response from us. Having heard God's word, we must now speak and make sense of what we say in order that others might hear and understand. Yet, on the other hand, it is precisely *because* this self-revealing takes *human* form (as it must if we are to hear and receive it) that the problem of a semantic *unio hypostatica* presents itself to us. For, however positively we may choose to construe the relationship between the uncreated and the created, it is a basic assumption of any doctrine of divine transcendence that the reality of God could never be accommodated *completely* within human language any more than within human flesh. And inasmuch as revelation takes place in human terms, therefore, it will always be as much a veiling as a revealing. There will always be an extent to which even those forms which God assumes and drafts into his service fall short of bringing the infinite to expression within the terms of the finite. It cannot be done, any more than we can give an adequate performance of a Mahler symphony on the triangle, or render the smell of fish and chips into verbal form. There is, in each case, something inherently inadequate about the tools at our disposal which renders even our best efforts little more than a pale reflection of the original, and such that we could never infer the original from mere familiarity with the copy. For Barth, as we have seen, the basic relationship between Creator and creature is certainly not to be construed as one of continuity but of radical discontinuity. On his view, therefore, the problem is not simply that language is *inadequate* to the task of speaking about God: rather, in and of itself, human language has no capacity whatever to speak of God, being fitted naturally to a realm with respect to which God is 'wholly other'. The force of Barth's use of the metaphors of veiling and unveiling,[2] therefore, is not to indicate that human speech about God leaves God 'partly' veiled, but that in the same instant God is both fully revealed and fully veiled by the form of the human. Thus, the fact that God becomes human and employs human modes of knowing in communicating with us, raises, rather than resolves, the question of exactly how those human realities may be supposed to refer beyond themselves and beyond their ordinary human context in their specifically theological application.

God, a theology which affirms an incarnational revelation insists, immerses himself in the messiness and contingency of history and the flesh in making himself known to humans. In doing so he does not lift us up out of our creatureliness, elevating us to some deified state in which we are able to contemplate divine realities directly, from a 'God's eye' perspective. This means, of course, that we cannot ignore or circumvent the familiar and ordinary associations which words and realities taken up into the service of divine revelation have for us. We begin, and remain, within the sphere of the human in theology. Insofar as we know God, we do so because he comes to be with us in this same sphere, and not because he lifts us out of it.

To this extent, a theology of the love of God cannot short-circuit or set aside the contribution which human experiences and understandings of love have to offer, but must take them fully into account. We may in due course wish to speak of God's love or Jesus' love as informing and transforming our thinking about human love; as, for example, when H.R. Mackintosh reminds us that in the Sermon on the Mount, Jesus presents God's love as a pattern for rather than a reflection of human love.[3] It is not that he loves like us, but that we are urged to love like him. But the hermeneutical realities of the situation are more complicated than beginning with God and moving to the human. First we have to obtain an understanding of the divine love; and such an understanding will already be fashioned

---

[2] See, e.g., *CD* 1/1, pp. 320f.; 2/1, pp. 234f.
[3] H.R. Mackintosh, *The Christian Apprehension of God* (London: SCM Press, 1929), p. 186.

from the messy stuff of human experience and ideas. That is what is entailed in the affirmation of incarnation. As George Newlands suggests, the Christian will certainly want to argue that the great gap between God's love and ours has been bridged in the person of Jesus, where the divine life is in some sense earthed in a human life. 'Through the humanity of God revealed in the humanity of Jesus Christ', he writes, 'we may come to understand the true nature of the human. But even Barth recognised on occasion that there must be something in our experience of the human which enables us to recognise a perfection of humanness in Jesus.'[4] We cannot, therefore, afford to overlook the obvious fact that that which comes 'from above' unless it remains above must at some point become incarnate in the humdrum reality of what exists here below, and as a consequence that reality must form some sort of resource for theological reflection and development.

But in coming down, in assuming the flesh, God does not, of course, leave it as he finds it. And this is a point of at least equal significance for our approach to theological language. For if in coming he does not lift us out of our creatureliness, God does, Christians claim, lift us out of our sinfulness. The process of incarnation does not entail change for God alone, leaving the familiar forms of the 'flesh' unaffected. That which is assumed is, as the Greek fathers suggested, in some sense healed or redeemed in the process, being taken up and reconciled from its sinful condition to a state in which it reflects more appropriately the being of the one who now indwells it. And this, we may suppose, is no less true of human language and conceptuality than it is of human flesh. Its assumption by the divine Word entails refashioning and recasting, a semantic shift which overcomes the incapacities resulting from its fallenness, even if those resulting from its creatureliness inevitably remain.

To say, then, that theology must begin and remain within the sphere of the flesh must not be supposed to mean that in making sense of the forms which revelation takes we can rest content with any simple trawl of our own experience and understanding in order to identify the common meanings and significances which ordinarily attach to those forms. As in christology we cannot simply

[4] G. Newlands, *Theology of the Love of God* (London: Collins, 1980), p. 132.

construct a portrait of the human Jesus rooted in our own perceptions of empirical humanity, but must always reckon with those
things which differentiate his humanity from ours, precisely
because it is in these very elements that his revelatory and salvific
significance resides, so too in this matter of theological definition,
while our starting point must inevitably be with our own creaturely
and sinful perceptions and experiences of love, fatherhood, righteousness and the rest, we must expect and allow the limits of these
perceptions to be ruptured and their content to be transformed as
they refer us beyond the ordinary and familiar to the humanity of
God, and beyond still, to God's own life and being.

In short, if we are to make sense of the claim that God is love,
then, precisely *because* this claim reposes on a revelation of God in
the flesh, we must come to terms with and seek to explore the
implications of the recognition that we are dealing with 'love . . .
but not as we know it'! There is both similarity and difference. A
claim that God's love both is and yet is not like ours. The task of
theological definition, whether we base it upon an appeal to revelation or not is, therefore, somehow to feel our way towards a grasp of
the shape and dimensions of the difference. And this is a task which
will involve us in a human intellectual activity the results of which,
whatever the quality of the raw materials, will and can only ever be
provisional and imperfect. It does not follow from this, however,
that all results must be equally (in)adequate.

Thus we arrive at the suggestion that the theologian must
function with some version of the doctrine of analogy. We
must recognize, that is to say, that words such as love, drawn as they
are from our creaturely language, arc applied to God neither
univocally nor equivocally, but in a way which involves both likeness and unlikeness to their everyday use. And, unless we consider
theology to be a matter of words and the relationships between
words alone, there will lie behind this supposition another; namely
that God's relationship to and action towards us is such that it is possible for human words and ideas sometimes and in some sense to
correspond and to refer us appropriately to who and what God is.
To say that such analogies between the divine and the human may
exist, however, is not necessarily to suppose that human beings as
such are ordinarily in any position to know of them, or to discern
their nature and contours. Assumptions concerning this epistemic

circumstance, and theological strategies constructed on the basis of them, may differ quite substantially.

Before turning specifically to Barth I want next to consider an approach to the question of what is involved in speaking of God's love which is radically different to his.

2. The metaphor of God as lover

Sallie McFague roots her so-called metaphorical theology expressly in the soil of human experience. Hence her particular reason for speaking of God's love (or, more specifically, of God as lover) is not tied specifically to biblical themes, or to any of the ways in which these have been developed in Christian theology over the centuries. It is rather because she is convinced that here she has identified a metaphor offering an imaginative construal of the God-world relation that resonates with contemporary experiences of relatedness to God. Theology, she insists, must be credible: that is to say, it must ring true for those whose assumptions and values are those of modern society.[5] But the theologian's task is not that of definition – so in the strict sense we do not define the nature of God's love, or anything else to do with God. Rather, the theologian is a philosopher-poet whose task is to try out new metaphors and models drawn from general experience in order to bring to expression aspects of the God-world relation as it is experienced by men and women today. Metaphors are imaginative leaps across distance, daring attempts to think differently and to express the quality of our experience of being related to God by borrowing human images and ideas. In this sense metaphorical theology is heuristic, experimenting and testing out new ways of thinking and speaking. It is by definition open to all possibilities. No metaphor can be excluded from consideration, although all must be tested, and there is always the risk 'that the leap across the abyss will be unsuccessful'.[6] The criteria of selectivity are not those of resort to the traditional authorities, although McFague insists

---

[5] S. McFague, *Models of God* (London: SCM Press, 1987), p. 32.
[6] Ibid. p. 35.

that some level of identifiable continuity with the past is important. But, since 'how language, any language, applies to God we do not know, what religious and theological language is at most is metaphorical forays attempting to express experiences of relating to God'[7] and it is the proven persuasiveness and appropriateness of a particular metaphor (which seems in practice to amount to its popularity and ready assimilation in the contemporary context) which eventually secures it a place as a legitimate expression of Christian faith for our time.

Although McFague eschews the normative role of tradition and makes experience her primary datum in theology, nonetheless, at the heart of the relatedness to God of which she speaks, the themes of salvation and of the 'transforming love of God' figure large. While the particular ways in which she construes these differ considerably from the mainstream of Christian theology, it is difficult to suppose that the basic categories themselves have not ultimately been borrowed, eclectically (and perhaps unconsciously), from that same tradition. What we must seek today, therefore, McFague suggests, are metaphors and models which speak to our generation of caring, mutuality, nurturing, support, empathy, service, and self-sacrifice at the level of ultimate reality. The metaphors she especially favours are those of Mother, Lover and Friend, to the second of which we now turn.

While the Christian tradition has from its earliest days wished to speak of love in God, McFague notes, it has been equally reluctant to engage the particular metaphor of God as lover. Yet such love, she notes, is 'the most intimate and important kind of human love'.[8] Surely, then, it cannot be irrelevant to an attempt to apply the language of love to God? While it is sometimes supposed to be the erotic associations of the idea which have rendered it inappropriate for Christian theological description, Eros as such, McFague notes, has its essence not in sex, but in finding value in someone else, and in being found valuable by them. To speak of such love between God and the world, she argues, while it may not have been tolerable to the classical Greek philosophy which so shaped and influenced

---

[7] Ibid. p. 39.
[8] Ibid. p. 126.

Christian theology in its most formative years, holds enormous potential for those who live in an ecological-nuclear era. In such an era, she suggests, we need to be told not that we are valueless in ourselves, that God has no need of us and showers his love upon us out of sheer grace, but that life is valuable and wondrous in itself, that God loves it because it is loveable, and that our reciprocal love is something which 'fills a need in God the lover', rather than something which he can take or leave. 'We need to feel that value', she writes, 'in the marrow of our bones if we are to have the will to work with the divine lover toward including all the beloved in the circle of valuing love . . . if we are to have any hope of attaining an ecologically balanced, nuclear free world.'[9]

While there are elements in McFague's protest against the abstract theism of the tradition which resonate fairly evidently with voices from across the theological spectrum, it is clear that her use of the lover metaphor takes her a very long way from the mainstream and its discussion of the love of God. Cutting herself loose from the moorings of Scripture and tradition, and appealing to experience and credibility as her guides, in effect she allows human experiences and construals of love to determine what she will say about God. Or rather, about human experience of God. For McFague, in a manner directly reminiscent of Schleiermacher, makes no profession to be able to say anything about God as such. The metaphors which theology fashions and develops are imaginative leaps across a yawning crevasse beyond which the mystery of God lies. Such metaphors, we should recall, are adverbial; they express ways of relating to or experiencing God. Of the nature of God they can and do say nothing whatever. They offer 'likely accounts', and the criteria of likelihood, like the selection of the metaphors themselves, lie in the hands of human beings and what they will find persuasive and credible.

C.S. Lewis writes that 'The human loves can be glorious images of Divine love. No less than that: but also no more.'[10] The danger which McFague's theology falls foul of, perhaps, is that of reversing the logic of 1 John 4:8. Throwing up conceptions of love drawn

---

[9] Ibid. p. 133.

[10] C.S. Lewis, *The Four Loves* (London: Geoffrey Bles, Centenary Press, 1960), p. 18.

directly from human experience and, lacking any objective standard of comparison by which to adjudge their worth, she effectively deifies them. At the end of the day such an approach seems likely to tell us little about God (even in poetic fashion), and rather more about the texture and colour of the human situation from within which it issues.

3.   Barth and the self-definition of God in revelation

To turn to Barth after McFague, while in historical terms anachronistic, is in many other ways an entirely appropriate and informative procedure. The theology which Barth set himself against in the early decades of this century was similar in some fundamental methodological respects to that which McFague espouses. Barth's contention, as we have already seen, was that every attempt to found human talk about God by pointing to the possibility and actuality of anthropological phenomena (whether latent rational truths, a sense of absolute dependence, an experience of the numinous or whatever) simply invites the Feuerbachian reduction of theological statements to anthropological ones, and ultimately traps theology within the confines of the possibilities and impossibilities of the human. For Barth, the utter transcendence of God and human sinfulness taken together render every and any attempt at an intellectual storming of the gates of heaven utterly futile. 'God', he writes, 'does not belong to the world. Therefore he does not belong to the series of objects for which we have categories and words by means of which we draw the attention of others to them, and bring them into relation with them. Of God it is impossible to speak, because He is neither a natural nor a spiritual object.'[11] At least, if it is *not* impossible to speak of God, if speech of him, if theology is in fact a possibility for human beings, then for Barth it is so only because God himself spans the gap which creation posits and human sin exacerbates. 'What if', he asks, 'God be so much God that without ceasing to be God he can also be, and is willing to be, not God as well. What if he were to come down from his unsearchable height

---

[11] *CD* 1/2, p. 750.

and become something different?'[12] This, of course, is precisely what the Christian tradition insists God has done, in a radical self-objectifying, giving himself to be known in cognitive, verbal and fleshly historical created forms. The possibility of human speech about God rests, for Barth, entirely upon this contingent fact. Theology, therefore, is not a matter of heuristics in the sense of some enterprising human exploration of the divine regions, but rather of obedient response to a given revelation.

For all his emphasis on revelation, however, Barth is anything but naive in his treatment of the problem of theological definition. The self-objectification of God involves God precisely in becoming 'not God', which means that the media of revelation, verbal, conceptual, fleshly, in their very mediation raise the problem of their own relatedness to God. In the event of revelation in which they are, as it were, united with God's Word by the Spirit, and given a transparency which in and of themselves they lack, they do not, nonetheless, become other than they always were. There is no transubstantiation, no docetic co-mingling of the divine and the creaturely which presents the divine to us immediately. Thus, Barth writes, 'what we see, hear, feel, touch, and inwardly and outwardly perceive is always something different, a counterpart, a second thing',[13] and never God himself and as such. Thus Barth realized that even in the light of God's gracious condescension in revelation, the problem of theological language must be addressed, and must finally be resolved by some version of the doctrine of analogy. Only thus, only if, notwithstanding the absolute transcendence of God over against the creature, there is some analogy created between God's existence and our language, can the truth of God's self-revealing in human form be safeguarded without compromising his transcendence. In short, when human beings, on the basis of God's self-revelation, speak of him as loving, it is either because he is loving in the precise way that we are (which is precluded by a due recognition of his transcendence), or else the love of which we speak has no meaningful relation to any ordinary human uses of the word (in which case it is a meaningless statement and tantamount to an untruth), or else it is because, in the event of revelation itself,

---

[12] *GD* 1, p. 136.
[13] Ibid.

God grants to this particular human language the power to correspond appropriately to himself, albeit in an analogous, and thereby
an indirect and veiled manner.

There is, of course, a vital difference between Barth's handling of
the doctrine of analogy and its classical development, for example, in
the theology of Aquinas. For Thomas, the doctrine of analogy is not
simply an account of what is going on in theological discourse; it is
also a means of acquiring knowledge of God and of his relatedness to
the world outside of the context created by revelation.[14] It is, in other
words, a tool deployed in the construction of a natural theological
metaphysic. In the metaphysical principle first aired by Proclus that
'Everything which by its existence bestows a character on others,
itself primitively possesses that character, which it communicates to
the recipient.'[15] Aquinas identifies a basis for theological speech
about God. Since creatures relate to God as effects to their cause, he
writes, 'we can be led from them so far as to know of God whether
He exists, and to know of Him *what must necessarily belong to Him* as
the first cause of all things, exceeding all things caused by Him'.[16]
Thus the analogical method renders substantive knowledge of God's
character. By analogical predication we name perfections which belong to God properly, even though, drawing our language from
creatures, the mode of signification is imperfect and falls short of
naming them adequately. This differentiation between the *perfectio
significata* and the *modus significandi* is crucial, since it allows Thomas
to avoid appearing to subsume Creator and creatures under a common category of being.[17] Hence God and creatures manifest goodness, for example, in ways appropriate to their quite distinct modes of
existence.

From Barth's perspective, however, the problem which looms
here is that analogy in its Thomist version lays claim just as surely as
McFague's metaphorical theology to a basis for human talk about

---

[14] George Newlands would seem to me to be incorrect in his denial that
this is so. See *God in Christian Perspective* (Edinburgh: T & T Clark, 1994),
p. 46.
[15] Proclus, *The Elements of Theology* 18 (trans. E.R. Dodds; Oxford:
Clarendon, 1953), p. 21.
[16] *Summa Theologica*, 1.12.12 (my italics).
[17] See Battista Mondin, *The Principle of Analogy in Protestant and Catholic
Theology* (The Hague: Nijhoff, 1963), p. 170.

God which is independent of God's self-revealing act in Jesus Christ.[18] Hence it lies within the grasp of human reason to discover what perfections must necessarily belong to God, and which cannot. But God, Barth insists, is not and could never be at our disposal in this way. That it must be possible for certain human words and ideas to refer analogously to God is clear, otherwise theology is either impossible or nonsensical. But they do not do so, Barth insists, by virtue of some natural likeness between the creature as such and God, but because God lays hold of them and grants them a capacity which exceeds their natural semantic range. Nor are human beings in any position to trace the precise nature and contours of the correspondence which God calls into being. In particular, Barth rejects the claim to have identified a basis for doing so via empirical observation and logical inference, as if the relationship between Creator and creature could be reversed and controlled to human theological advantage. In any case, he avers, since creation is *ex nihilo*, and God is not simply the first link in a chain of cause and effect, all we should find by such a method, were it in fact to be successful, would be the nothingness out of which we were first called into being.

While, therefore, Barth embraces a doctrine of analogy as a necessity, it is for him only a *factual* necessity, established by the contingency of God's creative and revelatory action, and not an *absolute* necessity determined by some metaphysical principle to which God and humans are alike subject.[19] Consequently human beings, Barth argues, are in no position to extrapolate from their own creaturely natures some account of the divine nature. The

---

[18] See, e.g., the discussion of analogy in *CD* 2/1, p. 232: 'The moderate doctrine of analogy in natural theology, as it has been and is represented in particular in the Catholic Church, stands in the closest material and historical connexion with the Liberalism which, under appeal to God's omnipotence, affirms all analogies . . . (and) shows a basic readiness in almost every connexion to discover new analogies in the world.'

[19] 'All kinds of things might be analogous to God, if God had not made and did not make a very definite and delimited use of His omnipotence in His revelation; that is to say, if the analogy of the creation and creaturely word effected by His revelation did not mean a selection, determined and carried out by Himself, from among the infinitely many possibilities and definitely referred away from others' (*CD* 2/1, p. 232).

analogy between God and human language, if such there be, can be known only by that which creates and drives us to speak of it in the first place; namely, God's revelatory and redemptive act in Jesus Christ, in the course of which we find human language and conceptuality taken up and permitted to refer appropriately to God in ways which transcend its natural capacity.

One recent account puts it thus:

> Barth's view is that human language in itself has no capacity for bearing witness to God. If human language is nevertheless able to bear witness, it will only be because a capacity not intrinsic to it has been brought to it from without. But that is grace, not nature. In a gracious and sovereign act, God takes up the language of human witnesses and makes it to conform to himself. God must therefore speak when spoken of by human witnesses if such witness is to reach its goal. He must reveal himself in and through the 'veil' of human language. It is at this point that the *inherently dialectical* character of the *analogia fidei* is clearly seen.[20]

It will be apparent that this is essentially the same dialectic that we have seen at the heart of Barth's christology and which characterizes Barth's whole understanding of the relationship between God and the creaturely. Human language, just as surely as any other creaturely reality, is in and of itself *non capax infiniti*. The fact that human speech which corresponds to God is actually possible, therefore, is a miracle of grace and not a natural state of affairs.

If, then, we are to speak of love in God, for Barth it can only be because this is how God has first spoken to us of himself, and we must be careful to allow our use of the term to be driven and guided from first to last by the particularities of that prior use. The verbal formula of 1 John 4:8, Barth notes, might at first sight encourage us to think in terms of an equation of God with some abstract universal idea, a Form of love in which he and others participate to differing degrees. But, he reminds us, the exegetical context makes it quite clear that we are intended to think not abstractly but concretely at this point.[21] 'This', the apostle makes

---

[20] McCormack, *Karl Barth's Critically Realistic Dialectical Theology*, p. 18 (emphasis original).

[21] *CD* 2/1, p. 275.

clear, 'is how God showed his love among us; he sent his one and only Son into the world that we might live through him. This is love . . . that he loved us and sent his Son as an atoning sacrifice for our sins. This is how we know what love is: Jesus Christ laid down his life for us' (1 Jn. 4:9–10). We must begin our reflection on God's love, therefore, not with some general concept of love, or with one of any number of different possible human experiences and exemplifications of love. Whatever role these may have to play in our subsequent thinking and theological development, they cannot be the dogmatic point of departure.

'It is not', Barth writes, 'that we recognise and acknowledge the infinity, justice, wisdom [and we might add love] of God because we already know from other sources what all this means and we apply it to God in an eminent sense, thus fashioning for ourselves an image of God after the pattern of our image of the world, i.e., in the last analysis after our own image.'[22] Rather, we must begin and continue for a considerable while with the testimony to God's love which is contained in the form of his revealing act itself. Of course this cannot mean any pure and simple reiteration, or a refusal to do more than receive and preserve in its original form the revelation which he bestows. We are called upon to interpret, to make sense, to present what we have learned in new and persuasive and compelling ways, to relate it to existing knowledge and experience in such a way that others may be able to hear and receive it. Thus 'The humility of our knowledge of God does not consist in the laziness of the servant who took his pound and buried it (Mt. 25.18), but in the fact that, invited and authorised by revelation to do so, we give God the honour which belongs to Him, to the very best . . . of the ability which He Himself gives us.'[23] But, in using and developing and translating the words in which he teaches us to speak of himself, we must ever seek to allow him to be the interpreter of these words, rather than cutting ourselves loose from the normative forms of his revelatory engagement with the flesh.

We need do little more here than list a couple of the things which Barth believes Christians are thereby compelled to say of

---

[22] Ibid. p. 333.
[23] Ibid. p. 336.

God's love in order to see how his contrasting approach leads him to a very different picture than that arrived at by McFague.[24]

First, God loves us as the one who loves in freedom. He loves us, that is to say, not out of any lack or need in his own being, but because he wills our existence as another over against himself and sharing in fellowship with himself. To be sure, God is love in his innermost being; but not an unrequited love which demands the creation of an object and a reciprocal response in order to find fulfilment. He is eternally, as Father, Son and Spirit, fulfilled in his love, and his love for us issues out of an overflow rather than a deficit of love. If, therefore, we may speak of a need-love in God in relation to his creature, it can only be with the proviso attached that this need, the desire for the creature's love, which also furnishes the capacity for pain and a sense of loss, is something contingent upon God's willingness to enter into such a relation in the first place, to place himself under certain relational constraints, to be limited in his freedom by the existence of a genuinely free other.[25]

Second, God's love for his creature takes a very particular form. It is love for the other which craves response, but a love which in itself is unconditioned by any capacity for response, or any inherent virtue or value, in that other. Indeed, it is love for those who are not only not loveable but who actively hate and reject and despise the lover. It is love which burns in anger at the existence and effects of sin and evil, yet never ceases to love those who are gripped by and the agents of sin, and which manifests itself supremely in the form of forgiveness.[26] It is, in other words, unlike any other love that we know, uniquely Holy Love.[27]

---

[24] See §28 of *CD*.

[25] See, e.g., *CD* 2/1, pp. 273–275.

[26] 'The love of God always throws a bridge over a crevasse. It is always the light shining out of darkness. In His revelation it seeks and creates fellowship where there is no fellowship and no capacity for it, where the situation concerns a being which is quite different from God, a creature and therefore alien, a sinful creature and therefore hostile. It is this alien and hostile other that God loves . . . That . . . is the miracle of the almighty love of God' (ibid. p. 278).

[27] See ibid. pp. 353f.

A careful focus on the form of God's self-revealing act helps us, therefore, to delimit the horizontal spread of different human options signified by our ordinary uses of the term 'love'. We whittle down the field, attending to the particularities and peculiarities of this specific application of the term until we are left with a pool of usable language and conceptuality which we may trust to refer us appropriately to their divine object only because he blesses our use of them. But what exactly do we mean by saying this? And where does it leave us? Specifically, what are we now to say of the vertical relation of these delimited human terms and ideas to the being of God? These may well be the most appropriate ways of thinking and speaking that we have, being the ones which God himself grants us and encourages us to develop and reflect upon, but may we say that in them we have the means to define God's love, or any other feature of his being and activity?

The truth is, surely, that the most serious problem of theological language remains, and we have not solved it simply by narrowing the field of language available for our use, and allowing our use of it to be controlled by the particularities of God's self-objectification in human and created forms. We are still faced with the vital question: just how does this human reality relate and refer to the divine reality lying beyond it? When we say that God's love is 'love . . . but not as we know it', we are saying much more than that the form which God's love takes on the human plane when it is incarnate differs significantly from any other human love that we are familiar with. We are also admitting that even *this* love is but a fleshly representation, a God-given analogy, of the divine reality itself. Barth writes: 'God is what man in himself never is, what man himself can only understand as he looks to Him, admitting that of himself he does not know what he means when he says it.'[28] And again, 'We may and must venture to bring the concept of love (the peculiar and final meaning of which we admit we do not know . . .) into the service of . . . the declaration of the act and therefore of the being of God.'[29]

Thus, while in obedience we are called to speak of God in *this* language and not other language of our own choosing or devising, the

---

[28] Ibid. p. 284.
[29] Ibid. p. 276.

fact remains that of ourselves we do not know what we are saying when we say that God is love, so far as its reference to God himself is concerned. We do not, in other words, know the nature of the dissimilarity between what our human words signify in ordinary discourse, and what they signify in theological discourse. Precisely because, in revealing himself, God takes human form, all revelation is at the same moment a veiling. It is never revealedness under the form of the human. The givenness of the humanity of Christ, and of the language and conceptuality which form its creaturely matrix for interpretation, do not in and of themselves, therefore, provide us with that which we seek, namely, a definition of God's love. Even in the light of revelation we cannot, as it were, climb up the vapour trails left by the divine descent, and find our way to heaven. The tangible forms of that revealing are but the opaque media of an event in which, in and through them, God opens himself and his truth to our knowing and our participation. But this event is not at our disposal. We 'know' how these human media refer beyond themselves as we are drawn into a relationship with the object to which they refer us, as we know him in faith, as the knowledge of God is granted us new every morning. Such knowledge cannot be pinned down, held onto, packaged and handed on to others. We can only point to the human media faithfully in order to direct others to the reality of which we speak.

At one level this situation is not unique to theology. Something analogous may be found wherever the semantic range of our language is extended metaphorically to refer to hitherto unknown and unspoken aspects of reality in order to grant us epistemic access. In the process of accommodating language to the world we are forced to borrow from our existing stock of words and images and to misuse them in order to draw parallels between the known and the only newly discovered. But precisely what the relation between the two is, what the analogy between them is, and what, therefore the familiar term *means* in its new metaphorical application, can only be discerned by those who are willing to submit themselves to the knowing relation. It is through our contact with the real that the meaning of our statements about it can finally be grasped. It would seem, therefore, that in this respect the problem of theological language provides a particularly clear instance of the problem of human language and its mode of reference to reality in general.

What does it mean, we might legitimately ask, to *define* anything? And can we do it? If creaturely reality is less mysterious than divine reality, it may be that it is nonetheless altogether more mysterious than has sometimes been supposed; and it is not inappropriate to suggest that every act of human speech entails the dialectic between 'it is' and 'it is not'. In the case of God, though, the matter does and must have a distinctive dimension which sets it apart if, with Barth, we seek to take fully seriously the meaning of God's transcendence with respect to the creaturely. For transcendence, in this context, means precisely that no ontological commonality whatever between God and the creature may be supposed to exist, and that, consequently, God lies utterly beyond the ordinary range of human saying and knowing. That the conclusion to be drawn from this is neither agnosticism nor some strategy of pure theological constructivism rests, for Barth, wholly and squarely on God's gracious decision nonetheless to call into existence a correspondence between our language and his own reality, a correspondence which is not rooted in or dependent upon nature, and which never falls within the range of human control therefore, but which depends from moment to moment for its existence upon a dynamic activity of the God who gives himself to be known. This is the 'inherently dialectical' nature of the analogy of faith, a dialectic which is and could never be resolved into a higher synthesis without the proper distinction between Creator and creature being dissolved.

4. Conclusion

To our original question 'How do we define the nature of God's love?' it would seem that we are driven finally in one way or another to respond that we don't, at least in any strict sense. For McFague, theology is not about defining God, but about fashioning metaphors which express our experience of relatedness to God, and none of these can be supposed in any way to penetrate the ether and speak of God as God is in Godself. They are 'likely accounts', pictures which may help us to think of our relation to the ultimate, but which lay claim to no specific knowledge of God as such. Even Aquinas, with his application of the analogy of intrinsic attribution, differentiating carefully between the perfection signified and the mode of signification, leaves us having to admit that, while we may specify which perfections God, as the cause of the world, must necessarily possess, we cannot specify *precisely how he possesses them*, and cannot therefore define precisely what the words we use to describe them mean in their specifically theological application. And for Barth, we have seen, *we* do not define *God*, but God defines himself for us, assuming our words and conceptuality just as surely as he assumes our flesh in order to reveal himself, and yet doing so in such a way that it never lies within our grasp to cash out the metaphors in literal terms, any more than we can capture the eternal Son simply by analysing the humanness of the historical Jesus. In both cases, the truth is known only as the event of revelation happens, and we are drawn into a triangular relationship with God himself through a transparency which the created media of that relationship do not possess in and of themselves.

The difference between Barth's account, and those of McFague and Aquinas, however, is that, at the end of the day we can trust that there is an appropriate analogy between human language and God himself at these points, not only because certain basic metaphors are, so to speak, of his making and choosing rather than ours, but crucially because God commits himself to an involvement with us through our use of this language, drawing close and drawing us to himself. We trust (we cannot presume) that as we speak of him he will be faithful and will speak of himself in and through our speaking, thereby opening out the ultimate reference and meaning of our words for us so that we 'know' through something resembling intuition how these words refer. Perhaps the fact that we cannot capture that meaning and pin it down in neat logical formulae bothers us. But is this anything more than our eschatological impatience which always seems to want certainty and clarity now, rather than resting content in the assumption that what we are granted now is sufficient, and being happy to wait for that time when we shall know fully, even as we are fully known?

Index of Names

Aquinas, St. Thomas 25, 114, 186, 193f
Athanasius 113
Augustine 142

Baillie, D. M. 1–6, 141
Baillie, John 165
Baxter, Christina 30, 129
Biggar, Nigel 84–87
Brunner, Emil 84, 88, 139f, 144f, 150–162, 164–166, 169–171
Bullinger, Henry 37
Bultmann, Rudolf 19, 42
Busch, Eberhard 144, 147

Dalferth, Ingolf 58, 60, 81
Descartes, Rene 121f
Diekamp, F. 103

Feuerbach, Ludwig 8, 14, 27, 29, 125f

Gogarten, Friedrich 157
Gregory, Nazianzus 100
Grundmann, W. 148
Gustafson, James 84

Harnack, Adolf von 139
Harries, Richard 20

Hart, Trevor 118
Hauerwas, Stanley 84
Hopkins, G. M. 19
Houston, J. M. 109
Hunsinger, George 127, 137

Isaiah, The Prophet 20, 33, 38

Jenson, Robert W. 109
Jüngel, Eberhard 56, 148

Kähler, Martin 2
Kant, Immanuel 7, 9
Kierkegaard, Soren 19, 40
Küng, Hans 48–50, 53–57, 63, 68–70, 72f

Lehman, Paul 84
Lewis, Alan 46f
Lewis, C. S. 183
Lindbeck, George 118, 122, 124, 137
Lossky, Vladimir 100, 110
Luther, Martin 40f, 54, 64, 122

MacIntryre, Alasdair 122, 133
Mackintosh, H. R. 178
Macmurray, John 20
McCormack, Bruce L. 14, 188, 190

McFague, Sallie 181–184, 186, 193f
McGrath, Alister 49, 61f, 108
Moltmann, Jürgen 102, 107, 109–111, 113–116
Mondin, Battista 186

Niebuhr, Reinhold 84
Newbigin, Lesslie 118–120, 122, 130, 137
Newlands, George 179, 186

Paul, The Apostle 33, 39, 54, 65, 81, 140
Polanyi, Michael 121f
Prestige, G. L. 112f
Proclus 186
Przywara, Erich 141f, 144, 153

Rahner, Karl 101–104, 108–110
Roberts, Richard H. 4, 5, 141

Schleiermacher, F. W. 7, 183
Schmaus, M. 54
Smail, T. 101
Stapel, Wilhelm 147
Sykes, Stephen 7

Taylor, Charles 75
Torrance, Alan J. 23
Torrance, Thomas F. 93

Ward, Graham 5
Webb, C. C. J. 105
Webster, John 60, 75–77, 80
Williams, Rowan D. 15, 105
Willis, R. E. 84

Yates, John 170
Yoder, John Howard 84

Zizioulas, John D. 105, 110, 113